Praise for *The Coaching Manual*

'No one has brought to life the nuts and bolts as well as the spirit of masterful coaching better than Julie Starr. *The Coaching Manual* is the definitive resource for aspiring as well as seasoned coaches looking to further refine their approach!'

Marshall Goldsmith, *New York Times* bestselling author of *Triggers, Mojo* and *What Got You Here Won't Get You There*

'Many authors claim that their books coach the coach about the process for how to coach; Julie Starr's *The Coaching Manual* actually delivers! It's practical, comprehensive, and eminently readable. For anyone entering the field – start here.'

L. Michael Hall, Ph.D., author and developer of *Meta-Coaching*

'Clear, accurate, well-written, and full of important information that all coaches just need to know! I would absolutely recommend this book to any coach, neophyte or experienced.'

Chérie Carter-Scott, Ph.D. MCC, author of *If Life is a Game, These are the Rules, Transformational Life Coaching* and 15 other titles

'*The Coaching Manual* is the most comprehensive, practical, best-illustrated coaching source I have ever seen. It compellingly teaches the mindset of keeping the responsibility on the coach combined with a powerful, realistic skill set.'

Dr Stephen R. Covey, author of *The 7 Habits of Highly Effective People*

'. . . the most comprehensive book on the practice of coaching that I have come across. If anyone wishes to become a one-to-one coach and only reads one book about it, this could well be that book.'

Sir John Whitmore, executive chairman, Performance Consultants International; author of *Coaching for Performance*

The Coaching Manual

The Coaching Manual

The definitive guide to the process, principles and skills of personal coaching

Fifth edition

Julie Starr

Pearson

Harlow, England • London • New York • Boston • San Francisco • Toronto • Sydney
Dubai • Singapore • Hong Kong • Tokyo • Seoul • Taipei • New Delhi
Cape Town • São Paulo • Mexico City • Madrid • Amsterdam • Munich • Paris • Milan

PEARSON EDUCATION LIMITED
KAO Two
KAO Park
Harlow CM17 9NA
United Kingdom
Tel: +44 (0)1279 623623
Web: www.pearson.com/uk

Previously published 2002, 2008 (print), 2011, 2016 (print and electronic)
Fifth edition published 2021 (print and electronic)

ISBN: 978-1-292-37424-6 (print)
          978-1-292-37422-2 (PDF)
          978-1-292-37423-9 (ePub)

British Library Cataloguing-in-Publication Data
A catalogue record for the print edition is available from the British Library

Library of Congress Cataloging-in-Publication Data
A catalog record for the print edition is available from the Library of Congress
10 9 8 7 6 5 4 3 2 1
25 24 23 22 21

Cover design by Two Associates

Print edition typeset in 10/14 Charter ITC Pro by Straive

NOTE THAT ANY PAGE CROSS REFERENCES REFER TO THE PRINT EDITION

Contents

About the author

Julie Starr is an expert and thought leader in the field of coaching. Since 2002, her best-selling book *The Coaching Manual* has supported the evolution of the coaching field through simple, powerful principles and practical approaches. With over 20 years and thousands of hours of coaching experience, Julie supports CEOs and executives from some of the world's best-known organisations. Her approach is challenging, compassionate and empowers clear leadership.

Julie's other titles, *Brilliant Coaching* and *The Mentoring Manual*, support managers and leaders to improve business performance by developing people. Her books are translated into many languages and are required reading on coach training programmes around the world. She lectures in universities and at industry conferences to inspire understanding and engagement. Julie is MD of Starr Coaching, a leading provider of coach training in organisations; check out **www.starrcoaching.co.uk** and **LearnStarr.com**.

Julie also writes novels for young adults and donates proceeds to charities that house, heal and educate street children and orphans; check out www.ruffdogbooks.com.

Acknowledgements

There are many people who have contributed to the development of the ideas and thoughts in the book, and I hope I've remembered to acknowledge most of them. So, I would like to express gratitude for the work of the following people: Richard Bandler, Brandon Bays, Kevin Billett, Deepak Chopra, the late Stephen R. Covey, Frank Daniels, Landmark Education, Milton H. Erickson, John Grinder, Byron Katie, M. Scott Peck, Anthony Robbins, Eckhart Tolle and Brian Tracey.

I'd also like to thank Eloise Cook, Dr Xanthe Wells, Rachel Raymond and Marcia Yudkin for their challenges, thoughts and ideas in preparation of the text.

Publisher's acknowledgements

1 and 130 Pema Chodron: Quoted by Sir Pema Chodron; **7 Socrates:** Quoted by Socrates; **17 Anthony Robbins:** Quoted by Anthony Robbins; **27 Noomi Rapace:** Quoted by Noomi Rapace; **39 Ram Dass:** Quoted by Ram Dass; **43 Genie Z. Laborde:** Inspired by Genie Z. Laborde; **56 American Psychological Association:** De Haan, E., Duckworth, A., Birch, D. & Jones, C. (2013), Executive coaching outcome research: the predictive value of common factors such as relationship, personality match and self-efficacy, Consulting Psychology Journal: Practice and Research, 65.1, 40–57; **79 Stephen M.R. Covey:** Quoted by Stephen M.R. Covey; **103 Steve Jobs:** Quoted by Steve Jobs; **126 Brandon Bays:** Quoted by Brandon Bays; **127–128 Journey Publications Ltd.:** Kevin Billett, co-author, Bays, B. & Billett, K., (2009), The Journey – Consciousness: The New Currency, Journey Publications; **129 Eckhart Tolle:** Quoted by Eckhart Tolle; **133 Elizabeth Kapu'uwailani Lindsey:** Quoted by Elizabeth Kapu'uwailani Lindsey; **163 William Shakespeare:** Quoted by William Shakespeare; **209 Dr. Wayne Dyer:** Quoted by Dr Wayne Dyer; **212 and 251 Daniel Goleman:** Adapted from Daniel Goleman's five components of emotional competence; **231 John C. Maxwell:** Quoted by Dr John C. Maxwell; **245 Marcus Aurelius:** Quoted by Dr Marcus Aurelius.

Publisher's acknowledgements

chapter 1

Introduction

'Welcome the present moment as
if you had invited it.'

Pema Chodron

Welcome to the fifth edition of *The Coaching Manual.* As always, this revised edition is informed by my ongoing enquiry, study and practice, both in the coaching profession and the field of human development. The intention of this book remains constant: to offer you simple principles, insights and practical guidance to support whatever type of coaching you choose to do.

The coaching profession continues to grow and develop in exciting ways. Coaching continues to ignite interest, as people are drawn to the impact, benefits and value of working with a coach. There is simply no relationship like it. Anyone coaching, or interested in becoming a coach, now has access to a vast store of knowledge, training, support and guidance as they navigate their unique development path forward. In the world of business, organisations sustain their use of coaches and coaching principles to create positive change by developing people. As a skill, a set of behaviours, or simply a way of being, coaching engages us personally and professionally, for at the heart of coaching is an awareness of our basic interdependency as people, and our need to evolve together. I see that much good is being created from this simple truth.

The Coaching Manual has been translated into many languages and supports the practice and development of coaching far and wide. Since the publication of the first edition, I continue to work and study within the field of personal development with a clear focus on coaching. With this fresh edition, the Free resources (at the end of the book) are available from the LearnStarr area of my website, www.starrcoaching.co.uk.

For readers keen to embrace coaching more personally, Chapter 9 Become a coach helps you decide how you will take these ideas forward. For example, as shaping your own behaviour in situations, or indeed by becoming a coach yourself. So, whatever your current interest is in coaching, I hope you enjoy this book and find that it strengthens the work that you do.

How this book works

This book explains the ideas and principles of coaching and shows you how to apply them in any coaching situation, from business coaching in the workplace to more holistic life coaching in a personalised setting. If you are new to coaching, the manual is a practical guide to support your learning and practice, often in everyday situations. For those already coaching, the manual offers fresh insights and thought-provoking ideas. For the busy manager, the manual provides ideas to shape your thinking and techniques to use with your team.

While I will often talk to you as though you are already a coach or are coaching in some way, please know that you do not have to be a coach to benefit from the ideas that follow. If you are in any situation where you are helping others to create change through learning, I am confident that this manual has something to offer you.

This book encourages you to adopt a collaborative style of coaching. By collaborative style I mean that the coach and the person being coached work together to create change. As a coach, you bring your specific skills to work with the situation, intention and need of the person being coached. To engage and empower the people you are working with, I will often encourage you to adopt a less directive style of behaviour and language. To help you to coach effectively, I'll cover the ideas and beliefs that underpin coaching and offer fresh views on the skills you need to strengthen. You will also have simple examples of positive coaching behaviour and language to help develop your self-awareness, such as 'I need to spend more time getting clear up front in conversations' or 'Right now I talk too much.' To help you navigate from the first 'hello' to a typical 'farewell', I have included the natural structure of an effective coaching conversation. In the barriers section, I will offer guidance on what to watch out for, in the shape of unforeseen blocks that hinder good coaching. To help you work with someone over several sessions, you'll find the common stages of a coaching assignment. Finally, when you're ready to leap into action, the Coaching resources will help give you even more confidence to get started.

A manual that works when you do

As you read, you will notice bite-size inserts that support your practice and learning. As you use them, you will increase your self-awareness and your ability to coach others. These inserts comprise:

Pause and Reflect

 These are a series of questions to help you link ideas to your experience, consider those and gain personal insight. You can write your answers down, speak them out loud, try them on to see how they feel, or just pause and think them through. The important thing to remember is that the questions are intended to provoke thought and action. By pausing and attending to the questions, you are letting the book go to work for you.

Story

 These are mostly fictional examples to illustrate a principle or idea and use imaginary situations and people. They are informed by my own work and often are based on real situations that I have adapted to make them appropriate to share with you.

Ideas into Action

 At intervals, you'll be asked to try an idea or approach for yourself, often in an everyday conversation. This is where you will begin to make progress on your ability to coach more effectively. Some exercises will be straightforward and help you confirm your understanding, while others will challenge you to do something a little further from your comfort zone. Although the exercises are clearly optional, I do encourage you to try more than you skip! Remember, only by coaching do we really learn to coach.

At a Glance

 In these you will find quick summaries of key points to confirm your understanding or create memory joggers for future reference. I will also offer hints, tips or advice to help you with key points – for example, how to acknowledge a coachee's emotions, or how to handle a negative response to your feedback. Again, these form bite-sized reminders of ideas that you can return to at any time.

Free Resources

 At the end of the book, you will find a Free resources section with materials to support you to develop your coaching skills and for your work with individuals. Content includes an overview of coaching to give to a potential coachee, and an example of the kind of notes you might take to accelerate your learning. You are free to use this content as part of your own personal practice and I request that you do not charge others for it.

Free resources are also available to download from the LearnStarr area of my website at: www.starrcoaching.co.uk.

What is coaching?

Put simply, coaching is a conversation, or series of conversations, that one person has with another. What makes the conversation different from others is the impact the conversation has on the person being coached (the coachee). An effective coaching conversation influences someone's understanding, learning, behaviour and progress. Coaching conversations can happen over different timeframes and in different environments. For example, you might have a coaching conversation during a face-to-face session that lasts two hours, or alternatively you could have a 10-minute telephone call that might also constitute coaching. This is because coaching is more defined by the impact of your conversation than the duration of it.

> **An effective coaching conversation influences someone's understanding, learning, behaviour and progress**

> **Coaching is more defined by the impact of your conversation than the duration of it**

Most often, the best person to judge if a conversation was a coaching conversation (or not) is the person being coached. If someone finds the following to be true after a conversation, then they would probably accept that it was coaching:

- The focus of the conversation was primarily upon them and their situation.
- Their thinking, actions and learning benefited notably from the conversation.
- If the conversation hadn't happened, they were unlikely to have had those benefits in thinking or learning within that timeframe.

How does personal coaching happen?

A personal coach normally works within arranged coaching sessions over time (often called an assignment). In conversation, the coach facilitates a process of enquiry and discussion, for example by listening, questioning, and offering summaries, observations and feedback. Through this distinct focus on them and their situation, the person being coached gains increased clarity regarding a situation or topic, which enables them to make progress in some way. A coach will also support an individual to decide on ways forward, for example by facilitating their decision-making process or by encouraging them to get into action and make change happen. In addition to tackling immediate challenges and opportunities, over time, the individual will often experience broader benefits, such as improved confidence, resourcefulness and emotional maturity.

Other coaching conversations might easily happen outside a formal coaching session. For example, a casual chat around a challenge, issue or goal might create a conversation that the individual decides has had a coaching impact upon them, such as 'He really made me think,' or 'That's it, I'm really clear on what I need to do now.' You have probably experienced this type of conversation yourself, where an informal discussion on a topic gave you unexpected insight or learning that helped you in some way.

A specific focus with a broader impact and benefit

Coaching helps people to develop and learn in ways that enable them to have or achieve what they really want. This is because a coach focuses on an individual's situation with the kind of attention and commitment that the individual will rarely experience elsewhere. Whether coaching is focused on someone's work life or personal life, this type of conversation often affects people's experience of both areas.

In a Nutshell

The activity of coaching brings together behaviours, techniques and methods that make a positive difference to the results a person is creating. An individual may have a specific goal or topic they would like to work on, or perhaps they have an idea of a general lifestyle they want to create. An effective coach facilitates discussions that increase an individual's awareness, insight and available choice in a situation. Coaches use effective listening and questioning; they offer constructive challenge or observations and give helpful feedback. For anyone, building an ability to coach is a rewarding challenge where we learn first about ourselves to better understand and support others. In a world where we face increasing complexity and challenge in combination with our goals, dreams and desires, a good coach can literally help us get better at life.

chapter 2

Collaborative coaching

'Life without enquiry is not worth living.'

Socrates

This chapter introduces the approach upon which this book is based –
collaborative coaching; please know that this term is less important than that
you understand its principles. As a foundation of your skill, I believe that the
best way to develop true mastery of coaching is to first learn this approach.
Once you have done so, you can then deviate from it, based on a wisdom that
gradually arises from your practice. The principles that follow are simple and
yet they are challenging, and many inexperienced (and experienced) coaches
are tempted to ignore these principles, and instead justify why they do so.
Perhaps they 'didn't have time' or 'this person needed something else from me'.
Unfortunately, if the real reason that you do not coach from these principles is
because you are unable to, then you allow your lack of ability/skill to influence
how you coach.

The success of this type of coaching arises from conversations that include
aspects of effective enquiry, the principles of which are covered throughout this
book. From my own experience, these principles are a combination of frustrating, revelatory, effective and, occasionally, delightful. That experience continues still, as I am challenged to remain trusting of the power of enquiry, in its
ability to create clarity, realisation and change, for the person I am coaching.

What does collaborative coaching mean?

A collaborative coach facilitates someone through a process of enquiry, learning and action. As in any form of coaching, our aim is to support someone towards a desirable outcome or to achieve an objective. However, in a collaborative coaching relationship, for the person being coached, the relationship feels like a partnership of equals, rather than anything parental or advisory.

A collaborative coach believes in the ability of the individual to create ideas, decide for themselves and move their situation forward. They use advanced skills of listening, questioning and reflection to create a highly effective conversation and experience for the individual.

> **It is often more effective to help someone gain their own insights into a situation than it is to tell them what they should think or do**

As you adopt this less directive approach, you are required to operate consistently from certain principles, for example, that it is often more effective to help someone gain their own insights into a situation than it is to tell them what they should think or do. A less directive, collaborative coach does not 'fix' someone, solve their problems or assume any position of superiority or higher knowledge. Although problems may be resolved during the process, our goal is always to help someone to reveal their own ability to do that.

The word 'coach' can mean different things, depending on the situation. For example, a vocal coach typically develops different strengths and skills, blending instruction, advice and guidance based on their distinct method of training. So, we need to distinguish the ideas in this book as a particular form of coaching and I am using the term 'collaborative coaching' to do that. Please know, however, that the term is less important than the principles that underpin it,

Less directive versus directive style

As a collaborative coach, your language and style are most often less directive, as opposed to directive. In Figure 2.1, you'll see this illustrated, while Table 2.1 shows how these two styles affect our language and approach in conversations.

Figure 2.1 Less directive versus directive style

Table 2.1 Directive and less directive style

Directive style	Less directive style
'You definitely need to act on this feedback.'	'How are you going to respond to the feedback?'
'Let's focus first on sorting the personal issues you say you've been having with Suresh and then we'll go through the change of direction on the project.'	'What seems more important to focus on first: what's been happening with Suresh or the changes in direction on the project?'
'I'm thinking that this is caused by a lack of planning.'	'What do you think is causing this?'
'If you want to improve your social life, you just need to join a club or group.'	'What options might you have for improving things socially?'
'This is really easy; you should jump onto a couple of online dating sites, get back in the game now.'	'What ideas have you had around meeting new people?' or 'What other options have you considered?'
'I think you need to revisit your original commitment to make the calls and act from that.'	'What do you think is stopping you from making the calls?'

A coach (or manager) with a directive style assumes that they have better knowledge in a situation and that they need to use it. So, they give advice or instruction with the expectation that the individual will follow or comply. The coachee might feel as if they are being 'told' to do something or receiving advice that they are expected to act upon.

A coach with a more directive style will feel responsible for coming up with most of the ideas and actions within the conversation. They might also imagine that they are working *on* the coachee rather than *with* them. A more directive style sounds like this:

Directive style of conversation

Coach: So, you say you need to stop procrastinating. What are you procrastinating about?

Coachee: Well, I guess you'd call it administration, I mean generally. I don't like paperwork, you know, filling in forms, sending stuff off – I've a desk covered with client notes and an inbox full of emails, it's all a bit out of control.

Coach: Right – and so you need to get it back under control quickly then?

Coachee: I guess I should.

Coach: So, there's a number of different ways you could do that. I'd suggest that first you sit down and make an action list of all the things that need doing, everything you're avoiding, and give each one a priority rating of high, medium and low. I can help with that. Then schedule a specific time in your day to review and work through the list. 'Just do it!', as they say.

Coachee: [hesitates] Oka-ay ...

Note that the coach did most of the talking and directed the content of the conversation. The ideas or solutions are given by the coach, and the coachee is expected to comply.

A collaborative style of coach trusts that an individual often has their own answers and simply needs support for their learning process. In this example, our procrastinating coachee probably knows enough about themselves and their own tendencies to be able to make progress. The coach's role is to help the individual enquire into the key aspects of the situation to surface ideas or insights that will create progress. This might sound like this:

Less directive style of conversation

Coach: What kind of things are you procrastinating about?

Coachee: Well, I guess you'd call it administration, I mean generally. I don't like paperwork, you know, filling in forms, sending stuff off – I've a desk full of paper and an inbox full of emails, it's all a bit out of control.

Coach:	What's the impact of being out of control with this type of stuff?
Coachee:	All sorts, from minor embarrassments when I have to apologise, to real dilemmas. I once had three credit cards in a row refused simply because I'd not switched payments over to my new bank account. I was left standing in Rome airport with no way to pay for my return flight home.
Coach:	How else does not dealing with this stuff affect you?
Coachee:	Well, to be honest, it makes me feel a bit of a mess. I mean, an adult who can't even complete an online form by the due date, and then I have to request another link because I've lost the original – I make myself feel pretty chaotic.
Coach:	Okay, we've talked a little about consequences; let's look in a different direction – what stops you from getting this stuff done?
Coachee:	You know I could say I don't have time, but I don't think that's strictly true. I think it's more to do with the fact that I just begrudge doing it.
Coach:	What is it about the administration and paperwork that you begrudge?
Coachee:	Oh, it's like being controlled, like someone else is making me do homework or something, when I'd rather be doing something else.
Coach:	That's interesting, isn't it? Is that true?
Coachee:	Well, no, of course not; in actual fact, the reverse is probably true. If I got this stuff cleared, I'd probably feel a whole lot freer and 10 pounds lighter – I could go and do whatever I wanted with a clear conscience.

Here the coach influences the focus and attention of the coachee, without telling them what to think/feel/do. As a result, the coachee comes to their own learning, gaining their own insights and new perspectives on the situation.

In this example, the individual is likely to feel that they've surfaced their own answers by being supported to explore their own thoughts and ideas in a focused way. As they reveal more of their inner resources, this naturally feels more stimulating and even fulfilling.

Directive language – advantages

It's important to acknowledge that a directive style has its uses and can be what's needed. An example might be the case of basic skill transfer. If I can work a food blender and you can't, you might not appreciate my exploring your thoughts or feelings about that! You simply want to know which button on the blender does what and in what order to use them.

At a Glance

You can't coach knowledge

Where someone has little or no knowledge in an area and needs to acquire that quickly, then simple instruction or advice works best. This is because we can't coach knowledge. If you don't know what the capital of Brazil is, it's pointless my asking you that. To help you maintain a position of responsibility, I might ask you how you could find that fact, but that might not serve your immediate need in the situation.

We can't coach knowledge

Sometimes, it is inappropriate for a coach to sit back or remain neutral in the conversation. For example, a gently worded piece of feedback may be more powerful for an individual than lots of less direct observations or questions. Consider an individual who constantly goes off at tangents in conversation and appears unwilling to stay on the topic they say they want to work on.

Examples of a more direct style include:

- 'Can I just note that you've moved away from how this is affecting you and we're now talking about something else.'

- 'I notice that you sometimes switch subjects, Josh, and I think you need to stay focused on the original topic of how this is really affecting you personally.'

- 'Josh, what he thinks seems less important that what *you* think – can we focus on that?'

To be effective as a coach, sometimes it's helpful to be a little more directive, for example less to tell someone what to do, and more to draw their focus of attention to something. When a coach offers an observation, which feels non-judgemental and timely, that can work well. In the previous examples, you'll notice some phrases seem more 'straight talking' than others. Obviously, for the above responses to be effective, the coach's relationship with Josh must be underpinned by trust and mutual respect. Josh is then more likely to view the above responses as helpful, rather than aggressive.

Directive language and style – disadvantages

Within coaching, a directive style has real disadvantages:

- The coach's intention feels like 'I must find the right answer here' instead of 'How can I help them find their answer?' and so valuable information or clues can be overlooked.
- The coach can experience unhealthy pressure in the conversation to know everything and be able to fix everything.
- The coach works from the principle that they have the best answers for the individual, and often they do not.
- The coachee may feel dominated or controlled, as the coach assumes a position of 'knowing better'.
- During the conversation, the focus and energy is more often on the thoughts of the coach – which reduces the ability of the coachee to access their own wisdom and learning.
- The coach's solutions may have little relevance for the coachee, and so become meaningless advice. This can reduce the credibility of the coach.
- Where the coachee is less engaged, for example with the coach's ideas, they remain uninfluenced by the conversation (nothing changes).
- If the coachee tends to avoid responsibility generally, they might enjoy the coach being in control as the coach's directive style allows the coachee to be more passive during the process.

Less directive style – advantages

When we encourage learning for the individual *from* the individual, we experience the following benefits:

- The coachee experiences being truly listened to and appreciates the effort the coach makes to understand them.
- The relationship is based on equality, which builds openness and trust. The coach does not claim to have all the answers and the coachee feels their contribution is worthwhile.
- Solutions are developed from the understanding of the person experiencing the situation, so they are normally of much greater relevance and effectiveness.

- The insights, perspectives and ideas that emerge are more relevant to the coachee and so they feel more ownership and responsibility for actions and results.
- If an idea does not get the result the coachee wanted, the coachee still feels ownership of the idea and so will be more willing to persist and get a better result.
- Being supported to think in different ways and to consider other viewpoints provokes ongoing learning in the mind of the coachee. As if the conversation is a pebble being thrown into a pond, questions are the catalyst that sets off a reaction. The ripples of a coaching conversation often reach beyond the actual conversation itself.

Less directive style – disadvantages

- Adopting this style and language demands a greater level of skill on the part of the coach. Statements, observations, summaries and questions are designed to influence, and not control (we'll cover asking effective questions more fully in the Chapter 4 Five fundamental skills of coaching).
- The coachee initially may become frustrated with a coach who doesn't direct the conversation or give them answers.
- The coach has much less control over what occurs during the conversation, and this can sometimes make them feel uncomfortable, out of control or less secure.
- Conversations might take longer, as the coach explores the thoughts and experiences of the coachee at the speed the coachee is comfortable with.
- The coach must help the conversation stay focused in a productive direction or balance a need to allow the coachee to explore their own views, while maintaining forward progress. So, the coach needs to distinguish digressions from valid topics of conversation. For example, when discussing your health, it's probably relevant to talk more about the food you eat than your partner's favourite restaurants – but not always.

Attributes of a good coach

Whether you want to develop your coaching skills further or are thinking of using the services of a coach, you need to know how an effective coach is noticeably distinct from a less effective one. Table 2.2 gives us an idea of what we are looking for.

To recap, the attributes of a good coach can be highlighted in three key areas:

- Principles or beliefs a coach operates from – for example, 'We are equal in this conversation', or 'I need to understand first.'
- What a coach can do – their skills and knowledge.
- What a coach does – their actual behaviour.

From the outside, a skilled coach can make the process of coaching look like an easy, natural conversation. Partly, that's because they remain comfortable during the coaching process, but mostly it's because they've learned to coach from effective principles of behaviour.

Table 2.2 Attributes of an effective versus less effective coach

Effective coach	Less effective coach
Handles discomfort, e.g., 'Look, I'm not sure this is working – can we look at why?'	May avoid discomfort, e.g. thinks, 'This just isn't working and I'm really not sure why.'
Makes someone feel valued, supported and acknowledged: e.g. 'Can we look more constructively at this? I'm wondering if you're giving yourself too much of a hard time.'	Makes someone feel isolated or strange, e.g., 'Hmm, you're a bit of an unusual case, really, aren't you?'
Supports the flow of the coaching conversation, so that the coachee feels able to talk and express themselves appropriately.	Labours to keep the conversation going or talks too much, or simply 'tries too hard'.
Through effective listening, can stay focused on the key parts of a conversation: e.g. 'Can we just pause and revisit that?'	Misses or disregards key information, perhaps wanting to 'press on' with the intention of getting a 'result'.
Remains impartial and objective throughout: e.g. 'I can see why you might think that, and I'm also interested to look at other causes of why she acted like she did.'	Introduces own judgement or prejudice into the conversation: e.g. 'I agree, she obviously wanted to teach you a lesson – you're right to be angry.'
Can clarify the drivers and goals of the coachee, e.g., 'When you say you want "more money", what specifically does that mean, and what's important about that for you?'	Leaves key thoughts or objectives vague or unclear, e.g., 'Okay, so you want more money, let's look at what you need to do to get that.'

▶

Effective coach	Less effective coach
Is encouraging, challenging and realistic about situations: e.g. 'Two weeks to make the calls would be great, and I'm wondering what would happen if you got that done in a week instead – what would that feel like?'	Creates either a lack of encouragement and challenge, or undue pressure, e.g., 'Aww, come on, how long does it take to make a few calls? You could have those done by tomorrow if you actually tried.'
Holds someone to account, to create a constant focus on the coachee's objectives, e.g., 'Okay, again you said by the time we next met you wanted to tackle the salary conversation with your manager – let's look at what's stopping you from doing that.'	Allows themselves to be 'fobbed off' or side-tracked from issues of broken commitment, perhaps to maintain rapport: e.g. 'Well, that's okay, you're really busy, so can you do it when things calm down a bit?'
Is happier to achieve lasting results over time than fast results that don't last.	Feels like they have failed if they don't see immediate results from the coaching.
Encourages a sense of possibility: e.g. 'So, imagine yourself speaking to an audience and this time you really enjoyed it – what would that feel like?'	Embeds negative language, causing the coachee to feel uncomfortable or stuck: e.g. 'Yes, your lack of confidence does seem to be the real issue here.'
Leads by example, e.g. shows up on time, calls when they said they would, keeps any commitments made, or makes amends when they do not.	Displays double standards, e.g. shows up late, uses weak excuses, is not prepared for the session, etc.

In a Nutshell

Collaborative coaching is a highly impactful coaching style because of its supportive, less directive approach. By facilitating a conversation based primarily on enquiry, the coachee surfaces thoughts, insights and ideas, which often frees up their sense of clarity and energy in a situation. After the session, wisdom and insight continue to surface as the coachee continues to make their own connections. From the coach's point of view, being less directive challenges our natural tendency to give answers or help by 'fixing'. This style appears highly skilful when done effectively. For the individual being coached, it can be a profound experience that, literally, can change their life.

chapter 3

Seven coaching principles or beliefs

'Your philosophy of life shapes you more than anything else.'

Anthony Robbins

In this chapter, I'll cover ideas that support your effective mindset as you coach; literally, the perspectives you choose to operate from that support your decisions and actions. These principles can help you navigate, perhaps to help you decide what to do when things become tricky, or when you feel compromised in a situation. Over time, they are also a way to review your progress and reassure your confidence, as you realise that these beliefs have become natural and comfortable for you.

Operating principles for coaches

As you decide to become a less directive, collaborative coach, you are also choosing to adopt a certain set of beliefs and principles, to ensure consistent standards and positive results. That is because there are certain perspectives and beliefs that support collaborative coaching. Adopting these principles does not mean that you give up your individual personality or style. Indeed, it's important that you don't; you need to develop an authentic style of coaching that feels comfortable and natural for you. However, as effective coaches, you and I operate from a common set of beliefs. For example, we believe that personal coaching is a positive thing to do and trust the process of a less directive conversation to create desirable results. In this chapter, I'm going to focus on seven coaching beliefs that support you, namely:

1 Maintain noticeable commitment to support the individual.
2 Build coaching relationships with integrity, openness and trust.
3 The coachee is responsible for the results they are generating.
4 The coachee is capable of much better results than they are creating.
5 Focus on what the coachee thinks and experiences.
6 Coachees can generate perfect solutions.
7 The conversation is based on equality.

This common set of beliefs become principles that can help your success over time. Because, when we compare them with our own behaviours and approach, we can often spot opportunities to improve. When our coaching is less successful, they can help us to understand why. For example, perhaps your coachee seems to be happy to spend the whole coaching session complaining about their situation at work. Perhaps they might also refuse to consider potential solutions or what they might be doing to make things better. As coach, you try in vain to help the coachee feel more positive about the situation and take action to sort things out. You might become concerned or frustrated and want them to make certain changes that you are sure will make a difference. However, when you revisit our principles, you remember that the coachee is responsible for the results they create and see that they are currently avoiding this idea. You also see that you have lost your belief that they can ever change their attitude or behaviour. Sometimes, we become so engaged/frustrated by a coaching challenge we forget to focus on the simple principles. Some issues in coaching can appear complex when a straightforward outlook creates the breakthrough you need.

Several principles occur as rules of behaviour, while others appear as an attitude of what, as a coach, you are there to do (or not do). Where you adopt these principles consistently, they will improve your ability to coach effectively over time. Let's look at each one in more depth.

1 Maintain noticeable commitment to support the individual

As someone's coach, your commitment to them and the coaching relationship must be noticeable (obvious) to them and you. If you are unable to maintain a supportive attitude and approach towards someone, I'd encourage you to consider withdrawing from the assignment.

At the beginning of the coaching relationship, this appears routine; as a coach, you are probably thinking more about how to set up the assignment to ensure success rather than whether you do or do not want to help the coachee with their situation.

However, as time moves on, you may experience factors that reduce your sense of support. This withdrawal may or may not be something that you are aware of. For example, simple fatigue with the coaching conversations or even the person you are coaching may creep in. Maybe the coaching process is showing little sign of progress or results and you feel that your coachee is not making enough effort. For you, this may show up as feelings of resignation, boredom or even frustration. As coaches, it is important that we are self-managing in this instance. We must regularly evaluate where we are in our coaching relationships and identify any negative thoughts or beliefs that may be impairing our own resourcefulness and, so, performance.

This reflection process can become a natural part of your coaching routine. For example, when I'm coaching, I take a few minutes' preparation before the session. In that time, I will read through my notes from previous sessions, reflect on what the individual's goals are and remind myself how I am contributing to that. It gets me into the mental mode of supporting the individual, regardless of how challenging the session might be.

Coaching from non-judgement

On a less comfortable note, you might decide that you do not like the person you are coaching very much! Remember, as humans, we have a natural tendency to judge others. We compare how someone else looks, thinks or acts with how we do. We might approve or disapprove of other people because of their appearance, their attitudes, the words they use, their tone of voice, etc. Our mind's thoughts and beliefs form a kind of 'cocoon' from within which we appraise other people. As our ego needs to maintain a position of 'I'm right', or a sense of 'I know best', our compassion for others can be lost. I can imagine that anyone new to coaching may struggle to believe that could be true; my experience is that life sends you a mixed bag of individuals to work with and some of them become lessons for us personally.

> **Our mind's thoughts and beliefs form a kind of 'cocoon' from within which we appraise other people**

As a coach, your role is not to judge and disapprove of the way your coachee behaves or how they live their life. A coach's role is simply to make clear links between the behaviours of the individual and the results they are getting. For example, your coachee might complain about people who work for him, explain how they lack ability and describe how often he's had to 'sack a muppet'. Apparently, his greatest frustration is when people lack confidence and won't take decisions or act without having to involve him first. He says he wants a high-performing team but 'I just don't have the raw material'. He explains, 'In team meetings, I give regular lectures and even tackle the main offenders directly – but people just don't seem to be learning.' He describes several confrontations with people who work for him and explains how little time he has for them.

As a coach, it's simple to make the link between the lack of a high-performing team and his potentially intimidating behaviour. However, if you adopt the position that his behaviour towards others is 'wrong' in some way, this is likely to reduce your immediate sense of personal support (or compassion) towards him, for example, 'He sounds like a bully.' In the moment, your openness also reduces as you make them 'wrong' for their behaviour. Maybe you voice your judgement: for example, 'It sounds like you're just too hard on people.' Sensing your judgement, the manager might become defensive, and so again close down to your influence. Given that the manager currently believes his assertive style is what is needed; you might also unwittingly put yourself in his perceptual group of 'muppets' (and again lose influence).

This manager will become engaged in changing when he decides for himself that his behaviour is not working and may actually be a reason he doesn't have a high-performing team. So, as a collaborative coach, your role is to help him to make links between his behaviour and his results, not to feel bad for being scary or a bully (or any of the other things you may have judged him to be!). Any disapproval impairs your ability to facilitate the process of a coaching conversation because it's simply distracting.

Work to stay more objective and neutral

Objectivity enables us to remain clear and constructive plus demonstrate noticeable commitment to support the individual. As a coach, you might hear of deception and cruelty, but it's not helpful when you are distracted by your own judgements of that. In addition, your disapproval usually communicates itself to the coachee – even when you don't voice it out loud.

When we do not regard someone with an open mind, we are less likely to understand them. This lack of understanding has a direct impact on our ability to relate to the individual and how things are for them. At the same time, we diminish the warmth and openness in the relationship, and reduce our ability to influence the other person.

A quiet mind can focus more objectively

Any judgement or evaluation of the person you are coaching creates a conversation in your own mind, or 'mind chatter'. When your mind is busy in this way, you are distracted from what's actually happening in the conversation. Your internal dialogue blocks your ability to focus and listen – it's like trying to watch television with the radio on.

Imagine that you are working with a coaching client who reminds you strongly of your own (difficult) ex-partner. Your client says something like, 'You see, I have really high personal standards and I expect other people to live by them,' and you recall that is almost exactly what your ex-partner used to say. Before long, you are comparing them to your ex-partner, and starting to dislike them. You might have thoughts or mind chatter about them – for example, 'You must be a nightmare to live with' – along with feelings of tension or frustration.

> **When we do not regard someone with an open mind, we are less likely to understand them**

As a coach, once we start to see someone as flawed in some way, we are more likely to adopt the role of 'fixer', for example making comments like, 'Isn't that hard for other people?' or 'What about other people's feelings?' Again, the individual is likely to sense disapproval and, perhaps, feel defensive or closed.

Your ability to relate to and understand someone is key to effective coaching; judgement is, therefore, a real stumbling block. Instead, we must work at simply facilitating the process of the conversation objectively – without judgement. When you maintain a more neutral, open posture, you can gather much clearer information and so gain more relevant insights into the situation. During sessions, your thoughts will be clearer, and you may even feel calmer, as you gradually begin to appreciate how it is for the person you are coaching. Instead of thinking things that you cannot say out loud, your mind remains quieter and more 'still'.

What does non-judgement feel like for a coach?

Put simply, to be in non-judgement feels like nothing, because there is nothing going on! During a coaching conversation, you are not having an internal dialogue along the lines of 'That's not right, that's an awful thing to say, etc.' Instead of being distracted by your own thoughts and views, you are really listening, and present, to the flow of the conversation.

As coaches, we move away from judgement by developing a sense of curiosity towards what is being said and what the individual is experiencing instead. Your overriding sense of purpose is to help the individual increase their clarity and awareness in a situation, to make progress in some way.

How do we let go of judgement?

Unless we spend years gaining the enlightenment of a Buddhist master, we must accept a lifelong journey with this one. It's part of our human condition to judge others, but the trick is to notice when you're doing it and stop. The way to do this is to build your mental ability to refocus, by combining awareness and intention.[1] Literally to develop the concentration to stay with what is happening in the present moment, rather than your thoughts about that.

2 Build coaching relationships with integrity, openness and trust

When you enter into a coaching relationship, you are also deciding to serve the individual in an open, straightforward and honest way. This is worth mentioning, as our integrity in this area becomes corrupted in subtle ways.

Integrity refers to the alignment between what we believe is right, wrong, good or bad and what we actually do. For example, if you believe that it's wrong to take something by an act of theft, then don't steal anything. Integrity is a simple, black-and-white principle. For all that, a constant alignment with integrity is not something that comes easily. For example, stealing logically covers all forms of theft, from taking someone's wallet to not putting a ticket on our car in the car park (which is technically theft from the owner of the car park). So, our integrity becomes a value we say we have and then something we negotiate with over time! When we are pressured, or not feeling resourceful, how easy is it to decide not to do what we say is 'right'? Like keep our promises: for example, 'I said I'd call, and I didn't,' or 'I would have told the truth, but it felt awkward.'

While our personal standards outside of coaching are less relevant, when in a coaching relationship we need to maintain high standards of behaviour in this regard. From experience, coaching situations present opportunities to test our integrity fairly regularly; it's just one of the many positive challenges we benefit from as coaches.

Your commitment to your coachee is a clear priority. It can be easy to fall into a trap when the person requesting and paying for your services isn't the person getting the coaching. This can happen in business, where a more senior individual has requested coaching for a colleague and asks you what is being discussed during the sessions, or what your personal judgements are of someone. One way to share the content of coaching discussions is for the coach to encourage regular conversations between the sponsor and the coachee. I find that this builds openness and therefore trust between them, which benefits their working relationship.

Another option is to discuss the update messages you intend to give a manager or sponsor with your coachee first, to make sure they are comfortable with those. Also, as a simple rule, never say anything about your coachee or client that you would not want them to hear about afterwards.

> **As a simple rule, never say anything about your coachee or client that you would not want them to hear about afterwards**

Pause and Reflect

Rating openness and honesty

Think of a work-type relationship. Ask yourself these questions to help you understand levels of openness and honesty in that relationship. This is especially useful if you can use an existing coaching relationship.

Q How comfortable are you in this person's company?

Q How freely do you express yourself when you are with this person?

Q Might you ever avoid talking about a subject or situation with this person?

Q Do you feel the other person ever avoids talking about certain things with you?

Q Did you ever hide an 'uncomfortable truth' from this person?

Q Have you ever said anything about this person that you wouldn't want them to hear?

▶

If you feel your answers are encouraging you to reflect further, and potentially improve your behaviour, please take the time to do that. For example, share your answers with someone you trust and whose opinion you value. Or repeat using different people and relationships – try to spot differences in your tendencies.

Maintain integrity of purpose: coach the individual

There is also a potential conflict between what the coachee wants and what the organisation wants and you need to balance those two things appropriately. I find that when you retain your primary responsibility to the coachee, that works out to be the appropriate perspective pretty much every time. I'll tell you about Ed as an example. This is based on a true story, involving three people, but with their names changed. Ed is the coachee, Carla is the coach and Lucas is Ed's manager (we might also call Lucas the sponsor of the assignment).

Story

A question of loyalty

Lucas asked Carla to give Ed a series of coaching sessions. Lucas felt that Ed needed to develop better relationships with his team to deliver faster results. During a briefing meeting, Lucas seemed fairly frustrated with Ed: for example, 'He's managing a really important area of delivery right now and yet he's just making no effort with his people.' He also explained that Ed knew nothing about the idea of coaching with Carla and that he was not sure how Ed would react.

To maintain openness, Carla explained that it was important to let Ed know the specific goals Lucas wanted him to work on, why coaching had been suggested and what Ed needed to do to be successful. Carla helped Lucas to identify constructive statements about the areas he believed the coaching needed to focus on and what the benefits of that might be. To maintain Ed's sense of empowerment, Carla requested that the coaching be positioned as a form of support that Ed could either accept or refuse at any point during the process. Carla also explained that, while she was happy to identify general topics of their discussion, she would disclose nothing of the actual content of her conversations with Ed. Any emails she might write that updated Lucas on the assignment would also be copied into Ed. Carla recommended that, if Lucas wanted any more information on the content of discussions, he should ask Ed directly.

In their first session, Carla and Ed spent time discussing the feedback from Lucas and exploring how coaching might be an opportunity that Ed could benefit from. Ed voiced scepticism of the process and wanted to understand more about the confidentiality of the coaching sessions. Carla explained what kind of updates she would be giving his manager and assured Ed that the specific content of conversations would be disclosed to no one.

Perhaps surprisingly, Ed welcomed the chance to discuss his situation. In short, Ed was questioning his desire to stay with the organisation, and especially doubted his ability to build teams, for example, 'I'm comfortable being a technician, this people stuff isn't for me.' He also acknowledged that, while his discomfort at dealing with people was becoming more apparent now, it was something he had always felt awkward about. Ed felt that the easiest thing he could do was leave.

Carla's focus during those conversations was first to establish what was best for Ed, and then to work out how that related to his manager and the company in general. They discussed several scenarios, including him applying internally for other positions or just leaving altogether. They also discussed the potential benefits and risks involved and how Ed felt about those. One of those risks included the idea that he might 'take the issue with him' or that the problem may occur again in the future.

If helping Ed to consider leaving sounds disloyal to our sponsor (Lucas), let's acknowledge that this is the principle that works more consistently, because you need to help an individual be successful on their terms, not anyone else's. Had Carla tried to influence Ed to stay, or to take on more of the responsibilities that his manager wanted him to, she would have corrupted the integrity of the coaching which should help Ed clarify his understanding, clarity and decision-making process.

In case you are wondering about what happened to Ed, well, he decided to stay and tackle the challenges in front of him. Time spent on balancing the different options, plus the potential pitfalls or benefits, enabled him to reach a decision he was comfortable with. He was also able to let go of thoughts of leaving, which he was using as a distraction to avoid issues that related to his style, rather than anyone else's.

▶

> By helping Ed to appreciate that he always had options, he was able to let go of the 'trapped' feelings he had due to the pressures he felt were being placed upon him by his manager. Through the process of discussion, Ed could hear that Lucas's expectations for him sounded more like encouragement than pressure. Without the coaching, that might not have happened. Two years later, Ed did leave the organisation but in a way that felt like a natural progression, rather than a hasty withdrawal.
>
> Life's not always quite so smooth, so it's good to be grateful when it is.

3 The coachee is responsible for the results they are generating

If we acknowledge that we are responsible for something, it follows that we have power and influence over it. For example, if I acknowledge that I am responsible for how good a job I have, or how much money I earn, then it's up to me to do something about it if I'm not happy. So, we coach from the principle that individuals are ultimately responsible for their experience and also the results they're getting. That includes their job, relationships they have chosen, where they're living, etc. We do this not because it is arguably always true, but because it is a more constructive viewpoint that enables a more resourceful perspective.

For coaching conversations to generate better outcomes for people, we need to maintain a sense of possibility

For coaching conversations to generate better outcomes for people, we need to maintain a sense of possibility – that better outcomes are available.

So, in coaching, this sense of an individual's personal responsibility is key if we are to empower them to act positively in their situation. The potential of the word responsibility is revealed when we break it into two halves, as it literally becomes 'response' and 'ability' – in other words, the ability to respond.

A typical example is the experience of redundancy, which often forms a crossroads for people. Some people respond resourcefully and take positive action, which reveals the potentially grey cloud of losing their job to contain a silver lining. People might change to a more fulfilling career, go and find a better job, enjoy a return to education, etc. Other people aren't so resourceful in their response to redundancy – they blame others, or argue their career/livelihood has been ruined, etc. By choosing to believe we can respond and make a positive difference to the situation, we are adopting a responsible perspective. This is ultimately more powerful than deciding we are unable to respond, for example, 'I'm not responsible for what's happening to me right now.' By saying this, we make ourselves victims of unplanned-for circumstance.

Victim postures – innocent or disempowered?

The opposite of a responsible, powerful posture can be called a victim posture. When we adopt a victim-like posture in response to a situation, we act as if life is something that happens *to* us, and we can do little to influence it. In our language, this might show up as statements like 'This keeps happening to me,' or 'They made me feel like this.' Along with the statement is a subtle denial of our ability to affect our experience.

> **'If I don't see myself as a victim then I'm not a victim.'**
>
> **Noomi Rapace**

When we reduce our sense of responsibility, we might also tend to blame others. For example, 'I can't do the type of work I really want to do because of my partner,' or 'My life hasn't worked out because of my childhood,' or 'Life's just not fair.'

In coaching, a victim-like perspective impairs your coachee's ability to imagine that they have real influence over their situations and results. As you facilitate conversations where this is an issue, your coachee will perceive fewer possibilities for themselves, for example, 'I just can't see a way out of this mess,' or 'I think it's all pretty futile really.' As coach, your role includes encouraging people to feel empowered and so adopt a responsible approach to their situations.

Responsibility is not blame

Sometimes, issues discussed in a coaching conversation can be emotive, and the principle that we are responsible for how our lives are going is not easy for some people to accept. For example, where someone comes from a violent background, has money problems and has just been fired by an unreasonable boss, it's difficult to encourage them to take a responsible view of their current situation.

So, as a coach, it's important that you remember that responsibility does not equal blame. Blame implies that someone has done something wrong because they have done something that is 'wrong'. Blame also implies a need for shame, guilt or suffering and, when a coachee takes on blame (instead of responsibility), they are likely to feel worse about something. Responsibility, however, is simply about acknowledging our own influence in situations. As a coach, it is essential to retain a clear distinction between the two.

Martyr – suffering for a cause?

A similar perspective to a victim perspective is that of a martyr perspective. A coachee with a martyr-like posture would tend towards feeling bad or burdened. In language, they adopt the perspective of a 'rescuer turned victim' – 'I tried so hard to make this all work out, but everything turned against me,' or 'I gave everything to that job/relationship and this is how I'm treated.' I'm using extreme examples to explain the point but, in real life, language and behaviour can be more subtle – for example, 'No, no, that's fine, I'm really okay with this,' (with a tone of voice that suggests otherwise).

Watch for the victim and martyr language in the following example:

Coach: Perhaps tell me a little more about what happened in your relationship.

Coachee: Well, basically, they dumped me with no warning. Things seemed absolutely fine when 'Wham!' I get a note on the kitchen table. No sorry, no nothing.

Coach: I guess you must have felt pretty bad at that point.

Coachee: Tell me about it – I feel terrible! I'm not sleeping, not eating – what am I supposed to do now?

Coach: What do you think went wrong?

Coachee: Who knows? It seemed like one minute I was living with someone and the next minute they've upped and gone. I wouldn't care; this is the third time this has happened to me. Life's just dealing me a rotten hand as usual.

From the dialogue, the coachee feels that this is something that's happened *to* them and that they are the victim in the scenario. As coach, it can be appropriate to ask your coachee to adopt a more powerful posture, by 'trying on' this principle of responsibility with you – acting as if it were true. When we examine the same situation from this perspective, we discover new insights or learning:

Coach: If you were to accept some responsibility for what happened in the relationship, what might you see?

Coachee: I'm not sure what you mean – why would I do that?

Coach:	Well, it might help get more information that might be useful, just by approaching the situation differently.
Coachee:	Okay. [Pauses] Well, my partner was always saying that I wasn't really committed to things working out, that I didn't put enough into it.
Coach:	Okay – what else?
Coachee:	Well, they kept saying we should talk more, about how things were going, if there was anything we weren't happy about – you know, all that feelings kind of stuff.
Coach:	What was your response to that?
Coachee:	Well, at the time I said I didn't see the point of that. I mean, who wants to have deep emotional conversations when you get home?
Coach:	What are your thoughts about that now?
Coachee:	Huh – yeah, I guess I should have stayed more aware of where they were at, at least that way I'd have known we had problems.

You'll notice that the coachee sounds more powerful and more in control later in the dialogue. With this fresh perspective, they cast new light on the situation. They are discussing things within their own influence, namely whether they committed to the relationship or didn't, whether they talked to their partner or not. They are showing us that learning is desirable, and suffering is optional. The purpose of doing this is simply to help the individual increase their awareness to promote a greater sense of possibility and choice going forward.

Pause and Reflect

Responsible or victim?

If you want to coach someone from a principle of responsibility, you first need to be able to relate to that idea personally. These questions can help you understand your own ability to take responsibility for yourself and your situation. Simply read through all questions once, then go back and consider each one more slowly:

Q How have you blamed other people or things for your problems?

Q When (or with whom) do you prefer to complain about problems rather than talk about solutions?

Q Are you able to link your own behaviours and the results you get? For example, 'I'm late because I didn't leave on time' or 'I didn't put a ticket on my car, so I got fined'.

Q In conversation, do you 'own' your own problems? For example, 'I need to do something about this'.

Q Do you complain that things 'aren't fair' or can you view situations more objectively?

If this is difficult for you to decide, maybe ask someone you trust for their opinion. Or next time you're discussing a problem or issue, notice how much you talk about that as a responsible, powerful person – or how much you simply moan and complain!

4 The coachee is capable of much better results than they are creating

To stay effective as a coach, you need to believe that the individual you are working with is capable of doing and being more, especially in relation to their stated goals. That might be anything from more ability in a certain area, a lasting relationship, better health, etc. If a coach secretly believes the coachee is simply not capable of progress and change, that belief is likely to undermine the coaching process.

For example, imagine your coachee says they want to be able to speak confidently and powerfully to groups. After initial discussions, you agree to work with them to achieve this goal.

As the coaching progresses, you help them rehearse and practise a presentation and decide that the person appears unable to stay calm or make a clear point and you can't imagine the possibility of them ever giving a successful talk in public. At this point, your ability to support the individual to achieve their goal becomes inherently flawed. Your negative expectation of the outcome of the coaching is likely to influence you during conversations.

You are probably already aware of studies that suggest that when parents or teachers have positive expectations of children, the children achieve better results than where the reverse is true. While it isn't an identical situation, the same principle affects coaching, especially where the coach's belief helps to reduce openness and trust.

As a coach, if you say one thing but think another, somehow that communicates. Maybe through expression, tonality or gestures, your coachee will sense that you don't actually believe that they're capable of achieving their goals. Maybe you'll encourage them to settle for less or learn to cope with their 'weakness'. In a worst-case scenario, you may even undermine their confidence and make the achievement of their goals less likely. Surely the reverse of coaching!

In some cases, coachees may set goals that you genuinely feel are unrealistic, or place too much pressure upon them. Please be careful, however, not to place your *own* limitations upon other people. In this situation, the question of integrity emerges. By integrity, I simply mean being true to your word – telling your truth and doing what you say you will do.

For example, imagine you are coaching someone who tells you they want to double their income within the next six months. While this kind of increase in income rarely happens, it is actually possible. It's up to you to decide whether you're willing to enter into a coaching agreement to support them to achieve this. To do so, you must believe that they are capable of creating the increase.

As a coach, if you say one thing but think another, somehow that communicates

Do you say yes to the work, secretly believing the coachee isn't capable? Do you tell them you think it's not possible, but you're willing to coach them into a more likely goal and risk losing the work? I suggest that where you're sure that something isn't possible for the person, you deal with it honestly. If you enter into a coaching relationship where you haven't told the truth about how you feel, then the integrity of the relationship is corrupted, and this will affect your ability to challenge and encourage the coachee in an honest manner.

For the coachee, having a coach who secretly feels that they are going to fail is not the kind of support needed!

Pause and Reflect

Are you a support or saboteur?

Think about an existing relationship where you coach or support the goals of someone else. The following questions will help you consider your levels of commitment to this person:

Q How do you feel about the goals this person has described?

Q How achievable do you believe this person's goals are?

Q Do you believe this person will really benefit from the results they want to produce?

Q How do you feel about the person you are coaching?

Q How committed do you feel towards their success with these goals?

If it seems appropriate, repeat the above exercise using a different existing relationship, and check the differences in your answers.

5 Focus on what the coachee thinks and experiences

The focus of coaching conversations should be on the coachee and not the coach. Does that sound obvious? Remember that a collaborative coach is not there to tell people what they should do or have them make choices based on the coach's life and preferences. In collaborative coaching, you are working with someone to help them get where they want to go. The principal focus must remain on the coachee's thoughts and objectives, as those are the reason the conversation is taking place.

Some people might imagine that a coach has sage-like wisdom, or limitless knowledge (a risky assumption). For example, a coachee may think a coach must have seen their situation before and so will know what to do. They may imagine that the coach knows more about life, how to be happy, how to be successful or fulfilled.

Perhaps your coachee asks you, 'What would you do in this situation?' This is an unintentional trap, laid to catch your coach's ego. Your ego hears this and purrs – perhaps imagining that someone wants to know what you think, so that they can learn from you, be more like you, etc. If, as a coach, you have experienced some great results with a few coaching conversations, it can be quite easy for success to go to your head. Maybe your ability to advise is something that you believe in (another risky assumption). Therefore, it's important that you remain very lucid and conscious (or present) to what's happening during a conversation, to enable you to divert attention back to the coachee's viewpoint.

Ideas into Action

Enough about me – let's talk about you!

Next time you are having a casual conversation with someone, notice the balance in the conversation between them and you. In other words, are you talking about your experiences and thoughts, or theirs? If it's appropriate, keep the focus of the conversation completely on them for a while – what they've been doing, what they've been experiencing, what their thoughts and opinions are, etc. After the conversation, ask yourself:

Q How comfortable am I when I'm not contributing my own thoughts and ideas?

Q How much did I have to resist adding what I thought or knew into the conversation?

Q What effect did it have when I concentrated only on what they said or thought?

As with all principles, occasionally you will have reasons to work outside it. For example, if an individual appears reluctant to share their experiences, then offering your own experiences or thoughts can create a greater sense of sharing and trust. What is important is that you have the awareness in the moment to understand what's happening: for example, 'Is it appropriate for me to share my views here or is that simply a distraction?'

6 Coachees can generate perfect solutions

As humans, we have an almost childlike wish to be the person who comes up with the best thought, the cleverest answer, or the winning idea. It is like it was at school, where praise and reward came to those with the 'right' answer.

In collaborative coaching, the rules of your game are subtly different. To continue the classroom metaphor, you apply all your learning and experience to make sure that the person next to you comes up with the answer. And that may or may not be the answer that you've thought of. Clear ownership of the answer rests with the other person, who will normally go and use it on their own, to get what they want, together with the praise and reward.

As a coach, you win when someone else does. Your pleasure comes from being part of someone else's process and helping them see different ways in which they can create the results they want. This becomes incredibly fulfilling for the coach and a huge motivation to continue coaching.

In practical terms, solutions or ideas spoken by the person being coached are often more reasonable, pragmatic, and likely to be formed into action. That person will usually feel greater ownership of the idea and link that to a sense of responsibility for its success.

For example, I might be coaching a working mother having problems juggling her life between work and home. We may explore lots of different aspects of the situation to understand the different values and factors involved.

I might have formed the idea that her childcare centre seems to be causing the problems. So, I suggest that she changes it. What could the consequences be?

The coachee might:

- seize on it immediately as it's a perfect idea for her
- reject the idea because she has a 'polarity response' to advice: she automatically takes an opposing view
- reject the idea because it doesn't feel right to her, or make practical sense to her
- initially accept the idea, then disregard it later
- accept the idea and switch to another care centre, but that makes things much worse and she then blames me
- accept the idea and disregard her own instinct, which is to involve her mother in the situation.

Remember, we operate from the perspective that the best-quality solutions come from the coachee, not ourselves. As coaches, we might still influence those ideas and insights; indeed, our involvement guarantees this. However, our most common tools of influence are still questioning, listening, observation and reflection.

Our most common tools of influence are still questioning, listening, observation and reflection

When we work with the rule consistently, we also develop an understanding of when to break it. Infrequently, I'll ask permission to offer a suggestion – for example, 'Can I offer a thought?' and then, 'How would switching your childcare centre affect the situation?'

By requesting permission, you're increasing the probability that the other person will accept your idea, while acknowledging the intrusion.

Once you've offered the suggestion, let it go. Do not become attached to their agreeing to it. They may or may not go with your idea and, if they do, it might be immediately or some time afterwards.

Above all, remember to give up the idea of appearing smart by having the right answer. In the above situation, the best solution for the coachee may well have been her own idea to involve her mother, because of factors the coach wasn't aware of. Her mother might welcome the opportunity to spend more time with her grandchildren, be flexible when and where she looks after the children and do all this for free. Until now, the coachee's mother may not have offered her services as she respected her daughter's need for independence.

A collaborative coach needs to temper the basic human instinct to be right about something. By giving up an attachment to finding a solution to a coachee's problem, we are actively encouraging them to find their own solution. Collaborative coaching encourages someone to be more powerful, more creative, and more in action around situations, by helping them to find their own ways forward.[2]

7 The conversation is based on equality

As coach, you are working with someone else to support them in achieving something that they want. Your relationship will feel more like a partnership of equals rather than anything parental or advisory.

As you continue to work with someone, you strengthen the process of coaching. Together, you explore situations, causes, barriers and ways forward. The person you are coaching must feel they are receiving constant support, while remaining your equal. At all times, they must feel free to make requests or contribute to the discussion.

Where coaches adopt a posture of superiority, for example, 'Trust me – I know about this,' or 'Hey, I really think you should listen to me on this one,' not only can they alienate the coachee, but they run the risk of giving poor or irrelevant advice.

Pause and Reflect

Are we equal?

Please consider a relationship where you support, manage or coach someone else. The following questions can help you determine the levels of equality between you and this person:

Q How much do you respect or admire this person?

Q If you weren't managing or coaching this person, how comfortable would you feel asking this person for advice?

Q If this person really wanted to do something and you told them you didn't agree with it, what would they do?

- Go ahead and do it anyway.

- Ask you more about your views before making a decision.

- Go with your decision, as they will assume you 'know better'.

As you notice your own thoughts and feelings in response to these questions, now ask them again of a second, different relationship – and notice any differences in that. This exercise is only for the purposes of your own awareness and reflection – what you choose to do with this information is up to you.

An imbalanced approach can also undermine the coachee's confidence, as they begin to feel subordinate in the relationship. Alternatively, they may dislike the inference that the coach is somehow 'superior' in matters relating to their own situation. Even when people are quite comfortable in a subordinate role, you diminish their ability to engage with their own problems or seek their own solutions.

By acting from a sense of equality and collaboration, we promote an environment where the truth can be told, mistakes made, and insights discovered. Use the testing questions that follow to explore the equality or equity in a relationship that is relevant to coaching.

In a Nutshell

Collaborative coaches operate from supporting principles or beliefs. To repeat the key principles:

- Maintain your commitment to supporting the individual.
- Build your coaching relationships on truth, openness and trust.
- Remember that the coachee is responsible for the results they are generating.
- Know that the coachee is capable of much better results than they are currently generating.
- Maintain your focus on what the *coachee* thinks and experiences.
- Remember that coachees can generate perfect solutions.
- Make sure that your coaching conversations are based on equality.

chapter 4

Five fundamental skills of coaching

'The quieter you become, the more you can hear.'

Ram Dass

This chapter focuses on the fundamental skills of coaching illustrated in our Skills Star, shown in Figure 4.1. While you already have a current level of ability with all of them, some come less naturally and so require practice. These primary skills distinguish a good coach from a not so good coach, and so you will want to work on each of these skills directly. In this section, and also in the Online resources, you will find simple exercises to help you do that. Please try these; I recognise that it is tempting to keep reading and promise yourself to get back to these at some point in the future. However, if you do miss out on practice, you may find yourself in a coaching conversation feeling ill-equipped and under pressure. In this way, you might unintentionally create an experience that is counterproductive for both you and your coachee.

Figure 4.1 Skills Star: Fundamental skills of coaching

Once skills are acquired, it's not like riding a bike – we coaches do forget! These skills are more like muscles; they must be used regularly to keep them strong.

Can anyone coach?

In theory, anyone should be able to coach. In practice, some people are better suited to coaching than others, perhaps because of their natural character, attitude and motivation. Some people find that coaching is a natural continuation of what they already do in conversation. Others find trying to coach someone laborious, frustrating or even pointless. However, anyone who is truly committed to developing these skills will find that commitment makes it possible. This is because the strength of our intention to develop these skills is more important than our existing level of ability with them.

> **Our intention to develop these skills is more important than our existing level of ability with them**

Many everyday activities contain several of the following skills – the most obvious being basic conversation! However, only in a coaching type of conversation are you likely to be focusing on all these skills at once. This is because to use the full set of skills in all conversations would be tiring for the individual and rather strange for those they were talking to.

Skill one – build rapport and relationship

Rapport – relationship in action

The foundation for all coaching conversations is the warmth and trust felt between the coach and the coachee. To be in conversation with a skilled coach is enjoyable; they are warm, attentive and easy to relate to. This is possibly because of their ability to build rapport.

Many people outside coaching have this skill; you can probably think of someone you know who is able to put people at their ease, or quickly build a feeling of familiarity or comfort when they speak to others. For others, building rapport is a skill they choose to develop. As a coach, you need to be aware of how rapport happens, why it sometimes doesn't happen, and what options you have to build or reduce it. You also need to develop a level of flexibility with the behaviours, to help you relate to the range of different people you will meet in coaching situations.

The word 'rapport' refers to the quality of a relationship during any interaction we have with another person. Rapport describes the amount of affinity and connection present in a relationship and is indicated by the warmth and comfort we feel. You will have noticed 'instant rapport' with someone in everyday life. Maybe the person next to you in a queue seems like someone you have a lot in common with. Or it could be the exact opposite – they are someone you just do not warm to.

When you have good rapport with someone, you will normally feel more comfortable and relaxed in their company. I say 'normally' because that, of course,

Figure 4.2 Building rapport and relationship

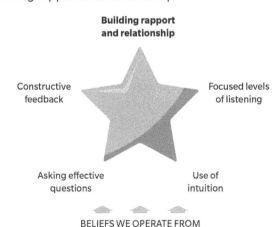

depends on what levels of rapport you want to have with that person. Certain situations of close rapport may be undesirable to you – for example, if you meet someone you instantly feel very attracted to and you already have a partner!

Pause and Reflect

Who do you have great rapport with?

Think of a friend or colleague with whom you believe you have great rapport. This will probably be someone with whom you have a good, easy-going relationship; someone whom you feel comfortable talking with; someone whose company you enjoy. As you think about them, ask yourself:

Q What does it feel like when I think about them?

Q What do we seem to have in common?

Q How do I feel when I'm talking to them?

Q What is similar about me and this person?

Q How does my comfort with them impact upon my behaviour when I'm with them?

You also probably know of someone who you simply cannot seem to relate to, even when you try. Here you find relaxed conversation more difficult or there is even a sense of distance or coolness between you. In this situation, you might imagine that you have no rapport at all, since that's what it feels like. However, because rapport relates to the quality of a relationship and there is some type of relationship happening, some quality of rapport, albeit negative, is still there. It's a little like assessing temperature in a room: while the room may be cold, it still has something you can measure. So, if you're in any kind of relationship, there will always be some sort of rapport. Figure 4.3 illustrates how a scale of rapport might look (inspired by Genie Z. Laborde).

Try the previous exercise and adapt the questions for someone you have less comfort or rapport with – for example, 'How does my discomfort with this person impact on my behaviour when I'm with them?'

What creates rapport?

Rapport is built on features of 'sameness'; where there is a high degree of sameness between two individuals, we build rapport more easily. Perhaps instinctively we feel less threatened by someone we feel is like us and are more easily

Figure 4.3 Scale of rapport*

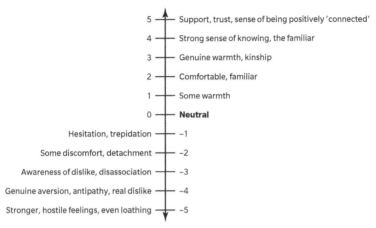

5	Support, trust, sense of being positively 'connected'
4	Strong sense of knowing, the familiar
3	Genuine warmth, kinship
2	Comfortable, familiar
1	Some warmth
0	**Neutral**

Hesitation, trepidation	−1
Some discomfort, detachment	−2
Awareness of dislike, disassociation	−3
Genuine aversion, antipathy, real dislike	−4
Stronger, hostile feelings, even loathing	−5

Note: * Inspired by Genie Z. Laborde

able to relax and open up to them. Categories of sameness can include many different aspects, for example:

- physical appearance/clothes
- body language/physical gestures
- qualities of voice
- language/words used
- beliefs and values.

Let's look at these categories a little more closely.

Physical appearance/clothes

For many of us, physical appearance has a huge effect on rapport. If we generally look similar, in colour, age, height, weight and features, we tend to be more comfortable with each other. If we dress in similar ways – for example generally Western style – again, we have an unconscious tendency to feel we are alike. For example, if a Kalahari bushman walked into a public event wearing only a loincloth and a few beads, feathers, and face paint, he might have little instant rapport with the other people there. Unless, of course, he was with the rest of his tribe in the Kalahari!

Body language/physical gestures

Where two people are shown to have good rapport, they can often have similar or coordinating body language. If seated, they might adopt a similar pose; if one person leans forward, so might the other; if one rests on an elbow, the other might easily follow. It's easy to observe this yourself, simply by finding some people and watching them. Have a go at the exercise below for a little harmless fun.

Ideas into Action

Check out levels of rapport

This is a nice easy one; go anywhere where there are couples or groups of people. Spend some time watching them talk and interact. Notice the 'dance' or interplay between them, how they move together, away from each other, how they stand or position themselves in relationship to each other. Ask yourself the following questions:

Q How do I know whether people are enjoying each other's company by how they move or act?

Q How can I tell whether people are old friends or strangers?

Q What seems to be affecting the way people move or behave?

Rapport isn't always obvious

The more prominent signs of rapport are easy to notice. Postures, gestures, range of movement and the level of energy they have – you'll easily guess which couples or groups have good rapport and which haven't. However, some signs of rapport are more subtle. For example, imagine you're watching two separate couples in a restaurant. The first couple is animated in their conversation, locked in frequent eye contact, using similar gestures and poses. You might guess that this couple has high levels of rapport and comfort with each other.

You then notice a second couple, sitting much more quietly, not talking very much, not looking at each other very much, moving with much less energy and animation. You might decide that they have a low level of rapport, as you interpret their lack of animation to mean coolness. You then see one of them rest a hand lovingly on their partner's and a momentary gaze of real affection pass between them. Then, as if nothing had happened, they return to their meal.

One explanation might be as follows. The first couple is in the first flushes of romance and just getting to know each other. Their energy and animation come from the excitement and anticipation of such a new relationship. Other signs of their rapport include matching facial expressions, movements towards each other – this is a dance of courtship.

The second couple has been happily married for many years; they are completely at ease and are simply a little tired that evening. Their deep comfort with each other is reflected in the similarities of their behaviour. There are signs of a dance; it's simply more of a steady waltz than a spicy tango. I'd also suggest that this second couple has a much richer level of rapport and relatedness than the first, based on a real sense of connection and intimacy.

Qualities of voice

During conversation, the way voices sound, namely our tone of voice, speed of speech and timbre (deep voice, high-pitched, etc.) also offers an indication of rapport. We convey a significant amount of meaning with our voice qualities and you are probably already aware of the impact that your tone, pitch and pace can have in a situation. Even a simple word like 'really!' or 'really?' can have multiple meanings in the way it's spoken.

Like physical postures, the amount by which the voice qualities of two different people match can also illustrate levels of rapport. Perhaps the speed at which they are talking and the amount of energy in their speech might all be similar or resonant.

Where key qualities of voice are not matched, you might notice a lack of rapport. One common mistake we make is to speak slowly and calmly to someone who's very angry and hope it will calm them down. This is 'mismatching' and can sometimes make them worse. Imagine you've stayed at home for the third day running for someone to come and deliver something and again the item has not arrived. After 20 minutes on hold listening to happy pop music, you finally get through to the delivery company's administrator. By now you're feeling really annoyed. You begin to explain the situation (angrily), only to be greeted by slow, warm tones cooing, 'All right, let's just take a moment ... first I'm just going to need a few more details from you . . . then [soothingly] we can get this whole thing sorted for you.'

As a caller, you're quite likely to feel patronised and as though your complaint isn't being taken seriously enough. After all, you're the only one who seems to feel upset by it!

The problem lies in the contrast of the operator's pace, pitch and tone. They would get a better result if they matched your speed of speech and character of voice. By speaking more like you, they could begin to build a sense of acknowledgement and understanding. For example (spoken quickly, with strength and purpose), 'Right, this obviously needs sorting out. I'm going to need a few more details – I want to get this fixed for you quickly.'

As a caller, you are more likely to believe your problem is being treated with a sense of importance, simply because the operator is using similar voice qualities to you. In turn, this is likely to have a calming effect and your own speech may relax. If the operator is skilled, they will continue matching you, and their own voice will become calmer as yours does.

Ideas into Action

Change your voice

Find someone who speaks in one of these ways:

- much more slowly than you
- much more loudly than you
- much more quietly than you
- if you want a 'stretch', you can also do it with someone who speaks much more quickly than you do, but be warned, it can be a challenge to keep up!

The first time you do this, I'd recommend you let the other person know you're doing an exercise without going into detail. Afterwards, you can then find out how it felt for them, how comfortable they felt, etc.

Step one

Have a conversation about something the other person is interested in, perhaps a favourite holiday location, or something that's happening at work. During the conversation, gradually match their manner of speaking more closely. If they speak more slowly, steadily slow down your speech; if they are quiet, speak more quietly. Notice how your focus of attention has to change in order for you to do this. Do this as smoothly as possible. Slight adjustments work better than becoming an exact match of the other person.

Step two

Afterwards, consider the following questions:

Q What did you have to focus on to be able to do this?

Q What effect did your matching seem to have (on you and on the other person)?

Q How did this affect the amount of rapport you felt?

If possible, ask similar questions of the person you were talking to. That way you'll gain a fuller understanding of how you altered the experience of the other person.

When you think you've mastered the technique, use it whenever it seems appropriate for rapport.

Language/words used

The words we use affect rapport in conversation, and we tend to notice their importance only when we get it wrong. For example, here is the initial part of a coaching conversation:

Coach: So, Jim, it's been nearly a month, hasn't it? How have you been?

Jim: Well, okay, I guess. I've kind of been feeling a little low, though, a bit under the weather as they say.

Coach: Ah, sorry to hear you've been miserable, that's not great.

Jim: Oh, I'm not miserable. I just said a little low – it's not that bad!

As coach, you're now in a mild recovery situation early in the session – not a great start! This could have been avoided by repeating the key words the coachee used: 'a little low' or 'under the weather'.

As a more positive example, have you noticed how groups or communities of people often adopt the same words or phrases as each other? We notice this within certain professions or occupations especially. For example:

Phrase	Meaning
'Let's take that offline.'	'Let's discuss that outside this group we're in now.'
'I just don't have the bandwidth for that right now.'	'I'm too busy to do that.'
'Break a leg.'	'I hope it goes well for you.'

Whether you're in tech, finance, the theatre or any other profession, you're likely to have your own words or phrases that help you feel related as a community. If you find yourself on the 'outside' of this kind of language, that is you don't understand it or can't use it – you might feel alienated when other people around you are using it. So, as a coach, you can use this simple principle to 'match' someone's language by using words and phrases from their profession or situation. Alternatively, avoid using jargon or acronyms that may alienate them in conversation, such as words or phrases from the coaching community, but not theirs.

Ideas into Action

Spot word games in your world

Over the next few days, observe other people talking in your work or social life (or simply go somewhere else and eavesdrop!). Listen to conversations, in particular the actual words and catchphrases that are being used. Judge for yourself the amount of rapport between people. Then consider:

Q What types of buzzwords or phrases are being used?

Q How much are these words being copied or repeated by individuals?

Q What effect is this copying having on the conversation?

A fun group to listen into is young adults. So, if you have the chance to listen to teenagers talk to each other, maybe try that (just don't expect to understand everything they say!).

Let's look at the previous coaching dialogue again – as the coach is more careful this time to match the individual's words:

Coach: So, Jim, it's been nearly a month, hasn't it? How have you been?

Jim: Well, okay, I guess. I've kind of been feeling a little low, though, a bit under the weather as they say.

Coach: You've been feeling a little low?

Jim: Yeah, I don't know if it's about anything specific, although to be fair I haven't really thought about it properly. There's something nagging me about it, though.

Coach: Okay, so if it's nagging at you, might it be useful to think more about it now?

You'll notice that the coach matches Jim's words in subtle ways, rather than copying exactly what he's said. This is because it's more effective to reflect key words or phrases, as gentle acknowledgement that the coach is listening and maintaining an appropriate focus.

At a Glance

Watch my feelings!

It is okay to mirror positive feeling words

Sometimes, we need to acknowledge someone's feelings as a way of empathising with them, or to demonstrate we understand what they have said. Here, it usually works best to use the exact words or phrase they use. For example, if they say they're really optimistic, say, 'It's great that you're really optimistic,' (not 'It's awesome that you're so buoyant'). If they say they're worn out, use the words 'worn out' (not 'fatigued' or 'dog-tired').

Avoid embedding negative feelings

Sometimes, however, you might want to reduce the significance of someone's feelings during conversation. Maybe you want to make them feel a little better about what they felt or help them stay more centred or resourceful. In these situations, use a diluted or reduced version of their word. For example, they might say, 'I'm scared rigid of making presentations,' and you don't want to get 'stuck' in that feeling. So, when you refer to these feelings, substitute the term 'scared rigid' for something more neutral like 'apprehensive' or 'uncomfortable': for example 'So might it help to look at ways you can reduce the discomfort here?' Notice also how using the phrase 'the discomfort' is less embedded than 'your discomfort' as there's a natural disassociation with the term.

Beliefs and values

What we believe to be true about our world and ourselves can separate people or bring them together. For example, watch a passionate meat eater debate with a vegan about their eating habits and you'll see and hear how beliefs can divide us! When we feel someone thinks like us, we are more inclined to like and trust them. For example, we tend to buy products and services from people we like and not from those we don't like. This is why an effective salesperson works to find common ground with their customer and often invests time to understand more about them, what they do, what they like and what they don't like. By agreeing with someone on topics upon which they appear to have strong views, such as the importance of a good education (or the irrelevance of one), we can build rapport based on their implied like-mindedness.

Balance awareness with integrity

In coaching, it's important to be aware of this potential influence and also to retain our own integrity. Pretending to agree with someone's belief about something (when you don't) lacks integrity. Most often and on most topics, I try to adopt a neutral posture, so literally not expressing a view. As a coach, we are not working to create influence by getting people to think more like us; instead, we are helping people to think more effectively by themselves. Remember, in conversation, focus primarily on what the other person thinks and believes, not what you think and believe.

> **As a coach, we are not working to create influence by getting people to think more like us; instead, we are helping people to think more effectively by themselves**

When to increase rapport

As well as knowing how we develop rapport, we should also know *when* to work at improving it. One point where you might work to build rapport is during the initial stages of the coaching assignment. At this point, the person you're working with may need to feel more comfortable before they can trust you and open up to the process of coaching. The other obvious place where you must make sure you build good rapport is at the start of each coaching conversation. No matter how warm or open your previous conversations have been, the time and distance between sessions create the need to reaffirm the coaching relationship.

Increase rapport through simple matching

One way to increase rapport is known as matching. This literally means being the same in some way as the person you want to build rapport with. In a coaching environment, simple ways of building rapport include matching posture, voice quality, speed of speech, physical gestures, etc.

When you are coaching and decide that rapport isn't as good as it needs to be, first look for mismatches or differences between you and the other person. Do a quick check on physical posture, voice qualities, amounts of energy you're both displaying – what are you doing that's different? A good place to begin is to subtly match physical posture, as this has multiple benefits, namely:

- It helps you to begin to focus more on the individual – to think more about what's happening with them and less about what's happening with you.
- It often improves rapport quite naturally.
- Once you begin to attune to the individual in this way, your concentration will increase or shift, so that at some level you might notice other behaviours by the coachee. With this heightened concentration, you will pick up or read other signals that previously you might have missed.

Your goal is resonance

To match effectively, do so gradually so that the other person is less likely to notice it and be made uncomfortable by it. For example, if your gestures are more animated than the other person's, calm yourself down a little. If you're speaking much more quickly than they are, gently decrease your pace. Make your movements resonant, not identical; to match someone who is leaning forward, incline your body slightly towards them. If someone is continually smoothing their eyebrow, touch your hand to your forehead. If they continually clasp or wring their hands, then occasionally bring yours together. This might sound strange, but it works!

When does matching become mismatching?

Be careful not to overdo it. That is, don't match someone so obviously, or to such a level of detail, that instead of building rapport you alienate them. Imagine having someone 'mirror' your every movement and gesture in exact detail. Instead of helping you feel more comfortable, you'd feel exactly the opposite.

The question of eye contact

Looking directly into someone's eyes and maintaining constant eye contact is unlikely to increase rapport. Most people do not like to be stared or gazed at, and some may even find it threatening. So, when judging how much eye contact is appropriate with someone, work at adopting an amount that is similar to their own. If the other person appears to make lots of eye contact with you, they will be comfortable with you doing the same. If they look at you less frequently, then they are likely to respond to a similar level of eye contact.

When to decrease rapport

There are times when it is entirely appropriate to decrease rapport or the levels of relationship during a coaching conversation. For example, when you want to close a discussion down, draw an end to the session and start to summarise the key points and agree on actions.

There are also inappropriate levels of rapport for a coaching relationship. Should too much familiarity or warmth occur between you and your coachee, the relationship can become one of friendship (and potentially collusion). Effective coaching is a purposeful arrangement between two people. So, as a coach, you must always be able to adopt a challenging posture in a conversation and too much rapport may create a reluctance to do this.

> **Effective coaching is a purposeful arrangement between two people**

When deciding to decrease rapport, the same principles apply as for increasing rapport, although often in reverse. For example, the session time is coming to an end and you need to summarise and complete the conversation. The person you are coaching continues to talk and appears unaware of the need to bring the topic to a close. First, notice where you are directly matching the other person and then begin to mismatch. Again, check your posture and then adopt one that is different (lean back, lean forward, etc.). Or, if their voice quality is relaxed and steady, put a little more energy back into yours.

If you've had good rapport, you may notice that they begin to match you: for example sit up straighter, begin to nod, etc. Normally, they will also become more aware of a closing conversation. Where you have done this subtly, and have had previously good rapport, this will normally be experienced as a polite gesture.

Ideas into Action

Increase and decrease rapport

This is a simple, basic technique to demonstrate our ability to increase and decrease rapport. It works by increasing or reducing a physical sense of 'sameness'. It's okay to play a little or have fun with this; you don't need to be hugely serious or professional in any way. To do it, you'll first need a willing partner and somewhere to have a conversation where you won't be distracted by your environment. A noisy bar or café can work as well as a quiet place – it's simply about you being able to relax and focus on what you're doing. Tell your partner you want to do a conversational exercise, but don't go into any detail.

Step one – talk and observe

Ask your partner to pick a topic they would enjoy talking about for a while, such as a favourite holiday or pastime. Begin the conversation, ask your partner questions, get them talking. Notice their physical posture and gestures as they speak.

Step two – increase rapport by matching

Continue the conversation and begin subtly to match their posture and gestures. If they are leaning forward, lean in; if they're moving a lot, increase your own level of movement. Continue doing this until you are comfortable that you're matching well, for example two to three minutes.

Step three – decrease rapport by mismatching

Now, as you continue talking, start to deliberately mismatch what they're doing. Fold your arms, turn or look away – be really different. Do this until you're sure it's had an effect – or until you can't carry on for laughing (it's not easy and they'll know you're doing it!).

Step four – talk about what happened

Explain to your partner the three-step process, and then ask them:

Q Did they notice when you started matching them?

Q What effect did matching them have?

Q What effect did mismatching them have?

The optional 'stretch'

If the exercise seems too easy, then match and mismatch on any (or all) of the following:

- their breathing
- their voice qualities – pitch, pace, tone, etc.
- the key words or phrases they use often.

Diversity, inclusion and unconscious bias

Within our workplace, when we use the term diversity, we refer to the unique differences within our communities. Those differences include gender, race, nationality, sexual orientation, character, religion, plus a mass of other ways we can point at differences. In the same context, when we use the term inclusion, we refer to the embracing of those differences, to enrich the whole community. As if we realise that, by valuing all differences present, we harness the true potential of those distinctions when they are gathered in one place. It's a little like saying that, if we want to build a retail shopping centre, we will benefit by listening to those people who dislike retail shopping centres with a passion, as well as people who totally love them. Inclusion acknowledges the principle that 'the whole is greater than the sum of its parts'.

Unconscious bias means that I instinctively attribute beliefs or characteristics to specific people, groups or even situations. For example, I think all people who are tall and appear to be physically strong must also feel confident. Or that people who are apparently homeless, for example live on the streets, are always victims of circumstance, whereas some will tell you that they chose to live this way because they prefer it. Unconscious bias is not automatically negative, but it can become so, for example we don't act sensitively to all people (just some people) or we forget to treat them as individuals with a unique set of preferences and needs.

Sameness, difference and unconscious bias

When we consider the topic of rapport within the topic of unconscious bias, it becomes a potentially tricky topic. For example, how does our unconscious bias impact our ability to develop good rapport with each other? Fortunately, the following principle of using our intention to drive our attention offers a way to solve the dilemma over time.

Combine intention with attention

One of the best ways to build rapport with someone is through your intention. Your intention during a conversation can have a tangible impact on the sense of relatedness you build with the other person. By 'intention' I mean your sense of purpose in a situation. This also counteracts unhelpful/ unconscious bias, as our intention naturally shifts our attention or focus. One way of doing that is to ask yourself a question to realign that focus. For example, during a conversation, you might

> **One of the best ways to build rapport with someone is through your intention**

want to increase your attention on features of sameness to increase the rapport between you and the other person. Do this by focusing on a simple thought, such as, 'How can I relate to you more closely?' or 'How are we the same?'

As you leave the question suspended in your thoughts, you will gradually surface insight. Maybe you will realise that you're staring too intently, or you're talking too much, or not enough. Quite often, your sense of rapport seems to increase naturally, as if by intending to increase relatedness you have done just that.

We have an innate ability to direct or concentrate our thoughts to create a specific outcome and asking ourselves positive questions can help us do this. Use the following exercise to try this idea for yourself.

> **We have an innate ability to direct or concentrate our thoughts to create a specific outcome**

Ideas into Action

Strengthen your intention

When we focus our minds using our intention, our thoughts can marshal themselves to show us the way forward. To explore this, go and have a conversation with someone you know quite well, but not very well. If you choose someone who you'd like better rapport with, that might work even better.

During the conversation, maintain an intention to have great rapport with the other person. Find a word or phrase that reminds you of your intention, such as 'I'm being warm and open' or 'we're in relationship' or just one word such as 'sameness' (whatever works for you). During the conversation, return to the thought or phrase regularly. Remember that you also want to be able to have a conversation; if the thought begins to act as a distraction, then forget it – let it go.

After the conversation, ask yourself:

Q What was the rapport like within the conversation?

Q How does your intention appear to affect your rapport?

Q How could you use this idea of intention in the future?

Develop the coaching relationship over time

Studies show that the quality of a coaching relationship has a direct impact on the effectiveness and results in that relationship.

> 'Client perception of the relationship may be the key active ingredient in coaching effectiveness.'
>
> **Erik de Haan, Ashridge Centre for Coaching[1]**

The duration of your relationship might be just one coaching session, or it could last for many months or longer. So, as well as being able to build initial rapport with someone, you also need to develop relationships over time. To enable this, we must consciously focus on the productive qualities within a positive relationship and build on them. To help you consider these key elements of the relationship further, I'm going to focus on factors of integrity, openness and trust.

Relationship factor: build upon a foundation of integrity

Acting with integrity involves us keeping our word. As a coach, what we say must match what we do. If you say you are going to call your coachee, then call them. If you say you are going to mail them some information by Friday, then mail it by Friday. As in life, this simple alignment of words and actions is very powerful within a coaching relationship. For example, when you keep your commitments to them, your coachee is more likely to trust and respect you and, over time, your relationship will benefit. This can also have a positive influence on a coachee's own behaviour. By setting high standards of personal behaviour, you become an example to the coachee of what works and what doesn't. The consistency of your behaviour forms a further support to the coaching conversations.

> **As a coach, what we say must match what we do**

As a coach, if you have not kept a commitment, then do whatever is appropriate to redress the situation. For example, if you didn't send information as promised, it's appropriate to acknowledge that (or apologise) and send the information if it is still needed. If you didn't call, then be open about that – apologise and do whatever is needed to make up for the call that didn't happen. Sometimes, it's appropriate to explain why a commitment hasn't been kept. Maybe you're late because your car broke down. However, don't over-explain your reasons, as explanations can become excuses that help us to avoid responsibility for our actions. For example, we use the excuse of heavy traffic for being late. A more responsible perspective is that we're late because we just didn't leave the house early enough!

> **Explanations can become excuses that help us to avoid responsibility for our actions**

The following guidelines help us keep commitments:

- Make commitments wisely: can I keep this commitment? Is this a good/reasonable commitment to make?

- Make commitments important: record them and check your list of commitments regularly.

- Deal with the consequences of any commitments you haven't kept – for example apologise, make amends if possible (this also encourages us to keep them in the first place).

If you are doubtful about whether or not you can keep a commitment, don't make it. Or simply make an adapted version of the commitment: for example, 'I'll post you the information on Friday if I get some free time, otherwise it will be either Monday or Tuesday of next week.' By building in an extension to the deadline, you increase your chances of meeting it.

Pause and Reflect

Are you keeping commitments?

Use the following questions to reflect on the current value of your promise in a situation. If you can't answer them, then use them to monitor your behaviour over the next few days, or even weeks.

Q How readily do you make commitments or promises to do things, for example saying, 'I'll do that/send that by . . . ' or 'I'll call you'? This includes doing things for yourself, such as 'I'm going to book that appointment this week.'

Q How many of your promises or commitments do you keep exactly as voiced, for example by the deadline you gave?

Q If you don't keep a commitment, what do you do: ignore the fact, or give excuses to avoid responsibility or put something right?

When you have some answers to the above, consider the following question:

Q Which of our integrity principles could you use to improve your performance in this area?

- Make commitments wisely – Can I keep this commitment? Is this a good/reasonable commitment to make?

▶

> - Make commitments important: record them, develop your own system or routine for completing them.
> - Deal with the consequences of any commitments not kept, for example apologise, make amends, if possible.

Relationship factor: openness and trust

A successful coaching relationship is built on a foundation of openness and trust between the coach and the coachee. As a coach, you encourage this by being open with your coachee and demonstrating that you are someone they can trust. The following are all ways you might do this:

- Keep your commitments.
- Act consistently in the coachee's best interests: stay focused on their goals and make their needs a priority during your conversations with them.
- Keep any confidences between you and the coachee.
- Mention trivial personal facts and details occasionally, such as your family, personal plans, a holiday, etc.
- Occasionally, share your own thoughts and feelings, for example about events outside coaching.
- Speak your own truth consistently: 'Here's what's true for me about that.'
- Support the coachee in conversation outside the coaching sessions (don't say anything about the coachee that you wouldn't want them to hear afterwards).

Skill two – focused levels of listening

The art of listening is generally misunderstood as a behaviour and underrated as a skill (we should teach it in schools). Good listeners obtain a better understanding of people and situations, meaning they can respond to situations more effectively than someone who hasn't listened. A good listener contributes to the speaker they are focused on, simply by the attention they place on them. In coaching, when you are listening to someone effectively, they are able to relax, express their ideas more clearly and generally feel understood.

> **A good listener contributes to the speaker they are focused on, simply by the attention they place on them**

Figure 4.4 Different levels of listening

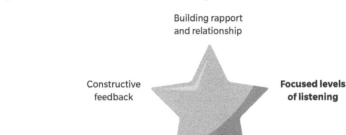

It's almost as though we grow larger in the conversation, simply because of the quality of the other person's listening.

So, in coaching conversations, the consequences of poor listening are important. As a coach, when you are not listening effectively you create an inability to understand your coachee and their situation. You also lose a sense of focused attention on your coachee, which is where much of the power and potential of the conversation arises. When any coach is unable to listen effectively over the duration of a coaching conversation, over time this becomes a real barrier to their success.

Selfless listening – beyond self

The phrase 'a problem shared is a problem halved' relates to the beneficial effects we experience when another person listens effectively to our concerns. Somehow, in the telling and the listening, a problem shared diminishes in size or significance for its owner. In this way, listening is a gift we can give others. As the listener, it is a gift because it requires your effort to put aside your own self for a while and focus entirely on someone else. In most conversations, this is not natural for us, as we place more of our focus on ourselves, our own thoughts and feelings, etc.

As a coach, regardless of what has happened before the coaching session, you must put personal thoughts or events aside and focus on the person you are coaching. Most people don't find this easy because of the attention it demands of us over time. Our minds tend to wander and become distracted and it is this tendency we must learn to reduce. However, with strong intention and practice, focused listening is a muscle that you develop over time.

Focused listening impacts on your effective influence

Listening to someone is a way to increase your ability to influence and yet, strangely, we often forget that. Instead, when we try to influence someone else, we tend to talk a lot. When we do most of the talking, we diminish our ability to draw information from other people. We also reduce the space and time available for us to process information and respond to it. When we stay longer in a mode of listening and appreciate what the other person is saying, or their point of view, we often gain relevant information and insight that benefits us.

For example, imagine you've asked a friend to go on holiday with you, but they still haven't given you a proper answer and are delaying committing to that. So, you spend a long time telling them how great the location, the facilities and the weather conditions are, before realising that they still don't appear convinced. When you spend time listening to what their objections to the holiday really are and what they really want, you are in a much better position to influence or accommodate their thinking. Or, more simply, to accept that there's no way they are going to say yes to the trip and you're wasting your energy trying to persuade them!

Listening within coaching

As a result of their listening, a good coach can go beyond what is actually said and begin to notice what is unsaid. This is not magical; it is simply that most of us are not fully listening most of the time. So, as a coach, you need to be able to sustain your listening in a more focused and effective manner than is typical in normal conversation.

> **Most of us are not fully listening most of the time**

For example, your coachee might explain how they are very excited about a forthcoming job move, saying it's good for them right now to be moving in a certain direction, and it's good timing, the smart thing to do, etc. However, in your listening, you might gain a sense of something else not being said that contradicts what your coachee is saying. Perhaps you hear a change in the person's tone of voice, or something about their words that doesn't quite ring true. In your active atunement, you can pick up on subtleties that can easily be missed by casual attention or listening.

You are then able to voice what you've noticed and check any reservations or anxieties about the job move. When we can deal with both what is spoken and unspoken, the conversation has much more depth for both speaker and listener.

What do we mean by levels of listening?

There are several different kinds or states of listening, although mostly we discuss the topic as though there were only one. We ask, 'Are you listening?' and expect the answer to be 'Yes', or 'No', as if there is a listening switch that we can turn on or off. Perhaps a more accurate response would be 'Sort of . . . ' or 'Yes, but just to your words,' or 'Totally! – with my mind *and* my body!' The quality of our listening changes with the amount of focused effort we direct towards what (or who) we are listening to. After all, if you are only half-listening, doesn't that take a lot less directed effort than listening intently?

Figure 4.5 shows different forms of listening as though they were levels. As our level of listening deepens, so does our focus and attention on the person we are listening to. Let's look in more detail at some of the ways that we listen to people.

Cosmetic listening

This you would probably recognise as 'pretending to listen'. That is, you're looking at someone and you might be nodding and adding listening noises such as 'Hmmm' or 'Yes' or 'That's interesting'. The other person may be unaware of your half-listening and may continue to speak; alternatively, they may have the sense of that which affects their own attention or mood.

In normal conversation, our thoughts are often elsewhere. During discussion, we might think about something different from what the other person is saying, or muse on thoughts or ideas prompted by what's being said. Occasionally, you

Figure 4.5 Levels of listening

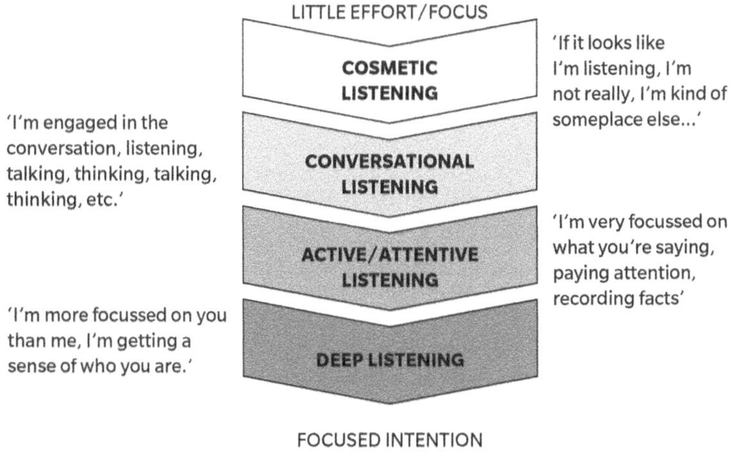

might miss something that the person has said, and lose track of the conversation, perhaps saying, 'Sorry, I missed that – what did you just say?' In some cases, we even intentionally tune out what someone is saying (as our own thoughts feel more important).

Circumstances and your intention for a conversation will determine whether you are using an appropriate level of listening. For example, when listening to a child's chatter, telling stories, or reliving events, cosmetic listening is sometimes okay and works for both you and the child. However, as you know, it can be great to really listen to children tell their stories as we are able to step into another, more playful world. It's also a great way to demonstrate your care for a child: when you listen to them properly, they will feel valued by you, which helps build their self-esteem.

And, if that makes you feel like a better parent/person, then it's probably good for yours too!

Superficial listening may also be appropriate when you sense that the other person isn't actually talking to you – they're just enjoying talking, letting off steam perhaps, and require little input from you. Of course, remember to check back into the conversation occasionally, just in case you've been missed!

This type of listening does not work in coaching, where your objectives for the conversation rely on you gathering information and understanding. However, most coaches occasionally drift off into their own thoughts and it's difficult to avoid. If it happens to us as a coach and we miss a key point of information, I recommend we are as open as possible: for example, 'I'm sorry, I'm still thinking about your ideas for the new job – can you repeat that last thought?'

By declaring that you lost your attention or focused listening, you reaffirm your commitment to listen. So, the person speaking knows that your primary effort is upon them and what they are saying. Since most people would acknowledge that they can lose track in conversation themselves, it's something that's normally easily excused.

Conversational listening

Conversational listening is the kind of listening that we do most of the time. In casual discussion, we listen, think, talk, listen, think, talk and so on. Our focus is on the other person, what they're saying and also on what we're saying, or thinking of saying. The balance between talking, listening and internally processing information varies from person to person. This balance relates to several factors, including our basic personality type, the nature of the conversation, how we are feeling, etc. Some people talk much more than they listen, some people prefer to speak less and listen more, and some appear to have an even balance of both.

Again, your intention during the conversation affects your listening. A police officer gathering facts at the scene of a road traffic accident is more likely to listen, register and internally process information before asking more questions or summarising to check facts. A person giving a

> **Your intention during the conversation affects your listening**

tourist some local directions is likely to be doing more of the talking and much less listening or processing of information.

For most of us, conversational listening is a natural activity. It requires little effort, is present in most of our normal daily conversations and can be tremendous fun and even energising. Coaching conversations are not the same as these day-to-day conversations, however, simply because of their purpose. Within coaching, we must develop a deeper, more focused state of listening.

Ideas into Action

Increase your self-awareness

To improve your ability in this area, you must first raise your self-awareness to create useful insight. So, you need to become more conscious of how you typically listen. Today, as you go about your day, use your conversations to consider the following:

Q How often do you pretend to listen to someone – and don't really listen?

Q How is your listening different within different circumstances, or with different people?

Q What effect does the quality of your listening seem to have on other people or the conversation?

Active listening

As an effective coach, you must maintain an ability to operate consistently at the level of active listening. As the name suggests, this requires us to listen in an active way; to acknowledge what is being said, restate messages, check our understanding, etc. When you are actively listening, the following is generally true:

• You have the intention of staying focused on what the other person is saying, to understand fully what they are saying.

• You are using more effort to listen and process information than to speak yourself.

- You are mentally registering and recording facts so you can potentially use them later (you might also take notes).

- You regularly confirm that you are still listening, by making appropriate sounds, gestures or expressions.

- You actively seek to understand what the speaker is telling you, by using clarifying questions, repeating or summarising information back to them or perhaps making observations or offering conclusions.

Here's how a conversation might sound where someone is actively listening:

Speaker: So, the whole interview with the conference and events start-up turned into a bit of a nightmare. I ended up wondering why the heck they'd invited me in the first place.

Listener: Really – why, what happened?

Speaker: Well, first, they kept me sat in reception for ages, so it was three o'clock in the afternoon before I got into the interview. My appointment was for two.

Listener: An hour late?

Speaker: Exactly! Anyway, then I got in and I'm greeted by someone from sales and some guy from the tech team – which was kind of strange. The least they could have done would have been to have someone in there relevant to the position they were hiring.

Listener: What was the position?

Speaker: Client development – not the sort of job that you'd think those two would be interested in. They started asking me about what type of events I'd run in the past, and how much I'd used video conferencing! Apparently, they were planning some new sort of offer in the marketplace. Then the sales guy starts getting interested in how I used the client data over time and the tech guy wanted to know about virtual delivery – they just kept going off at tangents.

Listener: Right – so how did you handle the conversation?

Speaker: Well, I just kept trying to focus on the importance of knowing your customer and staying aware of the overall costs of doing business, it really can build up.

Listener: Hmm – so what's happened since?

Speaker: Nothing, not a thing, no phone call, no email – nothing!

You will notice from the dialogue that the listener is focusing very much on understanding what's happened. The listener is gathering facts, filling in gaps, working to get a fuller picture of events. The listener is not spending large amounts of energy giving their own thoughts and views, not telling stories of interviews that they have had and not offering opinions or ideas. These behaviours would fit more into the scope of 'conversational listening' described earlier.

The listener is also following a logical time sequence, asking about actions or events in the order they would have happened. For example, the question 'What's happened since?' comes at the end of the conversation not the beginning. This enables the speaker to recollect information in a way that feels more natural to them.

Deep listening

This last category of listening is unlike any other, in that it goes beyond what it is logically possible to achieve by listening to someone. I have heard people describe good coaches as 'almost telepathic' because of their ability to listen to and understand another person from insights into what they have said, and even what they have *not* said. Let me be clear – coaches are not telepathic. But there is a highly perceptive level of understanding and insight that becomes available when you are in a state of deep listening.

> **There is a highly perceptive level of understanding and insight that becomes available when you are in a state of deep listening**

When a coach can achieve this quality of listening, they can experience the other person with a sense of who they are, as well as what they're saying. I can only describe this type of listening as a slightly altered state, where:

- you are totally lucid and present to the person speaking
- your awareness is entirely focused on the other person
- your mind is mostly quiet and calm
- you have a reduced sense or awareness of yourself
- you hold a sense of intention, which helps to clarify (hone) your state of listening, such as, 'I want to understand you/this,' or 'What's really going on here?'

This state of listening feels almost elusive in nature in that, once you realise you have it and are in it, the thought registers and it's gone again! As you listen, occasional thoughts or insights might pass through your mind and then you return your attention to the person in front of you. This heightened state of listening has similar characteristics to some forms of meditation, in that the listener's mind is essentially quiet and has an attention that is directed and focused.

Shift your attention

When we listen in this way, we move away from having attention on ourselves (our own thoughts and feelings) and instead focus on the other person. In terms of your ability to relate to the other person (what they are thinking and feeling about a situation), the quality of the information you receive is significant. For the person being listened to, as they speak, they are more likely to feel understood and perhaps experience a deeper sense of relatedness to you. In this way, deep listening becomes another method of building rapport.

Learn to listen with your body

Experienced coaches learn to use their bodies as well as their minds to listen to someone. So, they notice feelings or sensations and use those in order to inform their responses and approach. We notice this as a simple thing, such as a sense of wariness or a feeling of discomfort, which may even be physical, such as in our stomach or shoulders. While sometimes discomfort is appropriate and nothing to act upon, at other times signals from your body will further inform your listening and therefore the direction you take in a conversation. For example, maybe you have the feeling that the conversation seems a little shallow, or lacking in substance, and you might describe the signal of that as a tension across your chest. You decide to pause the conversation and check the thought: for example, 'Can I just check, is this a useful topic for you to be focused on right now? I want to make sure we're targeting your objectives for the session.'

> **Experienced coaches learn to use their bodies as well as their minds to listen to someone**

One of the best ways to increase your attention in this area is to practise staying present – to yourself, your situation, and the person you are with. That way, you will notice these body signals and communication more often. The exercise that follows will develop your ability to maintain present-moment awareness more often. If you know you tend to live in your mind, it's a good way of grounding you back into reality. It's also a way of reducing stress by learning to refocus on what's happening now, rather than your thoughts about what just happened, or might happen.

Ideas into Action

Practise present-moment awareness

Use this exercise anywhere and everywhere to practise being present. If you drive, try to practise in the car. Switch your music off, feel your hands on the wheel and begin the following sequence.

First, notice your surroundings. Focus on what's around you in more detail; shift your attention to that. What can you see around you? Look at things afresh, notice some detail, register where you are and what's happening (or not happening). Ask yourself, 'Where am I now?' to shift your lucid awareness.

Next, notice your body. How does your body feel its current position and posture? Alter that, if you want to, accept how your body wants to align itself to your surroundings. Notice how your body feels, scanning your torso, your head and your neck. Perhaps move a little more and get a stronger sense of being in your body.

Now, notice your mind. Acknowledge what's going on with it but do not analyse it. Knowing those thoughts are not needed right now, refocus on being in your body, in the environment you're in right now. Clear your mind by focusing on what's happening now. If any thoughts drift in, simply notice them and refocus on what's happening now.

Once you have gained a sense of what it's like to stay present, you should develop your ability to do that for longer periods. Practise the above exercise regularly and in different situations. Your ability to listen effectively during coaching conversations will increase directly as a result. Additional benefits for you will include improved mental clarity and stress reduction (tempting, surely?).

Combine your attention with your intention

During deep listening, staying present to the other person is an incomplete picture of what's actually happening. Also required is an intention that drives your attention towards the person you are listening to. We combine attention with intention to produce a deeper state of listening. In my experience, during coaching, this intention is often one of service – perhaps seeking to understand, seeking to help or provide support, something that contributes towards the individual and their objectives.

> **Combine attention with intention to produce a deeper state of listening**

It is neither possible nor desirable to stay in continual deep listening for extended periods of time. It is not possible because the coach cannot only listen; they must also make observations, ask questions and generally stay in the conversation. Plus, like meditation, it's a challenge to maintain a quiet state of mind. Long periods of deep listening are also not desirable, because the coaching process demands that you are more than a passive observer. As a coach, you must engage in dialogue to facilitate the other person's thinking. Your speaking, questioning, acknowledgements and physical gestures are all essential to this process.

Develop deeper listening

Deep listening challenges us in a different way from a lot of other activities, possibly because working harder can work against us. If you are seriously committed to the field of coaching then I recommend that you actively develop your ability to listen in this way.[2] Useful practice includes meditation, yoga, breathwork and mindfulness, because of the nature and strength of the attention (focus) you will develop.

Skill three – use of intuition

Intuition – within coaching

Watch any skilled coach and you will notice that they often seem to know the best direction to take a conversation, to gain relevant information or insight. As a skilled coach, sometimes you will spot what is missing from the conversation and become curious about that. You might then ask a question or offer an observation that shifts the conversation for the better. From one simple remark or phrase, you might unlock an issue for someone or cast fresh light on a situation. This is one of the distinguishing characteristics of a great coach, and one that makes the coaching role so valuable. The way we explain this behaviour is to call it intuition.

Intuition is an ability we all have, and one we can develop into a skill. For a coach, it becomes something they rely upon, to help shape and guide a coaching conversation. The following dialogue illustrates apparent intuition:

Coach: So, what is it about interviews that you don't like?

Coachee: Well, everything. I mean, the whole situation doesn't suit me. I get in there and everything seems to start going wrong.

Coach: Perhaps say a little more about that . . .

Figure 4.6 Using intuition

Building rapport
and relationship

Constructive
feedback

Focused levels
of listening

Asking effective
questions

**Use of
intuition**

BELIEFS WE OPERATE FROM

Coachee: Well, it's probably the questions; I know what I want to say, it's just that my answers don't seem to flow in the right direction. I end up talking too much about stuff that's irrelevant; I sound stupid. When I get out of there, I realise I could have done so much better.

Coach: You know, I keep wondering – who might you be proving right here?

Coachee: I don't understand what you mean.

Coach: Well, who might expect you to behave like this at interviews?

Coachee: Aaah, that's easy, my Dad, I guess. He'd say I just couldn't cut it under pressure. 'You're just not good under a spotlight,' he used to say. My sister was always so much better at this sort of thing; I guess I kind of live in her shadow a little.

You will see from the dialogue that there are several different directions the coach could have taken, many of which might seem more logical. What happened is that during the conversation the coach began to have thoughts and/or feelings that there was someone else involved in this issue. The coach also sensed something that felt like a sense of burden or resignation from the coachee. 'Who might you be proving right here?' is not a stock question for a coach. The question simply came to the coach as a thought and they went with that thought and asked the question.

Intuition – wisdom in action

Intuition is simply an access to our brain's potential to provide guidance and information free from the confines of our limited conscious mind. Through intuition, we can access vast stores of experience, knowledge and wisdom in a way that sometimes defies logic. Intuition is a way our unconscious mind has of communicating with our conscious mind and uses subtle means such as thoughts, feelings, sensations, imagery, sounds – or various combinations of those.

Intuition is a function of both our brain and our body – think of how we talk about 'gut instinct', or 'having a feeling about something'. Intuition potentially involves any part of our body, as it attempts to guide and direct our thoughts. Research arising within the field of neuroscience suggests that our stomachs contain a processing ability from a network of neurons that justify the name 'second brain' or 'little brain'. So, it's a potentially productive area to explore for yourself, by developing clearer access to your own 'gut feeling'.

In the earlier example, the options for the next question were far too many for the coach to consider, assess and decide upon. Rational, practical thought would probably have explored techniques of great interview skills, preparing and rehearsing answers, investigating the interviewers beforehand, etc.

Even if the coach decided to analyse how the individual might be stopping themselves from doing well during interviews, it would have taken a lot longer to arrive logically at the insight about the coachee's father. Instead, the coach trusted a sense that someone was 'being proved right'. During coaching, this sometimes causes a coach to risk asking a foolish question, or receiving an uncomfortable response, such as, 'I don't understand what you mean.' However, if our coach stays with their intuition, they will continue until their curiosity is satisfied.

Communicating non-verbally

Intuition incorporates the brain's ability to understand communication from situations or people by going beyond the more obvious signals we logically respond to. Typically, we respond to someone's language, tone, posture, obvious facial expressions, etc. In the same situation, there are also forms of communication that our conscious minds don't register, like someone's rate of breathing, or slight colour changes and micro muscle movements in their face. It's a bit like super high-pitched dog whistles – we're simply not tuned into them. Our unconscious mind, however, can gather, assess and interpret more and different kinds of information.

Sometimes, we communicate without language. For example, after walking into a room where two people have obviously been arguing, we might say, 'There was a real atmosphere,' or 'You could cut the air with a knife.' We mean that we have picked up signals or communication from within the room which suggests that an argument has just taken place. If we were to try to explain exactly what signals we got that caused us to decide this, we couldn't always give a complete answer. Maybe the two people were sitting quietly, maybe they weren't actually looking at each other – but does that totally explain the atmosphere in the room?

The overall capacity of our brain is a lot smarter than our conscious awareness. For example, while we struggle to compare more than three thoughts at a time, our brain's background processing can handle that easily. I hear stories of doctors or emergency workers who need to – and can – assess a situation much more quickly and accurately than the conscious mind can. They often can't say exactly what led them to an almost instant certainty of what the person's priority issue was and what to do about it. Clearly, the brain is operating in a way we aren't aware of or tapping into something beyond our conscious in order to gain access to and compare information.

Intuition is a practical reality

There's nothing mystical or spooky about intuition; it's something that we all use, regularly and practically. You might use it to choose the perfect present for someone, avoid scheduling something in your diary because you have a feeling something else might crop up, or know when someone is not telling the truth. Intuition simply builds on what you already know – knowledge you already have that is communicated to you via thoughts, feelings, images or sounds.

How do we develop intuition?

Within coaching, I'm aware that your trust in your own inner wisdom is something you must prove alone. Improving access to, and using, intuition takes practice, and it helps to acknowledge how you already use it. Consider for a moment how many decisions or choices you currently make with minimal rational thought. What happens with you before you do? Call it instinct, call it a gut feeling – you already have it. How do you know when you've left the house and forgotten something? How do you know when someone is telling the truth or not?

> **How do you know when someone is telling the truth or not?**

Because intuition speaks to us using subtle signals, imagery, feelings, sensations, thoughts, sounds, etc., we have to learn to become more receptive to this form of communication. Once you have an awareness of the forms of language your subconscious is using, practise tuning in. To tune in, you need to work to create a state of mind, body, breathing, etc. that enables you to hear, feel or imagine the messages arising from your subconscious. However, if you are feeling nervous, angry, or excited, or your mind is simply full of other thoughts, you are unlikely to be able to open up this channel for communication. Your strongest signals from intuition will come when you're feeling calm or relaxed.

Ideas into Action

Use your intuition

Choose or plan your next meal according to what your intuition is telling you. If you are in a restaurant, read down the menu of options and ask yourself, 'What's the best choice I could make here?' Relax into the question to make sure you can hear, feel or see the response. When you are relaxed, your breathing will typically be a little slower and deeper and you will tend to breathe from your stomach or mid-section.

Focus on one food option, imagine eating it and then check how your body feels, or what other images come to mind. Then go through the same process with a second option and see how that compares to the first. When you've imagined two or three options, use your comparisons to choose which one your intuition appears to be suggesting is the one your body would choose if it could. Of course, you can always override your intuition – and, yet, it's still good to be aware that you have done that.

Choosing food in this way can be a good strategy for anyone wanting to eat more healthily or lose weight. Maintaining a relaxed state gives you better access to your body wisdom. When your decisions are based on this wisdom, you'll often find yourself choosing something that is a positive choice for you and your body. Be warned, you may end up eating something unexpected!

The subtle nature of intuition

Intuition is not infallible; it is simply another source of thoughts and ideas. Because it is a subtle channel of information, it is easily interrupted, or drowned out, by the thoughts already going on in our conscious minds. It's a little like tuning in a radio to a particular station. If you hit two at the same time, the louder one is the one we tend to focus on.

The pitfall of intuition

Intuition also gets things wrong or eludes us when we would like it to appear. For example, I don't seem to be able to pick winning horses at a racecourse using intuition (and, yes, I have tried). Now I don't know if that's because my intuition is failing me, or I'm not using an appropriate intention, or that my attachment to winning distorts my access to wisdom in that setting. What's probably more relevant is that I don't have any knowledge, experience or skill for picking successful horses.

In other words, my subconscious mind has little information or experience with which to work. Which is probably why a trip to the races usually feels expensive!

However, I am confident of my ability to use intuition within a coaching environment because I do have experience and practised skills in this area. The same is true for many individuals specialising within a particular field. For example, I bet a plumber can find a random fault in a heating system using his intuition faster than appears logical. Based on years of experience and technical skill, what looks like magic is simply wisdom in action.

> **What looks like magic is simply wisdom in action**

An implied need to develop our own learning

If our intuition draws upon our latent wisdom and knowledge, then of course we benefit from increasing that knowledge. As coaches, continual learning, practice and self-development help us stay both effective and fresh. So, whether you learn by reading, attending courses or seminars, gaining supervision, seeking feedback, listening to audio recordings, writing reflection notes,[3] studying others, or a combination of those – I encourage you to remain both focused and committed to increasing your own knowledge and skill.

Skill four – asking effective questions

In any coaching conversation or a fuller assignment, as coach and coachee become travelling companions, the coach's questions provide the quality of light by which they travel. In coaching, a well-timed, simply worded question can remove barriers, unlock hidden information and surface potentially life-changing insights. Basically, to be a great coach you need to be able to ask great questions. Unfortunately, the ability to regularly ask great questions is uncommon enough to seem like a rare talent. Fortunately, it is a skill that can be developed, with concentration and practice.

> **As coach and coachee become travelling companions, the coach's questions provide the quality of light by which they travel**

What does a great question look like or sound like? Well, it has the following characteristics:

- It is simple.
- It has a clear sense of purpose.
- It influences the direction of someone's thoughts, without controlling them.

Figure 4.7 Asking effective questions

Keeping things simple
=====================

Simple questions often have the greatest impact because they allow your coachee to use their energy to form their response, rather than to try to understand the wording of the question. In addition, simple questions often get 'to the heart of the matter' more easily, because of their direct (straight-talking) nature: for example, 'What's important about that?' or 'What causes this?' We obviously need to balance 'direct' with a need to maintain rapport, and that is still possible.

Complex questions confuse people

When asking questions, being clever just is not clever. Unfortunately, for a coach, asking simple, straightforward questions isn't always automatic. Perhaps a coach hears the coachee say, 'Well, I need to earn more money, you see – that's important.' The coach might decide that they want to understand the motivation behind that and so respond with the following:

> **Too complex a question:** 'When you consider your motivations around this and what causes you to want to earn more money, what does this lead you to realise?'

This is not a great question. It's long and too complicated. The listener is asked to compare, analyse and then realise something. There is also an implied pressure to come up with a particular realisation, as though the coach knows the answer, and the coachee needs to come up with it. As a result of the coachee getting the answer 'wrong' or, worse, not being able to produce an answer, the conversation may become uncomfortable or laboured.

Alternatively, the coach's question might be:

Too casual a question: **'So, what's all this earning more money about, then?'**

Again, not a great question. Although it's brief, it's also too casual and lacks focus. The response to this question may be equally flippant, for example, 'Dunno – that's just me, I guess.' Additionally, there is a subtle tone that suggests the individual is 'wrong' to want to earn more money. The phrase is also like that used by parents discussing a problem with their children: 'So what's all this noise/crying/fuss about, then?' Remember when we make a person 'wrong' in the conversation, we begin to reduce rapport.

Another 'simple' option might be:

Questioning 'why': **'Why do you want to earn more money?'**

Easy to understand and straightforward to respond to, but it contains the word 'why', which has risks associated with it. When we ask someone 'why', it can be interpreted as a request for them to justify themselves. When a person feels that pressure, they can become defensive and begin to form a 'logical' case for their own actions: for example, 'Well, I just do. Why should I put up with the lousy salary this place is paying me?' If you really need to begin a question with the word 'why', make sure you soften your tonality a little to maintain rapport.

> **When we ask someone 'why?', it can be interpreted as a request for them to justify themselves**

Good questions are keys that open doors

The best question is one that the coachee can answer because it's simple to understand and inoffensive in its tone. If the question is helpful, it will surface the information needed to progress the conversation helpfully. Effective questions might include:

- 'Can you perhaps say a little more about the importance to you of earning money?' This is a gentle, respectful question, maybe a little general, but it's likely to create progress.
- 'So, money's important – can you say a bit more about that?' A little more casual, a little less direct and still might easily hit the mark. If it doesn't, you can be sure it's going to get you closer.
- 'What is it about earning more money that's important to you?' This is more direct, and relies on you having good rapport, and a fairly gentle tone of voice.

In coaching, simply worded questions encourage the smooth flow of a conversation, as the coachee can concentrate on their thoughts and respond naturally.

Keep the purpose of your question simple

When we ask a question of someone, or even of ourselves, the question normally has a purpose. For example, some questions gather information; some questions influence a person's thinking. In coaching, the questions that a skilled coach uses often do both.

Of course, as a coach, you may occasionally ask a question without really knowing why you have asked it. When the question combines instinct and experience, this is appropriate. However, this is the exception rather than the rule. If we frequently asked random questions with no idea of their purpose, we would create a very strange conversation indeed!

Table 4.1 illustrates examples of good coaching questions, along with their purpose.

Table 4.1 Effective coaching questions

Purpose of question	Coaching examples
Gather general information.	'Can you tell me more about what happened with her?' 'What other thoughts have you had about this?' 'What else is there to say about that?'
Gather specific information.	'Specifically, what was it about her that you didn't like?' 'When did she say this?' 'What were the words that upset you particularly?'
Help someone remember something more clearly.	'What else can you remember about that?' 'What do you remember seeing/feeling/hearing?'
Shift someone's attention to the present moment. For example, if they're becoming annoyed about something and you want them to stay objective.	'Okay, what else do you want to say about that to me right now?' 'So, what seems important about that right now?' 'Can you think of any other information that would be relevant about that for us here, now?'

Purpose of question	Coaching examples
Understand someone's values.	'What was it about her words that upset you?' 'What is important to you about that?' 'What would you have wanted her to say?'
Help someone appreciate another person's values.	'Why was that important to her in this situation?' 'What might be her reasons for acting like that?'
Get someone to link two thoughts or situations together.	'How does the earlier email you mentioned relate to what happened?' 'How does this situation affect how you're approaching work now?'
Help someone appreciate something from someone else's perspective.	'What do you think her experience was?' 'What might she be feeling at that point?' 'Why might she have said that?'
Help someone reach a conclusion.	'What are your thoughts about that now?' 'What conclusion are you drawing from that now?'
Influence someone to action.	'What needs to happen?' 'When seems right to do that?' 'What can you do?' 'What are your options?'
Prepare someone to overcome barriers to taking action.	'What might stop you from doing that?' [Follow-up] 'So how will you overcome that?'
Influence someone to think about a situation positively.	'How have you benefited from this?' 'What's the positive side/upside of this?' 'If you do resolve this, what will be different?'
Influence someone to think about the effects of an action on their environment.	'Who else is affected by this?' 'What are the potential risks associated with doing that?' 'How will this affect your other colleagues?'
Help someone learn from an event or circumstance.	'How has talking this through affected your views on the situation?' 'What learning have you taken from this?' 'If this kind of situation happened again, how would you react?'

There are obviously more reasons to ask a question than listed above. When you are learning to coach, it's helpful to notice your compulsion or intention before asking a question, and then construct the appropriate question that fulfils your intent. Do this in a direct and simple manner – for example, if you want to know what someone's partner thought about something, ask, 'What did your partner think about this?'

Avoid questions with implied judgement

Questions may do many positive things in a conversation, such as create clarity, explore different perspectives, etc. Unfortunately, they can also narrow options, imply judgement and leave the coachee feeling pressured or defensive.

It is important to ensure that the purpose of your questions is not corrupted by your own opinion. For example, a coach may hear a coachee describe his desire for a new job that involves more money and much more travel. The coach also knows that the coachee's wife is expecting their first baby. Logically, it seems reasonable to look at the effect such a move may have on the coachee's family. The following questions may appear to do just that:

- 'Won't that be difficult if your wife has just had a baby?'
- 'Isn't that a bit unfair on your wife right now?'

Both questions, however, have an implied outcome and strong sense of judgement. By using words like 'difficult' and 'unfair', the coach is expressing their own opinion. The potential benefit of exploring the impact of a job move may be lost as the coachee is pressed to justify his statement.

Asked with less implied judgement, the following questions work better:

- 'How will this amount of travel affect things at home?'
- 'Who else is affected by you changing jobs?'

By responding to more open and more neutral questions, the coachee can enquire into their own thoughts and awareness.

This is obviously an example of the less directive approach outlined in Chapter 2, where a collaborative coach seeks to draw insights and learning from the coachee.

Influence versus control

When you ask someone a question, you influence the direction of their thoughts. For example, 'What was the best holiday you ever had when you were young?' causes you to think about holidays in the past. Although it subtly implies that you have had a great holiday at some point in your life, the question is fairly neutral – it doesn't tell you what you should think.

Within coaching, a collaborative (less directive) coach works to maintain the balance between influence and control. Controlling questions narrow down options, imply judgement or create pressure on someone else to come up with the 'right' response. Occasionally, these types of questions can be appropriate, maybe to acknowledge what's obvious: for example, 'Isn't that date going to clash with your holiday?' Mostly, though, I would discourage the use of controlling questions. They inhibit thought and self-expression, and the coach risks missing information, losing rapport, or both.

> **A collaborative (less directive) coach works to maintain the balance between influence and control**

Table 4.2 illustrates controlling questions further.

Table 4.2 Controlling questions

Controlling question	Problem/issue
'And what did you feel about that – frustrated?'	Narrows down options of what the person may have felt, plus subtly assumes what they 'should' have felt – in this case frustrated.
'What made you act in such a hostile manner towards her?'	Implies both criticism and a requirement for the other person to justify their actions.
'How is that going to put things right if Priya's still so upset?'	Again, implies disagreement and requests justification.
'What is it about Priya that you aren't able to deal with?'	Assumes that the other person isn't able to deal with Priya, and that's a bad thing.
'What might you do to completely resolve the situation for everyone affected?'	Places pressure on the individual to get the question 'right' while implying subtle blame.

Avoid making someone wrong

Some questions make the other person 'wrong' in some way or imply blame. When we make someone 'wrong' about something, we create a sense of separateness between us: for example, 'Don't you think that was a little unkind?' When we do this in coaching, we risk damaging rapport and engagement.

> **'We judge ourselves by our intentions and others by their behaviour.'**
>
> **Stephen M.R. Covey**

Table 4.3 gives more neutral alternatives.

Table 4.3 Neutral questions

Coaching question	Benefit
'How did you feel about that?'	Open question enables the coachee to decide how they felt.
'What caused you to react like that?'	Helps the coachee disassociate to identify reasons for their behaviour.
'What was behind the way you acted towards her?'	As a follow-up to the above question, might uncover further information, such as values.
'What do you want to happen now?'	Helps someone disassociate from the past and associate with the future. Creates a focus on goals, a desired outcome, progress.
'What effect will doing that have upon Priya, do you think?'	Helps the coachee see the implications of their actions for others.
'What could you do to improve things now?'	Allows the coachee to consider options to improve things, plus imagine themselves carrying them out.
'What is it about Priya's behaviour that's important to you?'	Distinguishes Priya's behaviour from Priya the person. Also uses the word 'important' in a way that implies no judgement.

Ideas into Action

Change your voice and it changes the question

Any question is given further meaning by the quality of your voice when you ask it. Questions may be made clearer, colder, more supportive or more aggressive simply by the tone, warmth and speed of your voice. Try it yourself, using the question, 'So, what was important about that?' Speak the question out loud three times, and change the quality of your voice each time, using the following qualities:

- As if you don't care.
- As if the idea of 'that' being important is ludicrous.
- With genuine curiosity, as though the answer is important to you.

You will notice that a potentially helpful question can be wrecked by the wrong tonality. Alternatively, when you use positive tonality with a potentially risky or abrupt question, you're more likely to get a good response.

An appreciation of closed and open questions

Part of the flexibility any coach needs to develop is in their use of both closed and open questions. Closed questions can be answered with a yes or no and open questions can't.

Closed questions (Y/N)	Open questions
1 Did you enjoy your weekend?	1 How was your weekend?
2 Would you like that?	2 How would you feel about that?
3 Can you do that?	3 How will you do that?
4 Should he have called you?	4 What should he have done?
5 Did she agree to what you asked her to do?	5 How did she respond to what you asked her to do?

Open questions open up conversation

Open questions encourage more information than closed. They also encourage someone's participation and involvement, which helps us to explore their thoughts and ideas. For this reason, an effective coach will tend to use many more open questions than closed.

During a typical coaching session, I would expect the coachee to be doing at least 70 per cent of the talking. As a coach, using open questions is one way that you can enable this to happen.

Closed questions confirm or close down

Because they encourage a 'yes' or 'no' response, closed questions tend to reduce the disclosure and sharing of information. Nevertheless, closed questions may still be used to great effect, especially where we don't want a detailed response, for example:

- Confirming information: 'Have I got that right?'
- Moving the conversation along: 'Can we continue?'
- Closing a conversation down: 'Have we finished?'

The exception is when people don't respond to closed questions with a yes or no – this is especially common with politicians!

At a Glance

What if I can't think of my next question?

Sometimes, a coach will go blank, get stuck and not know what to say next! This is normal, human and happens to all of us at some time. Causes and potential options include:

You have lost concentration and so lost the thread of the conversation

Be honest, declare what has happened and move on: for example. 'I'm sorry, I need you to repeat what you just said, I lost concentration just then.' Then make sure you refocus on the conversation and what the coachee is saying, to regain involvement.

You are genuinely distracted by another thought, idea or insight

Here, it might be that your intuition has made a connection that's worth exploring. Again, be honest and declare what's happening, for example, 'I'm sorry, but I keep thinking about what you said earlier about not liking things too easy. Can we go back to that a little?'

The conversation seems to be leading nowhere or seems 'stuck' – maybe the energy has gone out of the conversation, or the conversation feels pointless

Be honest (again!). Say what you're feeling or thinking – after all, they might be thinking it too, for example, 'Okay, I'm kind of stuck now because I don't know where our conversation is heading – is this still a useful dis-cussion?' They might say, 'Yes, I'm actually getting a lot from this.' If so, find out why, for example, 'Okay, I'm interested, what it is that you're get-ting here?' You will then have a new focus for the conversation.

Alternatively, if they say, 'I know what you mean, I'm stuck with it as well,' you can then decide how best to continue, for example, 'Okay – do we leave that or do we want to know why we've got stuck with it?' or 'Okay – what could we be talking about?'

The coach's mind has gone blank because they are less confident or new to coaching

This one is helped by a little advance preparation or practice. You need to develop the ability to relax yourself and refocus, ahead of time. Develop the tendency to use your body to regain your sense of centredness and confidence. Try it now. Sit back a little, pull your shoulders back and move your breathing down into your stomach (so that your tummy goes in and out as you breathe). When you do this in a coaching session, use an interrupt-type phrase to enable you to refocus your thoughts, for example 'Pause and focus on what they just said,' or 'What do I need to do now?' Remember that pauses are often useful for the coachee as well as the coach – silences can be powerful! Alternatively, do a brief recap, using your notes if you have them, for example, 'Let's just recap a little – you began by saying that you wanted to . . . ' Usually, this is enough to reorientate you to the conversation and help you decide what you want to explore or discuss.

Powerful questions

Powerful questions are an invaluable tool for you within coaching and you can ask them in a variety of situations. Powerful questions have many potential benefits:

- They refocus thought, for example from problem to solution.
- They can help someone feel more powerful and constructive about a situation.
- They tap into creativity and create options.
- They can make a problem feel more like a challenge or an opportunity.
- They create a positive forward movement, that is towards solution or action.

Powerful questions are phrased in such a way as to encompass the problem and provoke an answer. The answer that they produce addresses the deeper problem, not just the surface issue. Table 4.4 demonstrates the journey between describing a situation as a problem and describing the same situation within a powerful question. The situation here is that the person is overworked and wants more support from their boss. They feel that their boss doesn't know much about their day-to-day situation and doesn't value the workload they are carrying.

When we ask a clear, powerful question in response to a situation, you can almost hear someone's mind crunch into gear. Our minds can't resist the challenge of a stimulating question.

Powerful questions are an invaluable tool for you within coaching

Table 4.4 Journey towards more powerful questions

Coachee's statement/question	Comment
'I'm really struggling with this job, and my boss doesn't support me – he doesn't even know what I do!'	This is a statement of complaint or problem; it focuses on what's wrong. It's not a question, and it produces no creative thoughts or ideas.
'Why can't my boss help me?'	This is a question, but it's not a powerful question. It's actually still a complaint. Also, if this question were answered, we'd get responses like 'Because he's not interested/too busy, etc.' Such responses are not going to help progress this issue.
'How can I get my boss to know more about what I'm doing?'	This question covers only the superficial aspect of the problem and so evokes only a partial answer. Remember that the person also wants their boss to support them, not just be aware of what they do. Responses to this question might include 'Spend some time with him so that he understands what you do'. A powerful question will produce answers to the deeper problem.
'How can I make sure my boss understands more about what I'm doing, and encourage him to give me more support?'	This is a good, powerful question. The question digs below the surface, to bring up a complete solution. The likely response would create ideas that address all parts of the problem, making the boss aware, and getting more support from him.

Powerful questions create possibility

These types of questions also create a sense of possibility in a problem situation, where previously it seemed lacking. For example, imagine you've been complaining relentlessly about needing a holiday but also needing the money to fix your car. You dislike your car, you would prefer something smaller, but it seems too much hassle to change it. Then someone asks you, 'How can you have *both* the car you want *and* the holiday you need?'

Hmm – gets you thinking, doesn't it?

Table 4.5 shows some further examples of powerful questions.

Table 4.5 Further examples of powerful questions

Coachee's statement	Powerful question
'I've moved jobs, I've moved home and now I've got no friends and no social life – I'm still feeling really unsettled here.'	'What could you be doing to feel more settled and meet some new friends?'
'I'm always worried about money. I'm worried about it regardless of how much I have. It's just always on my mind.'	'What's it going to take for you to feel more relaxed about money?'
'I want to go to night school but there's no one reliable to look after the kids. The situation's just impossible.'	'How can you get someone reliable to look after the kids while you go to night school?'

Ideas into Action

Let powerful questions work for you

The following will help you experience powerful questions for yourself, which is a good way to learn how to ask them by appreciating the impact they have upon our thinking:

Step one – identify three problem statements

Write down three problems that you think you have. Choose things that are moderately important but not earth-shattering, such as 'I want to exercise but I'm just too busy with everything else.' Leave enough space under each statement to write a few more sentences.

Step two – change problem statements into powerful questions

Under each problem, write down questions that provoke solutions to the issue, such as 'How can I be less busy and create time to exercise?' Remember, for a question to be powerful it must have the following attributes:

- The question assumes that there is an answer to the problem.
- The question provokes thought to begin to create answers or solutions.
- The question digs below the surface, and thereby invites a more encompassing solution.

For further support, look back at the previous examples.

> **Step three – answer your own questions!**
>
> Take a clean piece of paper and write your powerful questions down one side. Then, focusing on each question, produce ideas or solutions, for example, 'Get up an hour earlier,' 'Ask Sidney to pick the kids up from school on Thursdays,' 'Cook meals and freeze them on weekends.'
>
> Once you have some positive solutions, simply decide which you're going to commit to. Write down a list of actions, behaviours, habits or routines you want to make happen. Remember, it's great to have great ideas and yet only through your own actions can you bring them to life.

What if your question doesn't create progress?

Sometimes, no matter how many great questions you ask your coachee, they are just stuck and can't respond to your question productively. For example, you might ask, 'What else might you have done to help your team collaborate on this?' and your coachee can't think of an answer. You've asked the question because you want to help them understand their options or learn from a situation. You'd also prefer that those thoughts came from your coachee, if possible. However, they appear not to be able to think of a useful response, for example, 'I really have no idea'. The following are all potential options for you.

Option: pause, use silence to help them think

In coaching, silence is a powerful and underused tool, simply because of the space you create for the other person to relax into their own mental processes.

> **In coaching, silence is a powerful and underused tool**

Silence for the person experiencing it is often more comfortable than for the coach maintaining it, as our tendency is often to try to help move the conversation forward. It sometimes works to encourage people to be comfortable with going into silence, for example, 'Okay, so maybe take a moment to have a think about that?' Remember, keep your tone softer for it to feel more like encouragement than instruction.

Option: ask a vaguer question

Sometimes, a vague, less specific question helps as it reduces the pressure on someone to think in a specific way. Examples of vague questions include: 'What other options did you have?' or 'What have you been considering doing?' and 'What thoughts are you having about that?'

Option: use summaries and observations to free up someone's thinking

Please remember, there is more to coaching than just asking questions. When our questions fail to create progress, we can be tempted to offer an idea or suggestion, for example, 'Well, you could have spoken to the team about the bigger picture first.' For reasons discussed previously, this is rarely the best way to engage insight in the coachee, plus our idea may be irrelevant. Instead, I'd recommend that you learn to use regular summaries and observations, to help give someone more space to think and also to help them focus productively.

Summaries help people reflect and refocus

Using the earlier example, let's first look at how the gentle power of a simple, concise summary might work in this type of situation.

Coach: What else might you have done to help your team collaborate on this?

Coachee: I'm not sure . . . I don't really know.

Coach: [After a period of silence] Okay, so you said that you sent an email and asked them all to get together and build a project team to decide the best way of working with the new supplier.

Coachee: Right. So, I guess email might not have been the best way to do that.

Notice how the summary gives the coachee a rest from talking, and space to reflect on what they've been saying. By 'standing back' and listening to their own situation from another perspective, they can gain a more objective view about key facts or events. Now let's look at the slightly more directive nature of an observation.

Observations help people shift perspective

Coach: What else might you have done to help your team collaborate on this?

Coachee: I'm not sure . . . I don't really know.

Coach: [After a period of silence] Okay, so you said that you sent an email and asked them all to get together and build a project team to decide the best way of working with the new supplier.

Coachee: Right.

Coach: Can I make an observation?

Coachee: Of course.

Coach: Well, your email sort of assumes that everyone understood the background to the request, and also that they were comfortable to build a project team without your involvement.

Coachee: Well, I think they should understand the background because we've been talking about this long enough, but there is something in the idea about building the team without me being involved.

Coach: So, what thoughts are you having about that?

Coachee: Yes. I'm realising that the blocker might have been that Peter and Susie would both want to lead the team and that's always going to be an issue without me helping them to decide.

Notice how the coach's observation was only partially relevant for the coachee, but it still freed up thought for them. The follow-up question helped in combination, by encouraging the coachee to take the next logical step in their thought process. This is because when you ask a question after offering an observation or summary, you effectively hand the conversation back to the coachee.

It's important to remember that just because a coachee can't answer a question quickly and easily, you still have options. A period of silence, or asking a different or vaguer question, can often help. Summaries and observations can also create a subtle 'breakthrough' effect, simply because of the space they offer the coachee to reflect from a slightly different perspective.

Skill five – giving constructive feedback

Feedback to support self-awareness and learning

One of the many positive aspects to a coaching relationship is that a coachee becomes gradually more self-aware, for example of their own behaviours and tendencies. As a coach, one way that you support this is to offer feedback in helpful ways. This might range from making a simple encouraging observation in the moment, to offering a more considered, challenging view of someone's attitudes or behaviours.

As a coach, your ability to make helpful observations about your coachee and their behaviour is important to their coaching experience. Effective feedback can accelerate a coachee's learning, inspire them, motivate them, help them feel valued and catapult them into action. So, it's important that you learn to deliver feedback that is:

- given with a positive intention
- based on fact or behaviour
- constructive and beneficial.

What do we mean by feedback?

The term 'feedback' literally means to feed information back to someone. This information relates to the person receiving the feedback and provides data from which they can assess their performance or experiences. It can range from a general comment such as 'That was great/lousy' to more specific assessments of performance such as 'You overran the presentation slot by 17 minutes.'

Unfortunately, the term 'feedback' can also be associated with criticism, due to how and when people use it. This happens in the workplace, where praise can be rare, and frustrations or conflict must be handled professionally. So, the expression 'I'd like to give you some feedback' can be used to introduce fairly negative conversation. Sadly, the word 'feedback' can be used to give an illusion of professionalism to critical remarks. It's a shame, because while critical remarks do constitute feedback (they're information), often the same message could be delivered in a more supportive and effective manner.

For example, watch how the following statements comment on the same situation in different ways:

- 'You can really upset people because you're so blunt with your remarks.'
- 'When you told Markus he'd no chance of getting the job, he appeared upset.'
- 'When you told Markus he'd no chance of getting the job, I thought that sounded a little harsh, what do you think?'

All three remarks have a similar intention – either to change the way in which the person speaks to others, or at least have them consider they need to do so.

The first remark sounds like generalised, subjective criticism, and may easily upset the person hearing it. This remark is not a supportive way of giving someone feedback.

Figure 4.8 Constructive feedback

The second remark comments on specific behaviour in a more objective way and is less likely to offend the individual. The remark is fairly direct, although within a healthy coaching relationship this level of openness should be okay.

The third option uses a question to explore the individual's thoughts on the potential impact of their words or behaviour. This is a less direct attempt to influence someone's behaviour. This type of observation and gentle enquiry can be a supportive way to encourage further enquiry as to the coachee's viewpoint.

Of course, not all feedback relates to difficult messages. Praise and acknowledgement of good performance or progress are as important as observations of someone's need to consider different behaviours. When feedback messages are positive in nature, the benefits of raising self-awareness and encouraging progress still apply.

Knowing when to give feedback

Within coaching, an opportunity to give feedback may be prompted by you as coach or by your coachee. In either instance, you should offer feedback only in the genuine belief that it would benefit the coachee. Here are some valid situations to offer feedback.

Bite-sized feedback to raise awareness

Your coachee doesn't appear to have noticed something in a situation or appears unaware in an unhelpful way. Maybe they are using language or behaviour that you feel is interesting or relevant. By offering immediate feedback as an observation, you can often clarify their awareness. Examples of this include:

- 'I notice you tend to keep coming back to Eric's confusion over your job description and I guess I'm wondering why that is.'

- 'When you describe Eric, you use the word "chaotic" a lot and also "a complete mess" – did you notice that?'

- 'You know, you described a similar frustration with Eric in our first session. Is that related in any way?'

When you need to give a more considered message

Over a few sessions, you notice that your coachee seems unaware of a tendency they have to perceive conflict or adopt defensive positions of blame and complaint in a situation. You feel that some of the people issues they complain about aren't actually issues, but simply instances where they need to take some time to understand other people's views first.

This is potentially a situation where your coachee may be sensitive to your view or reject it if they are unable to appreciate it properly. To offer your thoughts effectively, you need to prepare, even if that simply means thinking your message through a little first. See the later section 'How to give effective feedback'.

When they ask for it

Sometimes, your coachee will ask you for feedback and you need to decide if it's appropriate or helpful to the coaching process. Your decision whether to offer your view needs to balance the need to maintain rapport and the relationship, with the need for your coachee to stay empowered and responsible. If you judge that it would be genuinely unhelpful to retain your view, then give it. For example, your coachee appears upset or frustrated and says, 'I just don't seem to be making progress at all. Why do you think that is?' If you refuse to comment, your coachee may view this as a withdrawal of some kind. Or they might even decide that you must have negative views that you are unwilling to share.

Knowing when not to give feedback

There are occasions where it would be less helpful for you to give feedback. For instance:

- When it seems to be an excuse for the coachee to avoid taking responsibility, for example, 'Oh I can't decide – what do you think I should do?'
- If giving feedback might interrupt the flow of a conversation or the thought processes of the coachee.
- If giving feedback may lead to an overly directive style, for example, 'Let me tell you what I think about your situation.'
- When you do not have enough information to give feedback effectively, for example, 'Well, I could guess what I probably think is . . . . '
- When, over time, the coachee is receiving excessive amounts of feedback, for example from people outside of the coaching process, or indeed the coach themselves.

When you input your view, you potentially confuse theirs

Imagine you are coaching someone who appears overly concerned with what other people think and it affects their ability to make decisions. Their first thought is to check what other people might think about what they do before fully exploring what they themselves want. In the past, this has led to them missing out on opportunities, or suffering in silence instead of expressing their views and needs. An appropriate approach might be as follows:

Coach: So, what will you do about the job offer?

Coachee: Well, I'm not sure. I've been asking around, doing a bit of a survey. Trouble is, everyone seems to be saying different things. I mean, you know me, and what I'm good at – do you believe I'm capable of doing the role?

Coach: Well, I can easily add my view, but what I'm really interested in is what *you* think about your capability to do it.

Coachee: What I think about it? Well, I'm not sure I've really considered that!

Notice how the coach chose to challenge the coachee's tendency to place too much importance on what other people think. In this way, you encourage them to use a more responsible (and so empowered) approach to decision making that relies more on what they themselves think and feel.

How to give effective feedback

As coach, you simply need to balance the pros and cons of giving feedback and to act accordingly. As I mentioned earlier, feedback should be:

- given with a positive intention
- based on fact and behaviour
- constructive and beneficial.

Feedback that is clumsily worded and badly delivered sounds (and feels) like criticism, for example, 'You're being arrogant about this'. As a coach, you can normally avoid this by taking care about what you say and how you say it. Some people are more receptive to hearing feedback than others and you must develop the ability to deliver a potentially difficult message in such a way as to maintain the motivation of the coachee.

Some people are more receptive to hearing feedback than others

While the following feedback guidelines apply in a coaching relationship, they also work for anyone giving feedback outside a coaching situation.

Feedback given with a positive intention

There are both positive and negative reasons to give someone feedback, for example:

Positive reasons:

- To help someone learn something that they would benefit from learning.
- To support someone to reach their goal or objective.
- To help someone overcome a problem that's bothering them.
- To acknowledge them and make them feel valued.

Negative reasons:

- To 'teach someone a lesson'.
- To control or dominate someone else, for example tell them what they should do.
- To help someone else avoid giving feedback – give a message on behalf of someone else.
- Where it would damage their self-esteem or self-confidence in a way that is detrimental to their ongoing resilience or well-being.

When our intention is clear and positive towards the individual, we are more likely to deliver a message that they experience as supportive and respectful. If it's a difficult message to deliver, then sometimes, by first speaking our intention, we can help the individual to appreciate the potential benefit of listening to it. For example:

Coach: I'd like to offer you some feedback, as I know you've been experiencing some frustration with the lack of support you say you've had from your colleagues. I have some thoughts that may help with a fresh perspective on that.

When giving feedback, maintain your integrity

Personal judgements, frustrations or a need to gain control of a situation are likely to impair our coach's ability to deliver effective feedback. For example, a coachee appears to be deliberating for what seems like an inappropriate length of time and the coach is becoming frustrated with what appears to be a simple decision for most people to make.

Coach:	Can I give you some feedback?
Coachee:	Er – Okay ...
Coach:	You seem to be procrastinating. I think you simply need to take the decision now and then stick to it.

If the coach were honest, they'd admit that their comment was born out of their own frustration for a delay that was annoying them. This is not an intention of benefit for the coachee or their ongoing success or well-being. The remark might disturb both the coachee's feelings and their decision-making process.

Given the coach's frustration and annoyance, feedback was an inappropriate intervention. Another option born from a more positive intention towards the coachee might be:

Coach:	Can I make an observation?
Coachee:	Er – Okay ...
Coach:	You appear reluctant to make this decision and I'm wondering what might be causing that?

By giving a more objective observation of the apparent delay plus encouragement to enquire further, the coach maintains a positive intention to serve the needs of the coachee in that moment.

Give feedback based on fact and behaviour

Feedback is more likely to be effective if it is factual and based on something a person can do something about (or change). It's often best to comment on behaviour, as a person can appreciate that they have choices about how they behave. Feedback that's non-factual or vague leaves them guessing, for example, 'That's really not working, is it?' or 'You need to get better at that.'

Feedback that relates to who someone is, their identity, is also difficult. While changing behaviour seems possible, changing who we are seems impossible. For example:

Coach:	Well, the Q&A part of the presentation didn't go well, did it? I do think you're someone who struggles in stressful situations. You seem to lack the natural confidence.

This remark is too general, subjective and vague for the person receiving it to do much with. They are left with the option of being someone who 'lacks natural confidence' – which may not be something they can do anything about. In the same situation, the following feedback is more usable and effective:

Coach: I noticed that some of your answers to the questions were fairly lengthy and I suspect that caused some people to lose the sense of what you were saying.

This is an observation of behaviour, plus a personal opinion of the effect of that behaviour. The person hearing it can disassociate from their behaviour enough to evaluate the situation more objectively. After all, most people know how to stop talking.

As a more positive example, if I notice that the coachee smiled a lot at the audience and they responded by smiling back a lot, I can give the coachee that observation. In future, they can choose to repeat the behaviour, in the knowledge that it's likely to produce a good result.

The difference between objective and subjective feedback

It's useful to understand the difference between a statement that is objective and one that is subjective. Objective statements are based solely on fact, for example something that really happened. Subjective statements contain the views and opinions of an individual person. For example:

Example 1: Objective	Coach:	Before you said 'yes' to that question, you paused and smiled.
Example 2: Subjective	Coach:	Before you said 'yes' to that question, you paused and smiled – for me, that's real progress.

The first statement comments only on behaviour, making it more objective. The fact that the coach chose to observe the behaviour at all suggests they think it is significant and that requires some judgement – but, for our purposes, we'll consider it an objective statement. The coach makes the observation to enable the coachee to respond with their own thoughts. The coachee is likely to comment on what caused them to pause and smile.

The second statement obviously adds the coach's opinion that progress is being made. The coach intends the statement to be supportive and encouraging and the coachee is more likely to respond to the encouragement, for example with 'Thanks' or 'Great'.

While both statements are similar in nature, notice that in their subtle difference they may create a very different result. However, let's be clear that neither form of feedback is right or wrong. What is important is that we appreciate the varying degrees to which we are being subjective or objective. The amount of fact and personal opinion within our statements affects the potential benefits, risks and results of feedback.

Subjective – it's a matter of your opinion

There are both risks and benefits to giving subjective feedback.

Potential risks include being inaccurate and directing or controlling the coachee in an inappropriate manner. When, as a coach, you say, 'I think', you use your own views and opinions, which can feel directive. As coaches, our personal views reduce an individual's ability to find their own solutions.

However, over time, the coach gains valuable insight into the behaviours and tendencies of the coachee that can help them to progress towards their goals. So, this risk of over-influencing the coachee must be balanced with the potential benefits of providing support, acknowledgement and recognition. Once the coach has established both credibility and rapport with the coachee, their input is often welcome.

Objective – it's a matter of fact

Objective statements reduce the coach's influence to a minimum and allow the coachee to respond only to facts. Of course, these 'facts' rely on the ability of the coach to observe behaviour correctly, or else the whole process is flawed.

Objective, factual statements are more likely to be accepted by the coachee as true than statements heavily laden with the coach's opinion. This is because there's less non-factual information to debate. For example, if I say, 'You raised your eyebrows when I said that,' instead of 'You don't believe me, do you?', my first comment is more easily accepted than my second.

> **As coaches, our personal views reduce an individual's ability to find their own solutions**

The potential downside of the coach making only objective, factual statements is that the coachee may want the coach's personal input to progress. Some behaviour might benefit from the coach interpreting it. For example, 'I sense that you're avoiding discussing your current partner,' might work better than, 'You've talked a lot about your previous marriage.'

The next examples illustrate the journey between objective and subjective feedback. The following coachee wants to become more influential in meetings. The coach has noticed a behaviour that they feel is relevant.

Example 1	Coach:	You said that you take comprehensive notes throughout the meetings.

The above comment is an objective comment.

Example 2	Coach:	You take a lot of notes. That might be relevant.

The above comment is still fairly objective and has a hint of the coach's views.

Example 3	Coach:	You take a lot of notes. That's likely to affect your ability to influence.

That one was less objective and contains more of the coach's views.

Example 4	Coach:	You take too many notes. It's got to be causing your lack of personal impact.

The example above has a hefty amount of personal opinion (subjective feedback) in it.

Example 5	Coach:	I'd say because you're taking notes all the time, it's causing you to lack presence. This is the real barrier here.

Example 5 is an extremely subjective statement that indicates strong opinion on the part of the coach. It's also very risky, as the coach is making a statement based on their understanding of the actual situation, which is likely to be limited. Also, by suggesting that taking notes is the most important factor, example 5 controls the direction of the conversation too much. Remember, collaborative coaching is a less directive, less controlling style of conversation. That way, we place primary responsibility for the conversation and the situation with the coachee.

Don't forget, there are no right or wrong options – only outcomes. As a coach, you need to know that you have choices and then stay aware of which is more appropriate: to offer your thoughts and views or stay with their process of enquiry.

Ideas into Action

True news or not news?

This exercise is a bit of fun with a twist; you will need a newspaper or online news source, a piece of paper and a pen. Choose a brief article you're interested in that describes a news event. Read the article once, so that you understand what is in it. Now, divide your paper into two columns, one headed 'objective' and the other 'subjective'. Using the columns, separate the objective facts in the article from the subjective or opinion-based statements. When you have finished, notice what and how much is in each column.

Q What does that say about the news source you chose?

Create constructive messages that benefit the individual

One of the signs of a skilled coach is their ability to make a potentially difficult or awkward message easier for the coachee to hear and digest. For the coachee to judge the feedback as constructive, the conversation must be, on balance, positive to them. They must feel that the coach has their success and well-being at heart, and that it was a worthwhile conversation to have in support of their development. Clearly, there must be some benefit from the feedback conversation for the coachee. Where feedback is directly related to the coachee's goals, this is fairly straightforward. Where the feedback does not directly relate to the coachee's goals, the coach should ensure that they can see some relevant benefit when checking their own intention for giving feedback.

Support their ability to hear a tough message

To enable the coachee to digest a potentially difficult message, as a coach you must support the emotional well-being of your coachee throughout the feedback conversation. Here are some of the ways to do this:

- Balance difficult messages with positive statements.
- Take personal responsibility for the views you are giving, for example, 'I notice' or 'I think'.
- Use open questions to encourage the coachee to shift perspectives or explore other avenues of thought.
- Use words/phrases with a neutral or diminished emphasis to describe difficult situations or emotions, for example 'some discomfort', 'slight resistance', etc.
- Communicate supportively using non-verbal signals, for example posture, facial expressions, tonality, eye contact, etc.
- Link observations to goals, for example, 'I'm wondering if, in the longer term, this might help you with your desire to build a stronger team.'

At a Glance

What if my feedback gets a negative response?

Sometimes, feedback isn't received in the way we wanted it to be. Unexpected responses might include the coachee being upset or angry, appearing shocked, or perhaps rejecting our messages completely. Causes of negative responses to feedback can vary, from a statement

---

we've delivered clumsily to a simple misunderstanding of what's been said. Maybe, as a coach, we're not feeling comfortable in giving the feedback; maybe we're feeling pressured or confused (these are not good times to give feedback, by the way!).

Or maybe we don't understand enough about the person or their situation to offer feedback. Maybe they are simply a lot more sensitive than you imagined. As a coach, the following can support you immediately after the coachee's reaction:

Make sure that this is a genuinely negative response that you need to act upon

For example, what you decide is a 'stony silence' might simply be the time the coachee needs to consider what they have just heard. It might be reasonable that they are experiencing discomfort and they simply need to process that feeling. During the silence, simply stay focused on your positive intention, for example to help, to serve their needs, etc.

Alternatively, if the coachee protests strongly, or becomes angry or upset, then listen to what they say before you decide what you need to do.

Take responsibility for your unconstructive feedback

If you realise that your feedback was clumsily delivered, then explain your meaning and intention once more. Acknowledge that your feedback hasn't worked out the way you intended. Apologise and express regret, for example:

'I'm sorry, I've upset you and I didn't mean to.'

'I've upset you with what I've said. I'm sorry, that's my fault.'

'I'm now really regretting putting it like that. I'm sorry.'

If you're not sure what it was you said that caused the upset, then still acknowledge your responsibility, for example:

'I suspect I've upset you with what I've just said – have I?'

If you find you're not responsible for their upset, then stay supportive – by allowing them time to think or facilitating their thoughts and feelings on why they've reacted in the way they have.

> ### *Make amends, explain if possible/appropriate*
>
> Explain your intentions, but don't excuse yourself; stay responsible. For example: 'My intention was to be helpful, but I haven't been, have I?' or 'I wanted to give you another way of looking at the situation – I hoped that it might give you another way forward.'
>
> ### *After the session: reflect and learn*
>
> While maintaining your responsibility, try to understand what it was you did that caused the response and learn from the experience. Your options for learning include:
>
> - When the coachee is in a better state of mind, ask them to help you understand what you did that didn't work. Be careful to maintain a position of full responsibility and ask them to help you learn. Be prepared to explain your intentions but avoid justifying yourself or making excuses.
>
> - Review the situation with someone you trust to help you learn from the situation (while maintaining the confidentiality of the coachee).
>
> - Read this chapter again and decide what principles or methods you might have used (or used more) to create a better response.
>
> ### *Summary*
>
> If we're going to learn to give feedback, we're going to make mistakes. So, it's important to know the principles of giving good feedback and focus on them. Where we give feedback that is unsupportive, then we need to acknowledge that and make amends, if possible. Then we need to learn from the experience. Please do not let a bad experience of giving feedback stop you from giving any more – as a coach, you need to give effective feedback if you are going to help others accelerate their learning and growth.

An example of constructive feedback

Obviously, the non-verbal element of giving constructive feedback cannot be demonstrated here, such as smiling, nodding, etc. The other principles are, however, illustrated in the following dialogue:

Coach: I wanted to discuss a little more your desire for less tension at home, which is proving more difficult now you've got your parents staying for a few months.

Coachee: More difficult? You can say that again!

Coach: I've noticed that, when you're speaking about your mother, mostly it's a complaint, for example, 'She's so moody' or 'She just loves being difficult'.

Coachee: Right – yes, I suppose that's true.

Coach: The other thing that seems to relate to this is the way you portray your father in the situation.

Coachee: How's that?

Coach: Well, you sound like you care for your father a lot. When you discuss him in relation to your mother, you say things like, 'Poor guy, I don't know how he copes with her,' and 'She must make his life a misery.'

Coachee: Yeah, I guess I do feel pretty sorry for him.

Notice how the coach is gradually constructing a picture of the situation that the coachee finds easy to accept. Observations so far are mainly objective, that is facts about what's been said.

In addition, the coach is careful not to use emotive or potentially sensational words that might cause the coachee to be uncomfortable or defensive. For example, instead of saying something like, 'You don't want going home to be such a nightmare,' the coach chooses to say, 'You want less tension at home.' It's a subtle distinction and an important trick to use sometimes.

The same dialogue continues:

Coach: You know, I'm wondering if how you talk about the situation, such as the stories you tell, is affecting your reactions to your mum and, perhaps, how you're feeling about the situation generally.

Coachee: Okay – go on.

Coach: What effect could the way you talk about it be having on you personally, do you think?

Coachee: Well, I guess I'm thinking about it more, I certainly seem to be complaining about it to people. Maybe I'm making the whole thing worse.

Coach: Okay, so I hear you complaining about your mother yet discussing your father as someone to feel sorry for or sympathise with. How does this actually affect your behaviour at home with them?

Coachee: Hmm, that's not a nice thought, actually. I guess how I am around my parents at home does mirror what I say. I'm very different around my father than I am around my mother.

Coach: How's that?

Coachee: Well, I'm much more patient, I guess.

Coach: So, what thoughts are you having now?

Coachee: Yeah – I need to work out how I'm really featuring in all this – that's the opportunity to affect the whole thing, isn't it?

Notice from the dialogue how the coach carefully builds an increased awareness of the situation in collaboration with the coachee. Open questions are used both to involve and to engage the coachee. Gradually, the coachee builds a fresh perspective on the situation that enables them to create other options for a way forward.

Remember the importance of maintaining the coachee's emotional state. This includes not upsetting them unnecessarily or putting them on their guard. In general, an understatement is more likely to be accepted than an exaggeration. Within coaching, I tend to use caution when describing problem-type situations. It's easier for a coachee to hear 'You have a situation that you want to change,' than 'You've got a big problem here.'

One good way of learning how to give feedback is to experience some feedback yourself. That way you will know first-hand what works and what doesn't.[4]

In a Nutshell

Whether within a formal coaching session, or simply as a style of behaviour or management, the following skills are core to coaching:

- building rapport or relationship
- different levels of listening
- using intuition
- asking effective questions
- giving constructive feedback.

These skills must be practised regularly to keep them available and fresh. Your coaching skills can be used in everyday situations and you will already have a level of competence with each one. By exploring and practising each skill directly, you will develop your ability beyond most people's. As coaches, when we can use these skills in combination, our coaching conversations flow naturally and easily.

chapter 5

Barriers to coaching

'**Deciding what not to do is as important as
deciding what to do.**'

Steve Jobs

There are several potential obstacles to effective coaching that can directly limit the quality of our results. We need to stay aware of both their causes and their consequences, as even the most experienced of us can fall foul of these sometimes. For example, we avoid fatigue as it impairs our concentration. We also need to avoid taking too many notes as it reduces the quality of our listening and our rapport with our coachee. In this chapter, the barriers we will look at relate to your environment, your well-being, and your behaviour, or they combine all three.

Environment: physical and situational barriers

One basic barrier to effective coaching is the physical situation that you coach in. The room or place you are in can make a real difference to how the conversation feels. Depending on the person and nature of the coaching conversation, it's possible for a space to be overly formal or overly casual. A quiet meeting room is normally preferable to a busy coffee shop, but you may not always have control over where you meet your coachee. So, keep in mind what kind of environment you want to create and try to negotiate where you can. Sessions should take place somewhere your coachee is able to relax, focus and be undisturbed during the session. Over time, you need to develop the ability to coach in a range of situations, and your skill of maintaining attention will enable that.

Of course, coaching doesn't have to happen in a room. Other potentially wonderful environments can be found outdoors – in a garden setting, on a park bench, etc. I know coaches who take clients on walks in nature; if you feel the potential distractions are worth accommodating, then that can also work. Also, for longer conversations, changing location or environment part-way through can work, for example get out of the office, go for a walk together, and then return to the meeting room. You have many options and I encourage you to consider them (and perhaps involve your coachee).

At a Glance

Is a location right for coaching?

Use the following questions to assess the suitability of a room or location you are considering using for a coaching conversation:

Q Imagine having a conversation in this setting – how does that feel to you?

Q How do you imagine your coachee will feel/respond in the environment?

Q Is the situation/room private, that is away from other people's hearing, out of view, etc.?

Q Is the environment comfortable and not too cosy? For example, luxurious sofas feel great but can put people to sleep.

Q Can you focus appropriately on your coachee, that is remain connected to them during the conversation?

Please remember that rarely is any location perfect and that some factors relate to personal preference, for example what is too cold for you may be just right for someone else.

Your well-being: avoid fatigue/tiredness

As an effective coach, you need to be able to maintain high levels of concentration and attention throughout the whole of a session. This means you must feel healthy and energised, rather than poorly or tired. Fatigue causes a lack of concentration, poor retention/memory, lack of patience and inflexibility. For your coachee, as you appear to lose concentration or 'drift off', they may view your low energy as lack of interest, boredom, or an inability to listen properly. When coaching sessions are long, or you have multiple sessions in one day, avoiding fatigue is your challenge.

One solution is to schedule only a reasonable number of sessions in one day, allowing time between sessions to recuperate. Avoid offering to stack many sessions into your day, with little or no gap between them. When a session runs over time and into the next one, you'll find maintaining good attention challenging or impossible. Try to give yourself time for at least one longer break in the day, for example lunch.

Whatever the circumstances, as a coach, you should do everything you can to stay as resourceful as possible during sessions. Simple things like drinking lots of water, taking regular breaks and eating the right foods help tremendously. Anything that creates a sense of tiredness – lack of sleep, alcohol, eating foods containing too much sugar, etc. – is best avoided. Our general state of health either enables us to coach effectively or impairs that ability and so I encourage you to look after yourself over time.

> **Our general state of health either enables us to coach effectively or impairs that ability**

Your well-being: maintain an appropriate state of mind/emotion

Your ability to listen, focus and think clearly depends on your personal state of mind as well as your physical state. As well as avoiding physical barriers such as general fatigue, pain or illness, you must also be in an appropriate emotional state to coach effectively. Appropriate mental or emotional states for coaching include feeling relaxed, aware, focused and objective yet optimistic. Feelings that are unsupportive of coaching include tension, stress, frustration, impatience, anxiety or simply boredom.

As a coach, you need to be able to manage your own feelings and emotions within a coaching session. Various factors may challenge your ability to do this and knock you off balance. Here are some of my own (real) personal examples:

- The coaching session is delayed by over an hour and you are left to sit and wait somewhere uncomfortable.
- You arrive for the session to find the room you planned to use is double-booked.
- You're coaching all day in the same room; it's freezing cold, there's no heating and you didn't bring a jacket.
- Your coachee starts the session by saying they want to quit their job (and the coaching) as they are deeply unhappy.
- People keep walking into the meeting room you're both in without knocking.
- A coachee talks about something traumatic that has upset them very deeply that resonates with you.
- An unplanned for fire alarm goes off just as your coachee reaches an important point in the conversation.

As much as possible, you must maintain a way of being during sessions that enables effective coaching. Whatever happens, you must respond resourcefully. For example, if the room is double-booked, go and find another (and keep smiling). If you are interrupted by a fire drill, respond in a relaxed manner, and resume the session when appropriate. If your coachee tells you they want to quit, stay calm and focused and gently explore their reasons why.

I find that a combination of commitment and detachment really helps. For example, I can remind myself I'm committed to the success of the coaching but flexible as to how that might happen. The fact that we must break the session to walk out as part of a fire drill may be just the interruption, we need to stimulate fresh conversation!

Let's continue with our topic of appropriate states of mind/emotion by looking at other potential causes of unresourcefulness.

Emotional states, sympathy and empathy

It's important that we understand the nature of both empathy and sympathy as they can create very different results. The word 'sympathy' means to share in an emotion or feeling with another person, so that two people experience similar emotional states at the same time. So, if you feel sad, that resonates with me so that I am sad too and, if you feel angry, so do I.

Empathy means the ability to identify mentally with another person. In other words, if you feel sad, I can relate to that; if you are angry, I can appreciate or imagine how you feel. Empathy does not mean that I feel what you feel, only that I can understand how you feel.

Sympathy can be debilitating

Imagine that a coachee is very angry or upset about something. Perhaps a work colleague has said something hurtful or unkind and we also become angry and upset, 'Well that's awful. That makes me mad just to hear about it and I wasn't even there!' We are sympathising and becoming personally involved in the issue in a way that's not appropriate. Through our emotional response, we support the coachee's anger or upset about the situation. As coaches, if we become angry or upset as well, then rational thought is difficult. We also become subjective about what we are hearing, and no longer hold a balanced perspective on the situation.

Another issue is that, as we sympathise with someone, we can imply that they are in some way a victim. When we make someone a victim, there is also a suggestion that they need rescuing in some way. These are clearly less empowering suggestions and are misaligned with the intentions of coaching.

In this instance, empathy is a more effective way to respond, for example, 'Look, you sound fairly angry about this and I can appreciate why. Do you want to say more about what happened?' By acknowledging the coachee's anger while remaining objective, we can continue to facilitate the conversation to enable constructive progress. We are also able to communicate an empowering assumption that the coachee can resolve their own situation.

Additionally, any coach who continually sympathises throughout sessions is likely to become emotionally drained. Taking on the emotions of others is something that counsellors and therapists are trained to guard against or deal with because of the debilitating effects over time.

When empathy seems cold

Empathy is fine in response to more typical emotions of frustration, annoyance, disappointment, etc. However, the risk of merely empathising with the coachee is that sometimes this can appear a little cold and unsupportive. There are times when empathy is not the best way to respond to someone who is emotional.

Sometimes, situations and events demand a more sympathetic response. For example, your coachee has experienced a significant loss of some sort and is visibly upset by it. For you to say, 'I can appreciate how that must feel,' seems inappropriate. So does exploring the situation objectively or looking for possible learning when someone is very upset. Maybe the coachee needs to know that their sadness is normal and that you genuinely care in that moment. In this instance, sympathy is entirely appropriate, for example, 'Scott, that's awful, I'm so sorry.' Sometimes, as a coach, you must be willing to show a personal connection to someone's situation.

Ultimately, your choice of response rests on a combination of factors. You must consider what the coachee might want and what seems effective for coaching at that point. You must also consider the potential impact on the ongoing coaching relationship. You need to stay resourceful throughout the conversation and it isn't helpful if you sink into a similar emotional state to your coachee.

Of course, sometimes this level of restraint just isn't possible. Some things strike such a chord with us that we are genuinely unable to control our response. That's human, natural and a real part of the coaching relationship.

Your behaviour: 'what not to do'

Some barriers to effective coaching relate to things we might think or do during coaching conversations. For example, we might ask too many questions for the coachee to respond to or display impatience when the coachee becomes confused or unclear. Many of these are matters of common sense and you can identify them for yourself, while others are less obvious and deserve our distinct focus.

It's useful to look at what causes these behaviours as a way of raising our own awareness which then enables us to avoid them. We will look at some causes in more depth later in this section, but for now I'll say that most of what follows is caused by our ego, as our mind makes efforts to sustain a sense of control or maintain a positive image or appear a certain way.

The behaviours we are going to explore can be both subtle and damaging to your results as a coach. They are:

1 Talking too much.

2 Adopting too much control over the direction or content of a conversation.

3 Playing 'fix-it'.

   3.1 Strategising in the conversation.

4 Looking for the 'amazing moment'.

5 Wanting to look good in the conversation.

   5.1 Needing to be 'right' or appear infallible.

6 Assuming previous knowledge and experience is relevant.

7 Focusing on what not to do.

As with most coaching principles, there are no rights and wrongs, only better results, or outcomes. For example, it's not wrong to talk too much; it's just unlikely to produce the results that you want to create. Some of these behaviours might resonate with you more than others. For example, you may think that you never try to control others in conversation and

> **We can often be unaware of a tendency, simply because of our familiarity with it**

don't 'need' to be right. In my experience, we can often be unaware of a tendency, simply because of our familiarity with it. So, please reflect on all the barriers, to avoid any unseen saboteurs from degrading the quality of your coaching practice.

At a Glance

Going beyond barriers

In all instances, the following three-step response will help you deal with barriers when they arise. The more you practise this, the more automatically you will relax and refocus in a situation:

1 Awareness: you notice that you are doing or thinking something that's not working.

2 Acknowledgement: you acknowledge this – and give it up (let the thought/action go).

3 Refocus: you shift your attention to a more effective thought or behaviour.

Remember, during coaching, you must retain a neutral or buoyant emotional state, so becoming annoyed with yourself during a conversation doesn't help! That's why we simply acknowledge something (accept it) and then let it go in order to refocus.

Barrier 1: talking too much

It may sound obvious for a coach not to talk too much during a coaching conversation, but it's actually quite easy to do. Perhaps we are feeling particularly enthusiastic about a point we're making and, 10 minutes later, we're still talking. Or our coachee may seem reluctant to talk and so we fill a potentially awkward silence by chatting.

The principles of collaborative coaching rest on the coachee being able to explore their own thoughts and experiences in a way that encourages insight and learning. This just isn't possible if they have to constantly listen to the coach talking. I recommend that, in conversation, your coachee does at least 70 per cent of the talking, perhaps more.

To encourage this, you will be listening, asking questions, offering summaries, making observations, or giving feedback. Occasionally, you may choose to further illustrate a point by telling a brief story, drawing a simple diagram or whatever seems appropriate. Overall, the balance of all the talking will still rest with your coachee.

Silence encourages enquiry

Periods of quiet are preferable to the chatter of a coach who feels awkward with gaps in the discussion, or silence. Remember, for the coachee, silence is often a wonderful thing. By not having to speak or listen, they can take time to reflect on their internal thought processes. Deeper thoughts and feelings take time to form and further dialogue with the coach may distract or pressurise the coachee's internal process. When much of the productive insight during the session comes from the process of enquiry, silence is a key factor in enabling that to happen.

> **For the coachee, silence is often a wonderful thing**

Learn to notice when the coachee appears to be reflecting on thoughts and ideas; it's helpful for them to do so. Maybe you've just asked a question and the answer is not obvious, or maybe your coachee has just made an internal connection and wants to consider it. By allowing the conversation to fall into silence, we offer time and space for the coachee simply to think.

The following exercise will help you explore your comfort with silence.

Ideas into Action

Try being quiet . . .

Go and have a conversation with someone about something they are comfortable or familiar with. You might ask them about their weekend or something they are doing at work: anything that they can discuss easily.

At some point, allow the conversation to fall silent, if possible. For example, when they pause, do not respond automatically. Use one or two moments of silence to deepen the conversation, by allowing them to think and then speak again.

After the conversation, consider the following:

Q What effect did your silences have on the conversation?

Q During any silences, how did you feel?

Q When does using silence not work?

Q What did you learn from this?

Barrier 2: adopting too much control over the direction or content of a conversation

Collaborative coaching involves encouraging someone to explore their own thoughts or experiences. It is important for the coach to maintain a balance between keeping the conversation focused and supporting its natural flow. The next dialogue illustrates too much control by the coach:

Coach: So, let's talk some more about the situation with your father. We need to find out exactly what the problem is and what's causing his behaviour. We need to get to the bottom of this, I think.

Coachee: Well, what is it you want to know?

Coach: Tell me about the most recent argument you've had with him and how he made you feel.

As you can see, the coach is controlling both the content and direction of the conversation. In this case, the coachee adopts a compliant, almost submissive, posture, saying, 'Well, what is it you want to know?' This places the coach in control of the conversation, which feels less like the equal partnership we need. Plus, there is little opportunity for the natural flow of the conversation to emerge.

The next dialogue demonstrates a coach maintaining a helpful focus, while enabling the flow of the conversation to emerge and develop:

Coach: So, you mentioned that your father's aggravating the situation and I wondered if it might help to talk a little more about that?

Coachee: Well, he's just being totally unsupportive of my efforts to get into college. He just keeps telling me to get out and get a job.

Coach:	What else does he say?
Coachee:	He says I'm wasting my time; that I'm going to be disappointed and let down when I can't get the course that I want.
Coach:	What might be his reasons for saying that?
Coachee:	I guess because he thinks I might do what my brother did when he was rejected. Mark ended up doing nothing for a year, just sat round the house being miserable.

You'll notice how the coach uses open questions to gently surface information from the coachee. If either party has the balance of control, it's probably the coachee. The coachee causes the direction of the conversation to emerge based on the information they are offering.

Closed questions increase control

The following dialogue shows how our questions can exert an inappropriate level of control:

Coachee:	So, I've decided that I'm not taking the job – they can keep it.
Coach:	Before you met the manager, didn't you say you wanted the job?
Coachee:	Well, yes – but things have changed now.
Coach:	And didn't you say you wanted a challenge?
Coachee:	Yes, I still do.
Coach:	Well, if you wanted the job and you wanted a challenge, isn't this the perfect opportunity for you?

In this dialogue, the coach used a series of tactically worded questions to close down the options of the coachee. The questions are closed questions, which leave the coachee little room to explain themselves fully. As a result, the coachee's own thoughts and insights are not explored and the potential of the situation is unlikely to emerge.

This type of control also places the coach in a superior position to the coachee. So, once again, the relationship feels more parental than adult-to-adult. A more collaborative version of the previous dialogue might be:

Coachee:	So, I've decided that I'm not taking the job – they can keep it.
Coach:	Okay, what's caused that decision?
Coachee:	Well, I don't seem to be what they're looking for, I guess.
Coach:	What are they looking for, do you think?

Coachee: Well, they seem to want someone energised and motivated. I've felt so low for so long in my current job I've forgotten what that's like.

As you can see, when the coach adopts a more open style of questioning, the conversation goes in a very different direction. As we notice we are controlling the content and direction of a conversation, we can reduce our influence quickly. In doing so, we open the potential for a natural flow of thoughts and ideas to emerge.

At a Glance

What causes your need to control?

There are a range of factors that increase our tendency to want to control a conversation. For example, we might:

✓ think we have spotted a solution to a problem and want to lead the coachee towards it

✓ think the coachee wants or expects us to take control

✓ have high energy for, or interest in, the topic under discussion

✓ be frustrated at the amount of time it's taking to discuss a subject/get to a point

✓ know a lot about the subject being discussed and want to display our knowledge

✓ have a naturally authoritative manner in conversation (maybe we are used to managing, or 'leading from the front')

✓ decide our coachee isn't 'getting something' and that we need to help them do that.

To practise reducing control in conversation, try the items 'Help someone else find their answer' and 'Develop deeper listening' in the Free resources section.

Barrier 3: playing 'fix-it'

Sometimes, in a coaching conversation, we assume that the coachee has a problem and it's up to us to help them find the answer. I call that playing 'fix-it'. We are focusing our efforts on finding a problem in what's being said and then trying to solve it (either in our own head or in discussion with the coachee). Drawbacks of doing this include the following:

- As coaches, we develop an inappropriate filter to listen only for problems.
- We are distracted by our own thoughts and analysis, which reduces our focus on the other person.
- Our solutions may be inadequate or less relevant than those the coachee could build themselves, given the time and support to do so.
- Our coachee can end up feeling frustrated or flawed – something of a 'problem case'.
- The person we are coaching disengages from the process as it feels more like 'training' than purpose-based enquiry.

Look at the following dialogue for signs of the coach playing fix-it:

Coachee: So, really, I don't know why I've taken on organising the party at all. It's typical of me to get stuck with something like this.

Coach: Well, why don't you cancel it?

Coachee: Oh, I couldn't do that, we'd lose money on caterers and flowers and things.

Coach: Can you get someone else to help you, then?

Coachee: Not at this late stage and, besides, why should I ask? They should be offering!

Coach: What about moving the date, then?

From the dialogue, the coach thinks that they have found the problem – namely that the coachee doesn't want to organise the party. The coach is playing 'fix-it', and is therefore reacting to incomplete information, guessing at possible solutions.

Instead, our coach needs to spend more time in enquiry to understand the situation and let the conversation develop naturally. The next example demonstrates a better approach:

Coachee: So, really, I don't know why I've taken on organising the party at all. It's typical of me to get stuck with something like this.

Coach: Okay, can you say a little more about that?

Coachee: Well, I seem to be the one who ends up doing all the work. I wouldn't mind if anyone actually acknowledged me for it. A simple 'thanks' would do.

The conversation has gone in a different direction, as the coach gently explores the situation. The problem (if there is one) may turn out to be entirely different from initial impressions. Maybe the coachee simply wants to be acknowledged for their efforts, or for efforts they've made in the past. By ignoring any temptation to find a problem and solve it, the coach helps both understanding and resolution emerge more naturally.

At a Glance

Coach the person, not the issue

In coaching, remember to focus primarily on the person in front of you, rather than their issue. Sometimes, we can get so involved in the engaging challenge of a situation that we forget that our role is not to solve someone's issues for them. By using behaviours such as silence, summarising and questioning, we support the coachee to find their own solution. Of course, at times it's okay to provide assistance in the form of the occasional observation, opinion or idea. However, please remember that your primary focus is to help the individual make their own connections. Only by providing them with the space and opportunity to do that will it happen.

Again, to practise your skills in this area, try the exercises 'Help someone else find their answer' and 'Develop deeper listening' in the Free resources section.

Barrier 3.1: strategising in the conversation

Another barrier to effective coaching is a subtle form of control known as strategising. By strategising, I mean when a coach starts saying or doing things to create a certain outcome. It links to the previous barrier of playing 'fix-it', as our compulsion to 'fix' something often causes us to strategise. For example, we may say something or ask a question to have the other person realise something or go towards an idea that we have decided is right. We might argue that our intentions for playing these mental tactics with the coachee are positive. Whatever our reasons for doing it – we are still strategising.

There are several ways a coach might strategise in a coaching conversation, and they all have one thing in common: when a coach is strategising, they are saying what they are saying 'to get a certain result' and they are not declaring this motive to the coachee. There is a subtle note of covert manipulation to strategising that enables us to distinguish it. Here are two examples of when we might slip into strategising.

Strategising to avoid appearing confused

Maybe a coach is thinking, 'This conversation just isn't working, and I don't know why.' The coach might feel uncomfortable about voicing that and so decide to take another route to explore the issue. They might say, 'Let's look at our original goals here.' This may or may not address the underlying issue – that the coach does not think the conversation is 'working'.

If the coach were being more truthful, they would say, 'I'm not sure that this conversation is working – how is it for you?' This is likely to open a conversation that exposes what's happening. If the conversation isn't working for the coach, it probably isn't for the coachee either. By approaching the subject openly and directly, the coach can explore what's really happening. Maybe the coachee wants to talk about a more random topic and has been preoccupied with that from the beginning of the session. If the coach hides what they are thinking and says, 'Let's look at our original goals here,' the coachee's other topic is unlikely to surface. By strategising, the coach avoided tackling the issue directly.

Strategising to avoid giving a potentially uncomfortable message

Here's how strategising looks when the coach is avoiding discomfort or potential conflict.

Coachee:	Well, I just don't agree with feedback comments. How can people say I withhold information? I think we should disregard that whole section of comments as malicious rubbish.
Coach thinks:	[I've heard you say, 'Information is power in this place' repeatedly and also that you don't tell anyone anything that they don't need to know.]
Coach says:	[In order to avoid giving more difficult feedback] What might have caused these comments, do you think?
Coachee:	No idea. There are lots of competitive people here; I think a lot of them just don't like to see others getting on.

The coach is effectively hiding what they are thinking. This may be to protect the coachee from potential discomfort or to avoid a confrontation. Or perhaps they are unused to giving feedback and so are less comfortable with that. Unfortunately, this may not create much learning for the coachee. One of the core coaching skills is the ability to give challenging messages in a constructive way, as supportive feedback. This skill enables the coach to say what needs to be said, to progress the coachee's awareness.

Being authentic – speaking our truth

The opposite of strategising is being authentic. When we are authentic, we speak our truth, we say what is there and this is not corrupted or changed in any way. For example, if we are worried about driving on the motorway, we declare, 'I'm worried about driving on the motorway.' We do not say, 'Let's go the country route, it's prettier.' In coaching, this level of honesty is needed to create openness and trust within the coaching relationship. It's also a more powerful way to communicate.

Example of being authentic

Using the previous example, let's look at a more authentic response from our coach.

Coachee:	Well, I just don't agree with feedback comments. How can people say I withhold information? I think we should disregard that whole section of comments as malicious rubbish.
Coach thinks:	[I've heard you say, 'Information is power in this place' repeatedly and also that you don't tell anyone anything that they don't need to know.]
Coach says:	That's quite a tough message, isn't it? Although, I can see some potential links to something you said in our last session – can I remind you of those?
Coachee:	Sure – I'd love to know what's going on here!
Coach says:	When we were discussing the management team meetings, you said you reported the minimum of your department's plans as 'Information is power in this place'. And, when we talked more about that, you said you saw no reason to tell anyone anything that they didn't need to know. I'm just wondering if we aren't seeing some of the effects of that here.
Coachee:	Yes, but everyone does that, don't they?
Coach says:	I don't know. And, right now, what's important to me is what works for you. Maybe, like this approach to reporting information might not be working. You appear to have created a perception that you withhold information.
Coachee:	Well, maybe I do but it's for good reason – but it's silly, isn't it? Do people really want to know this stuff? Maybe I need to think about this a bit.

Letting go of strategising

The way to avoid strategising begins with catching ourselves doing it. We need to develop an internal alarm bell for this behaviour. Using the previous example, maybe the coach thinks that the coachee needs to talk to the person who gave the feedback and express their concerns about it. The coach then starts to ask a series of questions to lead the coachee to that conclusion. The coach may or may not be right with their idea, and strategising with it can lead to trouble. It is more honest, and usually effective, for the coach simply to declare their thoughts at that point, for example, 'I keep wondering how speaking to Deborah about your concerns might help. What do you think?' Yes, you're being directive and so there's a need for you to notice that and switch back to a less directive mode quickly (which is helped by the 'what do you think?' part).

A good place to practise giving up strategising is in normal everyday conversation. Whenever we have an agenda for a conversation, or think we know how it's going to go, we tend to strategise. A simple example: your partner wants to go out for dinner tonight and you're too tired. You don't want to say so, because you think that sounds lame. So, instead, you start asking questions to change your partner's mind, such as 'Won't it be difficult to get a booking?', 'Aren't we supposed to be saving money?' or 'Who's going to drive and not drink?'

Once you have noticed yourself doing it, you can give it up. You might choose to declare your hidden thought or feeling, or simply let it go. Maybe a good night out is just what you need to refresh your spirits!

Ideas into Action

When are you strategising?

The following exercise can help you develop your own awareness of when you are strategising. It will also help you speak your own thoughts more authentically.

Use a conversation with someone to notice the difference between what you think and what you actually say. Pick a conversation with someone you're less close to – perhaps you're less relaxed in their company, or just never became really familiar with them. A colleague might work well – a partner or best friend might not.

Step one – develop awareness

During the conversation, watch that moment just before you say something. Maybe the other person has just said something to you and you're

---

going to respond. At that moment, you might first have a thought, maybe an opinion – do you respond with that thought? How much difference is there between what you're thinking and what you're saying?

Step two – practise authentic responses (optional)

Where you notice a difference between your true (authentic) thought or view and the response you might normally give, instead give a response that more accurately reflects your views. This will feel like you are speaking your simple truth, rather than what you think might sound right or appropriate. It's often easier to begin with something minor, like a true response to the question 'How are you?' or 'How was your holiday?' Say what you really think, rather than what you think might be expected.

Step three – focus on learning

After the conversation, consider the following:

Q How much did your speech match your real thoughts and views?

Q What causes the difference between what you think and what you say?

Q How does speaking your real thoughts and views feel?

Q What would happen if you matched your thoughts to your speech more often?

Q When might this not work so well?

This exercise draws our attention to times we might be strategising, simply to raise your awareness of that. Over time, you might choose to speak your truth on more significant matters, for example say what you think about a difficult situation or something you disagree with. Over time, I hope that you will find that staying more authentic helps you in other ways too.

Barrier 4: looking for the 'amazing moment'

Sometimes, in coaching, we experience a magical 'Aha!' moment between ourselves and our coachee. A fabulous idea or insight presents itself and the perfect way forward for the coachee appears. Problems dissolve, blockages are cleared, light dawns and the sun comes out. As coaches, for us this feels great. We know that, by the process of our conversation, we have really made a difference to someone. The 'buzz' of the whole experience can be quite uplifting and mildly addictive.

However, our barrier arises when we attempt to repeat this experience in other coaching sessions. We want to experience the high of that wonderful moment when the magical solution or insight is found. So, we assume that there's a great solution to every coachee's situation and attempt to find one in each session. We believe that, as a coach, we need to create tangible results in the form of amazing breakthroughs or ideas and so we form an attachment to doing that.

Amazing moments are fairly rare in coaching and usually occur when we least expect them – which means that trying to get the coachee to have a remarkable insight or flash of brilliance doesn't work. Personal coaching is a gradual process, where insights and learning emerge as much between coaching sessions as they do in them. For a coach to try always to produce fast or amazing results can distort their view of the conversation. Please remember that the coachee determines the value and effectiveness of coaching for them. Most coachees don't need amazing insights or breakthroughs; they simply need support with their ongoing learning and development processes.

> **Coaching is a gradual process, where insights and learning emerge as much between coaching sessions as they do in them**

Perfection is in the eye of the beholder

Sometimes, a great solution for the coachee does not look great to the coach. For example, your coachee explains how his studies at night school are interfering with his social life. The course that he's taking falls on the same night as his bowling club's match nights.

During the process of the coaching conversation, your coachee realises that, if he leaves the evening class 30 minutes early, he can still make the bowling night. At this point, the coachee seems pleased he's found what feels like a workable compromise. But you don't think that this sounds like a perfect solution. After all, the qualification the coachee is taking is important to his life goals.

At this point, as coach, you have options:

1 Accept the coachee's choice of a way forward.

2 Explore the potential risks and benefits of this option further.

3 Encourage the coachee to think of something else.

If you are still looking for the perfect solution, you will pursue option 3 and continue looking for another idea. This may cause your coachee to feel uncomfortable, as what feels to him to be a great idea is being disregarded.

However, if you genuinely feel that this is a flawed idea but simply accept it anyway (option 1), then you risk sharing the burden of the ultimate consequences. Maybe the coachee's coursework will suffer and he won't get the qualification that was so important to him professionally.

Bad ideas usually expose themselves very quickly when they are explored more fully. Likewise, apparently flawed ideas expose themselves as perfect by the same process of exploration. The following dialogue illustrates this principle, as the coach takes option 2 and explores the potential risks and benefits of the idea.

Coach: How will leaving the class early affect your studies?

Coachee: Oh, not at all. The last half-hour is always reading and reflection time. I can do that on the bus ride home.

Coach: And what will your tutor say if you request to leave early?

Coachee: Well, if I'm doing the reading, I don't think she'll mind. She's very easy-going as long as we keep up with our homework, which I always do.

So, ultimately, the coachee's idea appears workable. It may still not seem perfect to the coach. However, if the coach persists in pursuing a perfect solution, it may become a frustrating and pointless process for both parties. They may easily end up back where they started, with the coachee's first idea being the only practical way forward.

Barrier 5: wanting to look good in the conversation

We all have a need to maintain a positive image in the eyes of other people and ourselves (I call it 'looking good'). In coaching, this tendency can obstruct an effective conversation because it diverts our attention from staying fully present in the conversation. We may do or say things to impress, rather than for the actual benefit of the coaching conversation. When we are not fully present, the following can be also true:

- Our mind is focused too much on ourselves (how we are appearing) and not enough on the coachee.
- We are not as open and honest as we might be.
- Because we are less open and honest, we have less impact in the conversation.

When a coach devotes effort to look good in conversations, it reduces the quality of their attention and so their effectiveness.

> **When a coach devotes effort to look good in conversations, it reduces the quality of their attention and so their effectiveness**

Within coaching, there are various pressures upon a coach to look good. When a coach is delivering the service of coaching, it follows that the coachee may have certain expectations of them. For example, as a coach, you might imagine that you should appear to:

- be professional and business-like
- be very experienced/knowledgeable
- say clever or smart things
- have all the answers
- have a significant impact in a conversation
- know just what to say within the conversation
- have a happy, fulfilling life, free of problems or conflict.

Be yourself – everyone else is taken

Wanting to look good isn't a bad thing; it's a way we've learned to cope with some of the risks and pressures of life. We might assume that the alternative to looking good is looking bad – and that feels wrong to us. The alternative to using behaviours intended to make us look good is simply to be our natural selves.

For example, a coachee explains that they would really like to exercise more but they just don't feel like it. The coach just happens to have studied theories of human motivation, so spends the next 10 minutes describing Maslow's hierarchy of needs and drawing diagrams on paper as proof of this knowledge. The coach forgets the original point that led to the discussion of this theory, as they enjoy demonstrating how much they know. In the meantime, the coachee has become bored with the conversation and doesn't see how it relates to why he can't be bothered to go to the gym.

The coach has fallen into the trap of wanting to appear knowledgeable to the coachee. This may be to gain more credibility, or simply because they enjoy appearing knowledgeable. Unfortunately, the coach has diverted the conversation from something important and relevant, namely the coachee's lack of motivation. Instead, they focused the conversation on something less relevant – a lengthy explanation of Maslow's theory. If we'd interrupted the coach part way through his explanation and asked him, 'Why are you saying this stuff now?', a really truthful answer would be, 'Because I think it's impressive/sounds good . . .'

Confusion can be powerful

Another form of our 'looking good' trap arises from a real or imagined expectation from the coachee that the coach has all the answers and will always know the best thing to say. Sometimes, the best thing you can do as a coach is to acknowledge that you are as confused by a situation as your coachee. At least then you can work through the facts and issues together.

When we pretend we know or guess an answer, we can take the conversation in the wrong direction. So, after voicing your own confusion, one valid option is to give a brief summary instead. Remember, when you summarise the facts for your coachee, you'll give them space to reflect and think. However, giving summaries isn't something you'd want to do every few minutes as that can have the reverse effect of slowing things down. But a well-timed, 'Look, I'm not sure either, okay. Let's look at where we've got to . . .' can be the pause that accelerates progress.

Barrier 5.1: needing to be 'right' or appear infallible

This barrier links to the previous idea and yet deserves its own mention. Generally, we like being right and we don't enjoy being wrong. As coaches, we need to give up an attachment to being right – it simply gets in the way of the conversation. Oh, and because our attachment to being right is linked to our need to look good, to let go of an attachment to being right, we must also give up an attachment to looking good!

For example, a coachee may be considering setting up home with a new partner and complaining that they are having second thoughts. The coach may have a theory about why this is and become inadvertently attached to it:

Coach: Well, I think the reason you're having doubts is because you're anticipating everything that could go wrong. After all, it's a big step for you.

Coachee: No, it's not that. I haven't actually thought about what could go wrong.

Coach: Yes, but a lot of these things happen subconsciously. I think you're displaying a tendency called transference – that means you're transferring the real problem in order to disguise it.

In this example, our coach has made several mistakes. First, they've begun to play 'fix-it' as they try and produce a reason for the coachee's misgivings.

The coach doesn't actually understand the situation fully and needs to focus on enquiry to develop more understanding and insight. There's also some strategising going on – did you notice that?

Second, they appear to want to prove that their theory is right. Because of this attachment, they are taking the conversation in an inappropriate direction. From here, the conversation might develop into looking for things the coachee thinks might go wrong, or even why they haven't been thinking about what might go wrong! By using words like 'transference' the coach is also displaying some knowledge of psychology (that's the 'looking good' part). The effect on the coachee is likely to be one of confusion and/or defensiveness.

> **Remember that, when coaching, it's okay to sometimes make mistakes or get things wrong**

As coaches, when we make a mistake or get something wrong, we need to handle it in a mature, unattached way. There's a simple three-step approach that I use:

1 Acknowledge I'm wrong, either to myself or the coachee (whichever is appropriate).

2 Put the mistake right, if possible/appropriate.

3 Let go of thoughts of being wrong – move on.

For example, to show the previous example in a more effective way:

Coach: Well, I think the reason you're having doubts is because you're anticipating everything that could go wrong. After all, it's a big step for you.

Coachee: No, it's not that. I haven't actually thought about what could go wrong.

Coach: Okay, that's probably me jumping to conclusions. Tell me more about what you've been thinking.

Quickly and smoothly, the coach acknowledges their error and continues the coaching conversation. Both the coach and the coachee can carry on with the natural flow of the conversation uninterrupted.

Please remember that, when coaching, it's okay to sometimes make mistakes or get things wrong. All coaches do. What's not okay is for us to spend time and effort justifying or disguising errors or mistakes. To do so can confuse, disrupt or impair the coaching process.

Barrier 6: assuming previous knowledge and experience is relevant

This trap is an easy one to fall into and, when coupled with a tendency to want to fix things, can really inhibit a productive coaching session. Here we assume that what we know, our experience, thoughts or knowledge, is relevant to the coachee and then overlay that onto their situation.

Unfortunately, when we do a lot of coaching, the same or similar situations crop up. Sometimes, the situation or issue your coachee is describing sounds just like one you've heard before – a sort of flawed version of déjà vu. Because we hear that the conversation or the situation is similar, we can expect other aspects of it to be similar as well.

For example, your coachee explains a problem with their boss at work. They complain that their boss interferes too much in what they do, and they get really frustrated and annoyed by that. As you listen, you think you recognise the issue; you think, 'Aah, this is just like that session last week – they need to understand their boss's intentions.' From this thought, we jump to conclusions, for example that we understand the situation, or that we know what we need to do in the conversation. Our orientation to the person and conversation changes. We might then introduce the ideas that benefited the previous session, even though they are less relevant here. Remember, treat every new conversation as a new situation, no matter how familiar it feels.

> **Treat every new conversation as a new situation, no matter how familiar it feels**

Stay focused on the present reality

The other pitfall of assuming relevant knowledge or experience is that we reduce the clarity of our focus and attention. When we divert our thoughts to past coaching conversations, we lose our focus on the present. This impairs the quality of our attention and listening, which in turn affects our ability to appreciate fully what the coachee is telling us, and so coach effectively.

Barrier 7: focusing on what not to do

Now that we've discussed several things a coach needs 'not' to do during coaching sessions, we've created another. There's an obvious risk in focusing on 'what not to do' during a coaching conversation. For example, if I tell you, *do not think about* a blue rabbit wearing dark sunglasses – no really, *don't* think about his blue rabbit fur and his black sunglasses – what do you think about? (Surely, not a blue rabbit wearing dark sunglasses?!)

Coaches also need to not think about what they are not supposed to be doing . . . Confused? That is exactly the point.

When, as a coach, your head is full of thoughts like, 'Don't control the conversation', 'Don't treat them like they're a problem', or 'Am I strategising?', then you are distracted by your internal conversation rather than listening to the coachee. In addition, by focusing on what not to do, you may easily end up doing it. Did you ever have an awkward conversation where you knew you shouldn't use a word and, yet, that was the only word that would come? For example, 'Just don't say failure' – and the word failure is the only word you can think of.

Again, we need to develop the muscle of our attention to refocus productively. Use the earlier three-step process of awareness, acknowledgement and substitution to refocus your attention and let go of any negative or distracting thoughts.

The power of substitution

One way for us to let go of a thought is to replace it with another thought to refocus our mind. For example, if you find yourself playing 'fix-it', you might remind yourself, 'Just let the solutions emerge.' Alternatively, when you notice you are talking too much, you might remind yourself, 'Just listen and focus back on them.' It's like realising that a torch you have is shining on the wrong side of a room. You simply move the torch; as the light moves, you illuminate a better area, while returning the other side to darkness.

The ego – your mind's tendency to create barriers

Most – maybe all – of the behavioural barriers we've discussed are driven by our ego, which is formed by our mind's thoughts and tendencies, and borne from our sense of yourself. By our sense of self, I mean our ongoing concept of 'who we are'. This concept is indicated by the descriptive labels we give ourselves, such as 'I am a daughter, son, partner, father, mother, coach', etc. Some of our labels contain judgement, for example a good person/kind person, talented coach/rubbish coach, etc. Our ego also produces our self-consciousness (literally our consciousness of ourselves) and an inbuilt reluctance to appear vulnerable to others.

'Your ego is a false identity that your mind constructed and then you took up residence in.'

Brandon Bays

As a function of our mind, our ego creates our sense of ourselves as something separate and distinct from the world we live in. Some functions of the ego are practical, such as an ability to see ourselves as something different from the world around us. That means we do not walk into chairs or through half-open doorways. Other functions are less helpful and based on our ego's fear-based need to protect and survive. This causes an often-unconscious drive to move away from imagined threat, discomfort or pain, both physical and emotional. For example, in winter, I might get angry because my partner keeps turning our central heating down – as I fear being cold. Or, in a social group, I might avoid sharing an embarrassing experience, to avoid revisiting the emotional discomfort of that.

> **Our ego creates our sense of ourselves as something separate and distinct from the world we live in**

The illusion of size and the relevance of influence

We often imagine that ego is defined by size, for example, 'He/she has a huge ego,' but it is more accurate to assess our ego and its impact in terms of its effect upon us. By that I mean how strong the influence of your ego is on you in situations and how much choice you have over that. For example, if you fear rejection, can you still approach a situation where you might get rejected? Your ability to stay free from the influence of your ego might look like, 'Okay, I'm uncomfortable asking for this in case they say no – and I'm still going to ask them.' A healthy relationship with our ego is to be aware of its influence and still have free choice in situations.

The three horsemen of the ego

Our ego is driven by base human emotions such as fear, guilt and shame. In our everyday life, we may experience these emotions only mildly, if at all. The strongest versions of these emotions we feel only rarely. For example, a mild version of fear may be apprehension or tension. Other emotions may surface as a sense of discomfort, resistance or 'stuckness'. Our mind forms strategies to move away from these emotions so that, literally, they are not experienced or felt. The avoidance strategies of the ego can be better understood (and related to) using the following three-part structure:[1]

1 **Inflation** – building ourselves up, boasting, exaggeration, etc. Here our strategies away from discomfort cause us to develop 'showy' or ostentatious behaviour.

2 **Deflation** – reducing ourselves, being shy, withdrawing, 'playing small', etc. Here we diminish emotions by efforts to negate or contradict them, for example, 'I don't really care.'

3 **Rigidity** – becoming stuck, inflexible or intransigent, stubborn, refusing to change or adapt, etc. Here we barricade ourselves from emotions using lots of rules and formulas, which act as a shield against emotions.

Use the following checklist to notice how some of our common (human) tendencies link to the previous strategies for yourself.

Ideas into Action

Spot signs of your ego

Consider the following to identify the influence (or fixations) of your ego:

✓ *Inflation:* How conscious are you of your own need to portray yourself in a certain light or image? For example, 'I'm a good person/smart person/attractive person etc.'

✓ *Inflation:* How much might you exaggerate your successes, or compete in conversation with others?

✓ *Inflation:* How strong is your need to control or dominate a situation, person, or environment?

✓ *Deflation:* How much do you play down your own strengths and achievements, perhaps deferring to other people instead?

✓ *Deflation:* How much do you focus on your own weaknesses, or criticise yourself (rather than compare your weaknesses objectively and in true proportion to your strengths)?

✓ *Deflation:* How easily do you become shy or self-conscious in situations (and how do you react when that happens)?

✓ *Rigidity:* How defensive and stubborn are you when you are wrong in a situation? For example, how easily do you say sorry?

✓ *Rigidity:* How much do you worry unnecessarily about things that might go wrong?

✓ *Rigidity:* How adaptable are you in situations? For example, how willing are you to change your position or point of view?

While the above questions can be uncomfortable for us to consider, they do help us become more self-aware and that is generally a positive thing. However, it is less helpful if we then criticise ourselves because of our responses. Please be kind to yourself when you reflect on the above and remember that everything is progress.

The ego in coaching

In coaching, our ego shows up as unhelpful thoughts, urges and, sometimes, actions or behaviours. For example, to avoid feeling uncertain or exposed intellectually, we might tend to stay in topics of conversation where we are knowledgeable. The barriers of playing 'fix-it', looking good and strategising can relate to our ego's drive to do this. Another example is that our need to stay in the known might make us only ask questions that we imagine we know the answer to, whereas, of course, we need to be willing to ask questions that we don't know the answer to!

> **We need to be willing to ask questions that we don't know the answer to!**

For us to fulfil the potential of the coaching process, we must be willing to go beyond the false limits and boundaries that the ego wants to place upon us and the conversation as it happens. We do this by simply staying present.

'The ego's greatest enemy of all is the present moment.'

Eckhart Tolle

Don't use the ego to try and fix the ego

Once we become more aware of its tendency to influence and limit us in situations, our ego can be frustrating. For example, in coaching, you might see how you sometimes don't ask plain and simple questions. Instead, you over-complicate them in an attempt to sound clever until your questions actually sound confused and lack impact. When you analyse the session afterwards, you realise that you simply need to stop worrying about sounding stupid and just ask a potentially foolish or obvious question.

What doesn't work is noticing what we've done and then giving ourselves a hard time about it. Remember, self-criticism is simply more mind chatter (thoughts) and, ultimately, a symptom of the ego's deflation and rigidity! Practise our earlier three-step routine of 'awareness, acknowledgement, and refocus' to let negative thoughts quieten down.

'Compassion for others begins with kindness to ourselves.'

Pema Chodron

Stay present in the conversation

Much of the ego's influence upon us arrives in the form of mind chatter, or compulsions (feelings) linked to our thoughts. For example, in a coaching session, the other person becomes visibly upset and they begin crying, which makes you feel awkward, or unsure, or both. So, you fill the uncomfortable silence with talking, and try to make the other person feel better. You switch subjects to something they can discuss without being upset and the conversation continues as if their becoming upset didn't happen. Only afterwards do you realise that, at the 'upset' point, the topic being discussed was probably useful for the individual to work through. What stopped you from pursuing it were your uncomfortable thoughts and feelings, for example, 'Oh no, now they're upset, and I did that, this is getting really bad.' What you needed to do was stay focused on the other person and notice what they needed and what would work best for them.

When we are present, to ourselves, our situation, and the people we are with, our minds naturally fall quiet, which means the influence of the ego lessens, as it ceases to generate thoughts and feelings from imagined risks, anxieties or needs. As a coach, you become more authentic, as your behaviours align more with your own true values, rather than the fear-based drives of your ego.

Use the exercise that follows to practise staying present.

Ideas into Action

Are you present?

In conversation, we focus quite a lot on our own thoughts, what is being said, what we are thinking of saying, etc. This exercise demands that we let those thoughts go, as we focus solely on what is really happening. This is a challenge and, yet, also incredibly rewarding!

Step one – present to yourself

Becoming present requires us to refocus our attention into the here and now. Do it now. Lift your head up from reading this and focus on wherever you are – your surroundings. What can you see and what can you hear? Let your mind go quiet, as you become acutely aware of what's actually going on. See what you are seeing, hear what you are hearing, feel what you are feeling. Breathe. Notice. Ask, 'Where am I now?'

Step two – present to someone else

Go and have a conversation with someone and practise being 'present' while you're talking to them. Really focus your attention on them and what they are saying. The more present to them you become, the more your mind will fall quiet as you notice them properly. Notice any mind chatter (thoughts) or compulsions. Any time your mind drifts off, wanders, or starts thinking of something else, bring it back to what's happening there and then. Practise our three-step routine:

1 Become aware (notice).

2 Acknowledge (I'm present).

3 Refocus (open and attentive).

When you speak, stay present to what you're saying, experience your own words and the impact they have.

Step three – focus on learning

After trying this, congratulate yourself for staying present for an extended period of time (that's unusual). Then ask yourself the following:

Q What is different about a conversation when you remain present?

Q What did you have to do to become present?

Q If you remained present more in your conversations, what impact would that have?

Practise becoming present regularly, until it feels very natural as a place to operate from. When we are more present more often, we notice our situation and circumstances more lucidly. We literally become more conscious to our reality; and, if that sounds grandiose, the everyday benefits include fewer mislaid phones and keys, fewer forgotten appointments, and lower stress levels generally!

In a Nutshell

Much of the skill of coaching lies in what a good coach doesn't do, as well as in what they do. Some behaviour is counterproductive to the coaching process and gets in the way of a great conversation. Some of these are simple behaviours, like talking too much, while others relate to the coach's belief, such as a need to be right, or to find the perfect solution.

Once we become aware of these behavioural barriers, we are able to let them go.

The way to avoid these barriers is to develop an intuitive sense of when you're implementing them. This begins with increasing your awareness, including understanding the pitfalls, which you are doing by reading about them here.

Over time, you won't have to wonder if you're doing something that's not working, as your unconscious will let you know. Intuitively, you may get a feeling or thought that you're not content somehow, as something in the conversation feels uncomfortable. When you attend to that thought, you'll notice what it is that you're doing. At that point, just acknowledge the realisation, give up doing whichever counterproductive behaviour you've slipped into and move on (let the thought go).

chapter 6

Coaching conversations: The Coaching Path

'True navigation begins in the human heart. It's the most important map of all.'

Elizabeth Kapu'uwailani Lindsey

This chapter offers you a supporting structure, or guide, for a typical coaching conversation. By typical, I refer to most formal coaching conversations, as well as many casual or unplanned conversations. My coaching path is intended to help you navigate through a conversation. It is not intended to provide a definitive formula, or to inhibit your natural creativity and flexibility. So please use what follows to support and encourage your coaching, rather than be restricted by it.

Figure 6.1 illustrates the basic path that a typical coaching conversation might follow. Although you will see five stages illustrated, please know that that the first and last relate to opening and closing the conversation and require only basic skills. Plus, you are already familiar with greeting people and ending conversations, so you simply need to adapt your current approach slightly to ensure you do that effectively in a coaching situation. It's the middle stages of

Figure 6.1 The Coaching Path

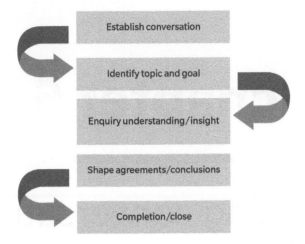

two, three and four that actually distinguish this as a coaching conversation, rather than any other type of conversation. To guide you along, at each stage, you will find principles and example dialogue that follows the complete path of a conversation.

The coaching path: guiding principles

To continue the idea of a journey, imagine the different stages as places to dwell or stay a while. By that, I mean that this is not a sequence of 'tick boxes' that you need to complete. During conversation, these activities expand and contract naturally. Also, activities along the path may be returned to or combined. For example, you may initially agree on a topic the coachee wants to work on and then need to revise that when you surface a more important issue or topic. Or you might return to an activity, for example go back into enquiry as you find that something about a topic or situation is unclear.

These are activities, not tasks

The coaching path is a series of activities that blend, rather than a list of tasks to get done. Please remember that, if you approach the phases as tasks, you're more likely to focus on completing tasks and so allow a mechanical feel to the conversation to develop. You may also feel more determined to get to the end and could miss subtle cues from the coachee that you need to backtrack, or simply stay where you are a while longer.

For example, you are at the stage of 'enquiry and understanding' where you imagine your job is to gather a description of a problem related to why someone is unhappy in their work situation. Your coachee tells you the cause of their frustration is the long hours plus too much pressure and stress; however, you may still not truly understand what is really going on. But, if you think your role is simply to collect an answer to the question, then you may move on to the next phase, 'agreeing ways forward'. You may facilitate your coachee to come up with ideas for a way forward, which include refusing to work overtime, or even quitting the job completely. However, if we had stayed in enquiry a while longer, we might have surfaced the person's underlying reluctance to ask for help in an area of the job they find particularly difficult. We needed to let go of our urge to move forward or make progress in the conversation and relax into the activity of enquiry even further. Then we'd have noticed that, actually, the coachee had more to say about the topic. On hearing about the issue with long hours, we might have picked up a note of discord, or something not quite ringing true. Remember, our focus should be on the coachee and what they are saying, rather than getting through the stages.

> **Our focus should be on the coachee and what they are saying, rather than getting through the stages**

Let's work an example through The Coaching Path
Coaching Trey

The following scenario demonstrates how The Coaching Path unfolds during a discussion. Trey is our coachee and it might help if you could imagine yourself as the coach. For the purposes of this example, let's acknowledge that it's a distilled version of a conversation. This means that we have reduced the dialogue to leave the key principles exposed. Normal conversation when written down would not make for great reading! In real life, I would expect much less 'coherence'. For example, from the coachee, we'd hear more stalls, half-sentences and repeated information, or even nonsense. From the coach I'd expect more 'umms' and 'aaahs', plus more questions that didn't add much value, a few blind alleys, etc.

In this scenario, the coach will be using principles, behaviours and skills outlined elsewhere in this text. In particular, the skills described in Chapter 4 Five fundamental skills of coaching, will provide support for your reading. So, let's use the scenario to travel along the coaching path.

Stage one – establish conversation

This first stage is about you building the basics of a conversation, for example saying hello, having the other person feel comfortable, welcoming them into the conversation and creating a good balance between warmth and formality. You will see we're at the start of the path in Figure 6.1.

Our objectives at this stage include:

- Greet your coachee in an appropriate manner.
- Establish warmth and rapport.
- Deal with any housekeeping, such as duration of session, any potential interruptions, etc.
- Create an appropriate atmosphere – 'We're beginning a coaching session now.'
- Create a sense of leadership in the conversation, for example, 'You're in safe hands.'
- Identify a future point for the conversation to end.

Let's assume familiarity

The following dialogue shows how a coach might build the foundation for a session in an ongoing relationship. We are assuming the coaching has been happening for a while and the coach and coachee are comfortable with each other. Where this is the very first session of an assignment, this stage requires more preparation, and we'll discuss that more directly in Chapter 7 Coaching assignment: in three stages.[1]

Figure 6.2 Establish conversation

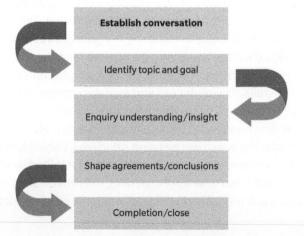

In this example, I hope to illustrate the balance between warmth and professionalism in the coach:

Coach: Hi Trey, how's it going? [shakes hands] You're early, I think! Have you been waiting long?

Trey: Aaah, you know me, I'm keen to get on . . . [laughs] Sorry, do you need time to prepare or something?

Coach: Nope, I'm all set. I've read through my notes on the train. Just let me grab those and we'll get started – can I get you a drink or something?

Trey: Actually, I've ordered some coffee to be brought in; it should be here any minute, hopefully.

Coach: Lovely. Now let's see where we are. [pauses] We've scheduled around two hours for this – is that still possible?

Trey: Yep, I'm fine until four o'clock.

Coach: Great. Let me just check my phone is off. Yes. Okay, perhaps we can begin with a brief recap from last time, and then we can focus on what you want to get from this session – how does that sound?

Trey: Sounds good.

Coach: Okay, so this is session three out of six, and we last met on 21 March, didn't we? Let's look at what came up in that conversation.

Trey: Well, you'll be pleased to hear I did actually talk to Mike and Yannis after last time; those were good conversations, actually.

Coach: Really? That's great; I look forward to hearing what happened. Okay, last time we covered three main areas, didn't we . . . [coach begins to run through simple headlines from the previous session, plus any actions agreed].

That is obviously a fairly fast set-up to demonstrate the principles. Some sessions need more set-up than others, for example maybe the coachee needs to query something, or introduce a new piece of information. I have omitted Trey's update from the previous session to maintain our flow.

Be willing to navigate the conversation for both of you

Notice how the coach is willing to lead the process of the discussion, by keeping time, performing the recap and focusing the coachee, Trey, on his goals for the session. This light touch is probably all that's needed to enable Trey to relax into the conversation. Remember, your coachee needs to feel that they're in safe hands in order to do this and so there's a need for you to step forward in the conversation at this point. When you navigate the process of the session, then your coachee only needs to focus on the content. I must stress that navigating is different from controlling the direction of the conversation. It's a little like helping someone to go clothes shopping. Occasionally, you may need to remind them that the purpose of the trip was actually to buy trousers not shoes or help them find what they want. Then all they need to do is try on clothes, while you offer the appropriate challenges and feedback.

At a Glance

When taking notes becomes unhelpful

Writing for recollection

Note-taking can be a valid method to maintain an appropriate amount of information during and after coaching sessions. So, as you are coaching, it's fine to occasionally write key facts or phrases. During a session, I tend to write brief 'memory-joggers' and then add other points from memory I feel I need after the session has ended. I also record any agreements made, so they can be reviewed during the next session. I'll check those as we are closing the conversation, for example, 'Let me just make sure I have a note of your key thoughts and actions here' (and finish writing those down).

However, be aware that, as you write, your ability to listen to, or observe, your coachee is reduced. Your attention shifts from what is happening with them (what they are saying, how they appear and the gestures they make) to your own thoughts and the physical act of writing. When we are new to coaching, we tend to take too many notes. We are worried that we may miss an important point or lose track of key facts. Actually, it's just as likely you will miss something important because the quality of your listening is reduced.

So, while it can be valid to record something that you feel is relevant or that you want to mention later, I encourage you to question your own need to do that. If it's that you fear you might forget something important, then my own experience suggests otherwise. I find that as the quality of my listening increases (and I stay present to the conversation) my need to take notes reduces.

Stage two – identify topic and goal

During this activity, you will agree a place to begin plus a desired destination. It's a gentle orientation to where your coachee wants to work during the session, rather than a rigorous, detailed assessment. You are balancing clarity and a sense of direction, while maintaining pace with the coachee. Our progress from the previous stage is illustrated in Figure 6.3.
Our objectives at this stage include:

- Help the coachee to decide what they want to work on.
- Encourage the coachee to 'own' the direction and content of the conversation.
- Help the coachee to 'expect' a potential solution, for example encourage a sense of possibility.
- Have the coachee feel comfortable that the coach is facilitating the conversation in a professional, structured way.
- Give you, the coach, a clearer sense of what you need to do in the conversation, for example where you need to navigate towards.

Right now, our role is to agree a topic and goal for the conversation, without putting pressure on the coachee to know everything. For example, the coachee is likely to arrive with a general idea of what they want to talk about – a topic. Maybe they will also have an idea of what results they want from the session. The coach needs to help refine these a little at this stage, to distil one or more threads for the conversation. With gentle questioning, some clarity is gained at this point, while more might arise later. Again, a light touch is often best. For example:

Figure 6.3 Identify topic and goal

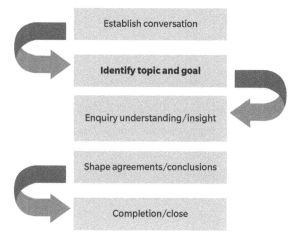

Coach: All right, so what is it you'd like to get from this session?

Trey: Well, I'd like to talk a bit more about my impact in meetings. Since our last discussion, I've noticed that I am actually a bit unpredictable. I want to look at that a bit.

Coach: Okay, so . . . thinking about your impact in meetings, what would you actually like to get from this session?

Trey: I guess I'm just looking for ways to be a bit more consistent. I do want to understand what goes on with me, but really, I want some ideas as to how to come across as a bit more confident . . . a bit more of the time.

Coach: Okay, right, I've got that [takes short note]. What are our other topics, then? What else would you like to work on?

Get clarity, rather than detail

The dialogue above gives enough clarity to continue, without the coach getting pulled into the next stage ('enquiry and understanding') too early. You may disagree and I encourage you to decide for yourself when you are happy to continue. I think that without the coach asking, 'What would you actually like to get from this session?' the initial objective is too vague. The response to the question – 'I want to understand . . . I want some ideas . . . ' – creates the clarity we need at this stage.

Vague leads to drifting

At this stage, if you hear a statement from your coachee that you feel is too vague, don't continue without getting more specific. You are the best judge of what is vague. Vague is indicated by the sense that you sort of know what they mean, but not exactly. For example, the following are vague answers to the coach's question, 'What would you like to get from this session?'

- 'I thought we could maybe work on my confidence a bit.'

- 'I need to look at me and what I do in presentations.'

- 'I want to look at how I'm coming across in top-team meetings; I'm just not making progress.'

Hopefully, you will be alerted to the potential for misunderstanding. The coachee is using vague terms that could mean something different from what the coach assumes. In the first statement, their need to work on their confidence may refer to a specific event in the future they want to prepare for, or a past incident they are upset about. The coachee could be referring to a range of topics, from speaking to large groups to a recent argument they've had. Or they may not mean confidence at all. Most of us would feel the need to dig deeper at this point.

Where you continue with a vague topic and goal, you risk misunderstanding and mistakes later. If a coach takes too long to realise what the conversation is really about, the coachee may become confused and feel adrift (and so not in safe hands). If the coach continues without clear direction, the conversation may go round in circles. The best option is to gain sufficient clarity at this early stage from the coachee. This requires that you ask your coachee what their objectives for the session are and probe further, if that's appropriate. In the following dialogue, the coach encourages the coachee to relax and explain further, without suggesting they've been misunderstood:

Coach: All right, so what is it you'd like to get from this session?

Trey: I thought we could maybe work on my confidence a bit.

Coach: [gently] Can you say a little more about that?

Trey: Well, it's to do with presenting in meetings . . . sometimes, everything's fine, great actually, but then, in the senior team sessions, I just don't seem to be able to function.

The coach makes a gentle request ('Can you say a little more?') and that helps the coachee open up. With little additional prompting, the coachee normally will continue talking around the topic and offer further insight into what they want to talk about. If they don't and we still need more specific information, the coach may continue to question the coachee to gain further clarity:

Coach: All right. So, what do we need to do in this session? I mean, where would you like to get to with this topic?

Trey: I guess I'm looking for ideas, hints and tips. You know, how do other people do it? Even just to understand what happens with me in these situations. I did one last week and really messed up.

By now, we are getting much clearer about what is in the coachee's mind. Once our coachee has offered a little more information and explained their need further, I'd normally summarise what I think our start-point for the conversation is, before moving on to the next activity. For example:

Coach: Okay, Trey, let me just check – you want to look at presenting in meetings with a view to gaining some ideas, or hints and tips. You would like to know a little more about why, in other meetings, you can present well and also why that's not always true in the senior sessions. You'd like to be more consistent. How does that sound?

Trey: Yes, that's it.

With our initial questions, we're simply identifying broad topics and goals, such as consistency, senior meetings, understanding, etc. Normally, you'll further refine what Trey actually wants during the next stage in a natural way.

Of course, there may be other topics and goals for the session, so you'll want to check by saying something like, 'What other topics would you like to work on?', 'Is there anything else you'd like to cover?', etc. You may end up with a list of things to work through. Simply note those down and agree a suitable order to work through them. For example, 'Right, where seems the best place to start?' If there's something you feel they may have forgotten, then it's okay to offer that, for example, 'You said last time you'd like to discuss the charity day – is that still relevant?' (And be willing to let the topic go, if it's not required.) For the purposes of this scenario, we're only using one topic – Trey's consistency in meetings.

Remember the person within the process

It's important to balance your need to get a detailed objective with a consideration for the feelings of your coachee. When a coachee arrives ready to tell a big story about a recent incident and the coach wants to spend a long time identifying detailed goals, we mismatch the coachee in a way that might be counterproductive. The coachee may feel that too much time spent 'preparing to have a conversation' is pedantic. We need to balance both positions. In these circumstances, you could let the coachee talk a little, release any tension or emotion for a while, before referring them back with a statement, such as:

'So, you've talked a little about your frustration with your presentation to the senior team last week and the disappointing feedback since. That's obviously important and something we need to focus on. I wondered if I might just confirm before we continue . . . what specifically would you like to leave with following this conversation?'

Again, it's down to your own judgement. As coach, you need to have enough sense of direction to navigate confidently, without getting stuck in detail.

How to decide you need a more specific goal upfront

Of course, there are exceptions to every rule. Sometimes, you'll decide you need a specific goal much sooner. For example, if the individual does not really know what they mean themselves by the term 'confidence'. Maybe they're confused and feeling a bit emotional about something that hasn't gone well. Or maybe they don't seem to have any real goal. You may then decide to be a little more rigorous at this initial stage:

- 'Tell me a little more about confidence. What does that mean to you?'
- 'What specifically is it about confidence that you'd like to work on?'
- 'So, Trey, by the end of this session, what would you like to have achieved?'

The goal for the session is not the same as the goal for the situation

Please remember that the goal for the session is not the same as the goal for the topic. During the session, Trey's goal is to come up with some ideas to help him perform better in meetings. That is what our coach needs to help him produce. But that session goal relates to Trey's broader (overarching) objectives, like gaining the respect of the senior team, being promoted, or just feeling great about giving presentations. As coach, you need his session topic and goal to serve him in the conversation. You are then likely to enquire into his overarching goals later. As you work through the next stage of understanding his issue, you might ask questions such as, 'How do you want to feel while you're giving presentations?' or 'What kind of impact do you want to have?' It's often inappropriate to try to gain that goal early on, as your coachee is unlikely to have the clarity of thought yet. That will come later, as we enquire into what's happening, and what Trey thinks or feels about what's happening.

Strangely, in some situations, you may hear a goal that seems definite, but you suspect it needs thinking through. For example, 'Operating at this senior level just isn't right for me, I'm just messing things up. I need a role that's more in line with my strengths. So, I've given myself three weeks: I want to find a new job by the end of this month.' In the next stage, you may find further enquiry into that goal renders it redundant. The coachee may find that, actually, it's a hasty decision based on an uncomfortable experience. For now, you need to capture it and, perhaps, check if the individual has other goals for the session.[2]

When you feel you have got enough mutual clarity and agreement to continue, simply go to the next stage.

Stage three – enquiry understanding/insight

This stage begins the real process of enquiry, to surface understanding and insight for the coachee. As the coach, you will also become clearer about the situation, although the primary aim is to support the awareness of the coachee. I'll whisper that, sometimes, this stage is where the magic of coaching reveals itself. As we gently surface someone's thoughts, feelings and realisations, we may uncover a perfect idea that moved unnoticed in the swirl of other thoughts surrounding it. Remember, however, that your job is not to spot what that is (and then strategise towards it); instead, you simply need to facilitate an effective process of enquiry.

Please avoid fixing, advising or jumping to quick conclusions. Instead, seek to understand, look for gaps or contradictions, and gently probe into what seems to be happening.[3]

So, we're now at a key place on our path, as illustrated in Figure 6.4. Our objectives at this stage include:

- Enquire into the situations that relate to the coachee's topic and session goals.
- Paint a 'fuller picture' of the situation.
- Increase the self-awareness of the coachee, in relation to the topics being discussed.
- Deepen understanding/insight for the coachee, leading to clearer thought.
- Help the coachee begin to form ideas or decisions based on clear thinking.

Revisit the facts

Remember, there is a subtle trap to fall into during this stage, which is to hear a familiar situation and imagine we understand it. Let's continue the thread from the previous examples. So far, you know that Trey wants to improve his confidence when he's presenting, particularly in meetings with senior people present. He had a bad meeting the previous week and really wants to improve his performance at the next one. But, actually, you still don't know much about what's really going on. After all, Trey is a unique person with his own experiences, beliefs and values. So, begin by assuming there's still lots to learn about Trey, and lots of opportunity for Trey to get clearer about himself.

Figure 6.4 Enquiry, understanding and insight

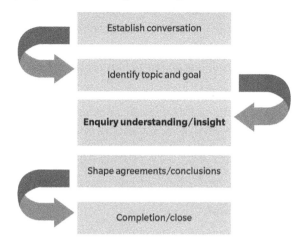

Build an understanding

Start by asking for some simple, factual information about the situation (whatever the situation might be). Be curious, assume that you don't know everything and ask questions that build a clearer picture of what's going on. Remember, as coach, while you are laying out the facts for you to understand, you'll also help the coachee become clearer about the situation and how they feel about it. For example:

Coach: So, can you tell me a little more about what happens in meetings?

Trey: I guess it varies a lot. Sometimes, everything's fine. I come across completely naturally. But then, sometimes, I just don't seem to be able to find my voice – it's like I can't even express a simple thought or piece of information. I come out wanting to kick myself. It's horrible, actually.

Coach: Okay, so what actually happens?

Trey: Well, it's like last week. I'm presenting our progress to the top team and it should have gone well. I'd got some good figures, after all. But, somehow, my whole presentation was a complete mess. Then, when it came to the questions, I couldn't even remember basic data. My boss had to jump in and help. Later, he told me what I already knew, really, that I didn't do myself justice at all.

Coach: All right, so you also said that sometimes you come across completely naturally, and everything is fine – can you tell me more about those situations?

Notice how the coach is gathering basic information, without going deeply into anything, then shifting the balance from an unpleasant situation to a better, more pleasant one. It's a little like emptying someone's pockets onto a table. We're just getting items onto the table at this point, not studying any of them in great detail. If something troubling comes to light, simply observe it and move on. Let's continue:

Trey: An easy example would be my client meetings. I presented a similar update to those guys yesterday and it's fair to say we really shone. I mean, by the end of it, the client sounded delighted with how it was all going.

Coach: So, can you tell me what was different from the session last week, with the top team?

Trey: Well, with the top team, the whole thing seemed more pressured somehow. I mean, it shouldn't have been – I knew our results were good. But I guess I'd worked myself up a bit before going in. When those guys start drilling you with questions, they can really chew people up.

Coach: And how was that different from the session with the client?

Trey: [pauses] I think really that's about what we are there to do. My focus is different. At this stage, it's to make the client feel comfortable that we're doing a good job, and we are. Also, I'm there to support some of my team. I want them to have a good experience that gives them confidence.

Hopefully, as you're reading this, you're developing your own questions about what you see is happening. Your natural powers of observation will have you comparing facts, seeing differences or even illogical statements you want to explore further. Avoid jumping to conclusions; don't try to fix anything; stay in enquiry mode. For example:

Coach: What else was different?

Trey: [pauses] Well, I guess because I'd had the run-through the previous week, I felt more prepared. I mean, I know it didn't go well the first time, but at least it all felt familiar.

Coach: Familiar?

Trey: Yeah, you know, the running order of the slides, the questions I was likely to get. I felt more prepared.

Keep building information

Again, by now you may think, 'Oh, I can see what his problem is – I know how to fix this.' Please challenge your own automatic response. You may have seen one potential solution: Trey needs to rehearse more. But, remember your objectives at this middle stage:

- Enquire into the situation and increase clarity.
- Help Trey increase his self-awareness around the situation.
- Encourage Trey to surface any insights or ideas that may help him.

As coach, you must avoid spotting an obvious quick answer and 'fixing' it. Stay relaxed and focused and you'll realise there is more to find out. For example:

Coach: So, you've got two meetings where both audiences are important, and you're presenting basically the same material.

Trey: Yes.

Coach: And, in one meeting, you feel under pressure and in the other one you don't?

Trey: Well, not exactly, I mean I'm under pressure with the client but that's a good sort of pressure.

Coach: Can you describe a 'good sort of pressure'?

Trey: Well, you know, when you know there's a high expectation and you also know that you've met that expectation. It's kind of like . . . it's already gone well. Does that make sense?

Now we have a little more information – Trey appears to perceive the pressure of the top team differently from that with the client. He imagines a high expectation from the client and also imagines that he's met it already. Again, it's all useful in the process of enquiry. But you are still interested to know more, to increase Trey's understanding:

Coach: That's interesting. How do you perceive the pressure in the top team meeting, then?

Trey: [pauses] It's definitely different. I guess, when I think about it, it's totally different. It's all a lot heavier; there seems more at stake.

Coach: More at stake?

Trey:	It's funny, you know, now I'm thinking about it, I'm imagining something like the lion's den, you know. Like whatever happens I'm going to get chewed up.
Coach:	Right. That's quite a contrast between the two sessions, isn't it? In client meetings you appear to relish the challenge, but with your senior team you're anticipating something very different. How do your own expectations affect things, do you think?
Trey:	[pauses] Well, that's the key, isn't it? Or certainly it's one of them. Basically, it all becomes a self-fulfilling prophecy. I need to think more about that.

Summaries alleviate pressure and enable reflection

It's important to remember that this stage is about surfacing understanding and insight – not simply about asking a series of questions. Continuous questions can fatigue a coachee and perhaps feel a little unnatural. Notice how the coach added value by simply reflecting the coachee's own statements back to him. Used sensitively, a brief, well-timed summary can have the following benefits:

- gives the coachee a rest
- demonstrates accurate listening by the coach
- enables the coachee to hear for themselves what they have been saying, and check for themselves how they feel hearing that now
- enables the coachee to form links in the information they have expressed
- creates a natural pause which enables both the coach and the coachee to reconsider progress and decide the best way forward
- might prompt the coachee to surface additional, relevant information or insights.

Remember also that a conversation has different elements to it. As a coach, you want to be as natural as possible with the coachee, so remember to smile, nod, gesture, etc. while you ask questions, check facts, summarise, pause and reflect. Over time, you need to develop a style that's natural for you.

Let's imagine the coach has let Trey rest in silence for a while before continuing:

Coach:	Might it be helpful if I just summarise where I think we've got to?
Trey:	Sure. Although I think it's already dawning on me.
Coach:	Okay. So, as we started, you talked about confidence; although, when we looked at that, really you mainly focused on this recent topic of the top-team meeting.

Trey:	Right.
Coach:	Can I just check: have we narrowed this down too much by focusing on just these two meetings?
Trey:	[pauses] Well, no, not really, I mean there are other occasions, but I'm starting to suspect that it's all wrapped up in the same stuff. This is just a good example.
Coach:	Okay. So, you're describing the two sessions quite differently, although the broad content of the presentation is the same – you're presenting good results that relate to the performance of your team.
Trey:	Yup.
Coach:	In one session, the top team, your focus is more about you, your performance and the fact things may go badly.
Trey:	[laughs] Yeah.
Coach:	And, in the other, your focus is much more about your team, supporting them – plus you expect a great outcome.
Trey:	Yes, I do – I just imagine the whole thing differently. [pauses] Like actually the thing in the top team is all about me, but with the client I'm much more about everyone else, you know, looking after my team, helping the client feel comfortable and confident – what I think I'm there to do is rather different.
Coach:	You also mentioned that you felt more 'prepared' in the client session, partly because you'd had the experience of the first one.
Trey:	I did. Partly that's because I knew it was unlikely to go like the first one, but, more importantly, I'd just had a run-through.

Where are we? (A quick summary for you and me)

Let's take a quick look at where we are with progress in this stage of 'surface understanding and insight':

- We've focused on what Trey seems to want to talk about.
- We've laid out some facts of the situation: two meetings, different start-points, different outcomes.
- We've dug a little deeper to create clarity: how are the two meetings different? How does he prepare differently for them?

Remember, I have shortened the investigation for the purposes of this written example and your own enquiry process is likely to be more thorough. So, we've reached a point where Trey appears ready to make his own links, come to his own conclusions and decide on his own realisations. Again, as coach, our role is to support him with this, not do the work for him. Rather than drill him down into what we think he should be deciding, instead you can ask a question that's general enough to encompass wherever his thoughts might be, but one that also encourages his conclusions to surface:

Coach: So, what thoughts are you having now?

Trey: Well, I think a lot of it is in the way I set things up. I mean, both practically and also in my head. I just imagine the two things as completely different experiences.

Coach: And how does that affect what actually happens?

Trey: It means that what I'm doing in the session is different. Like in the top-team session, my whole game plan is about not screwing up. But, when I'm in front of a client with my team, I'm on a roll, I feel so sure of myself.

Coach: So, how can you feel that sure of yourself in the other meetings, the top-team meetings?

Trey: I think there's a fair number of things I can do. Some of it's in practical preparation and some of it's to do with mental preparation. Some of it's simply about staying relaxed, making that more important.

Coach: All right, so how would it be if we work through some of those things you can do and get them down on paper?

Trey now seems ready to list some of his ideas and options. Let me just acknowledge the question that helped him reach that point: 'How can you feel that sure of yourself in the top-team meetings?' This is what I call a 'powerful question', a question that encompasses the problem, while assuming a solution. For further explanation, please look at Table 4.1 Effective coaching questions in Chapter 4 Five fundamental skills of coaching.

Develop a sense of possibility

What's also occurred is that Trey seems to have moved from a perception of no possibility to one of possibility. By the phrase 'no possibility', I mean not being able to imagine that a better way might be available or possible. For example, when Trey first began talking, he was focused on what had gone wrong and also his feelings about the situation: 'I just don't seem to be able to find my voice' and then, 'It's horrible, actually.' At an extreme, he may even have imagined that it was impossible for him to perform well in a top-team meeting.

Trey may have been feeling so frustrated about the outcome of the bad meeting that he was a little stuck. For example, maybe in his mind he was replaying what went badly, focusing on the negative feedback, dreading the next meeting, etc. Through gentle questioning, comparisons and observations, the coach helped Trey regain the sense of possibility that he could actually perform well in that kind of meeting and enjoy doing so. It's a subtle form of magic, but magic, nonetheless.

Regain a feeling of influence

Trey also moved fairly quickly to a sense of influence over his situation: 'I think there's a fair amount I can do.' At the beginning of the session, he made comments such as 'I want to understand what goes on with me,' and then, 'Somehow, my whole presentation was a complete mess.' His words suggest he feels a loss of influence over what happened during the meetings. I might wonder if he was operating from more of a victim posture in regard to the issue. By this, I mean he thought something was happening *to* him rather than he himself was the cause of his own experience. For further discussion of this key principle, see Chapter 3 Seven coaching principles or beliefs.

While acknowledging that our enquiry with Trey has been brief and feels incomplete, let's leave the stage of 'surface understanding and insight' and continue.

Stage four – shape agreements/conclusions

Ideally, this will feel like a natural progression from the previous activity. Here we shape the previous elements of the conversation into conclusions, or raised awareness, or maybe actions to encourage further progress. Figure 6.5 shows where we are on our path and your objectives at this stage include:

- Acknowledge what insights or conclusions the coachee has gained.
- Refine and/or summarise ideas and options.
- Surface any additional conclusions, ideas or options
- Agree specific actions, if appropriate.
- Create a sense of the future, for example help the coachee find the motivation to act.

Figure 6.5 Shape agreements/conclusions

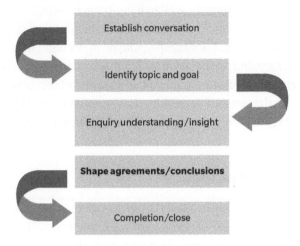

Pulling the conversation together

The key to this stage is actually the previous stage. As a coach, when you have effectively surfaced the relevant information, feelings, contradictions, comparisons, etc., this stage is more straightforward. The previous discussion has helped your coachee clarify what's actually happening, what they think about what's happening and also what they might want to do about it. Our role now is to help distil, refine or build on their thoughts so that they can maintain progress after the session.

Using the scenario with Trey, let's continue:

Coach: So, you've mentioned that there's some practical preparation and mental preparation for the top-team meetings that would help. Can you tell me more about those things?

Trey: I think I need to involve my team more: either by having them present or simply by rehearsing with them in advance. As a minimum, I need to rehearse with them in advance.

Coach: That's interesting. What effect would rehearsing have?

Trey: It would mean that I felt prepared, that's a big one. But also, I think I'd remind myself that the whole team is involved, that I'm presenting 'our' results, not 'my' results. More 'we' and less 'I' – I think that's quite important to me.

Coach: Can you say a little more about that?

Trey: Yeah . . . well, it has to do with why I'm much better in client situations. Basically, when my focus is also on them, I don't feel so on the spot.

Coach: Okay, that sounds like real insight . . . great, and how feasible is it that they can be present?

Trey: It's certainly possible. Maybe not all of them, but it's up to me who I invite in. I think, actually, it might reflect well on the whole team. Certainly, my boss would be supportive.

Coach: Good. Okay, so what about when they can't be there – how else can you prepare?

Refine ideas

Our coach is obviously drawing Trey's ideas out, testing them for practicality and creating more clarity about what Trey is deciding to do. In addition, the coach is also creating a sense of the future. By asking the question 'What effect would rehearsing have?' we are testing the validity of the idea: after all, it might not be the full solution. We're also encouraging Trey to imagine doing something practical to create a benefit. Hopefully, Trey's optimism will increase as he becomes motivated to make the effort of rehearsing. Notice also how the coach challenges a potentially 'imperfect' solution: 'How feasible is it that they can be present?' Of course, Trey may say that simply rehearsing is enough. But let's not assume he will. Maybe there's something else. After all, he's hinted earlier that there's 'lots' he can do.

Let's continue:

Coach: Good. Okay, so what about when they can't be there; how else can you prepare?

Trey: You know, a lot of it is mental. It's the way I'm drawing it in my head. I think I need to set myself up for success, rather than anything else.

Coach: How might you do that?

Trey: It's simple things, like focusing on a positive outcome, reminding myself what I'm there to do. Making sure I stay relaxed.

Coach: Right, and I guess I'm wondering how you'll do that practically, you know. What will you be doing?

Trey: Well, the rehearsal will definitely help, help me relax. But, actually, just the realisation that I let myself imagine the worst, predict failure – I just need to stop myself doing that, see it more like I see the client session.

Coach: Okay, so instead of predicting the worst, how do you want to see the session?

Trey:	You know, like I'm on a home run, on a roll, like it's already gone well.
Coach:	Great, I get that, 'like it's already gone well . . . ' You've said that a couple of times. And, you know, you do seem a bit brighter about this whole thing now.
Trey:	Yeah, I feel brighter. That's silly, isn't it?
Coach:	[laughs] Well, not so silly if it helps you do well. Okay, let's just check what we've got.

Agreements and actions

It's often appropriate for a coachee to agree to actions following a coaching session. Certainly, in the above scenario it seems relevant that Trey take action. However, this is not always true. For example, imagine that, during the conversation, Trey had realised that he wasn't actually happy in his current job. Obviously, that would be an entirely different (and longer) conversation than the one we've portrayed. But, if Trey had reached that conclusion, is it wise to move straight to action by perhaps looking for another job, telling his boss, etc? Probably not. Maybe the most Trey should commit to doing is to go and reflect on the situation further, before meeting his coach again. That doesn't sound perfect either, but I'm sure you get the point. Sometimes, progress is made through direct, positive action – but not always.

Summarise and agree

When, as coach, you feel that you have mutual clarity about what the coachee has decided and also what they are going to do, it's time to summarise and agree on the next steps. As mentioned previously, a summary may release further thoughts for consideration, so please be ready for that.

Let's resume:

Coach:	You've said you want to prepare in two ways, both practically and mentally.
Trey:	Right.
Coach:	Practically, you want to rehearse with your team, get them involved earlier and maybe even take some of the team in with you?
Trey:	Yes, probably just one person, that would be fine.

Coach: Okay, are there any other ways you might practically prepare?

Trey: [pauses] Well, I do keep thinking about my boss, Mike. I keep thinking I should involve him more.

Coach: That's interesting. How might you involve Mike?

Trey: Well, I think I need to show him the presentation in advance, get his thoughts and ideas. Maybe not all the presentation, but some of the slides that I think will provoke questions.

Coach: How will Mike respond when you approach him?

Trey: Fine, I think. He won't want too much detail, but he's brilliant at anticipating what those guys will do.

Coach: Okay, I've got that one. Let me just check, are there any other practical ways you want to prepare?

Trey: [pauses] No, I don't think so. I'm happy with that . . .

Precision in language

Some of you may be noticing a slight repetition in the conversation. In written dialogue, it's probably more noticeable than in real life. You'll see that the coach seems to be covering the same topic more than once, or simply using Trey's own words and phrases. This is all normal, and part of an effective conversation. The coach is using repetition to confirm the coachee's thoughts and as a way of navigating through the conversation.

Using someone else's precise language and phrases can be fundamental to building rapport and also clarifying meaning. For example, when the coach says, 'You've said you want to prepare in two ways, both practically and mentally,' it serves as a reminder, a clarifier and a prompt to focus on doing that. Trey doesn't need to wonder what the coach is referring to; he can simply relate to the point. The coach might have said, 'Okay, so there were two significant ways you wanted to get ready in advance,' but Trey might hesitate, thinking 'Did I?' or 'What were those, then?' The phrase doesn't have the same impact on Trey, since it's not Trey's phrase. It's a simple, yet effective, option to use the coachee's terminology where possible, to keep things clear between you both.

Let's continue with the scenario:

Coach: All right, so, in your mental preparation, you want to imagine the top-team session in a similar way to how you imagine the client sessions. You mentioned 'on a roll' and 'like it's already gone well'.

Trey:	Yes, absolutely.
Coach:	You also said you wanted more of a sense of 'we' in the conversation than 'I'.
Trey:	Yes. I want to remember that, actually, I'm there to represent my whole team, not just my own efforts.
Coach:	Okay, great. So, are there any more ways you might mentally prepare?
Trey:	[pauses] Well, I'm not sure. To be honest, it's all mental preparation really, even the rehearsals and asking Mike for advice. It's all to help me be in the right frame of mind on the day.
Coach:	I can really see that. I guess I'm just wondering if there's anything else you feel you want to do?
Trey:	[pauses] No, I'm happy. I think the realisation of what's been happening, plus the actions we've got . . . it's enough.
Coach:	Great. And when do you next have a chance to put this preparation into practice?
Trey:	Oh, very soon; we've got another review three weeks from today. I probably need to start getting that ready from Monday.
Coach:	Sounds like perfect timing.
Trey:	[laughs] You could say.

So, a little more refinement, confirmation and encouragement. Hopefully, you'll get the sense that the coach has gained sufficient agreement to suggest that Trey is both engaged and enthusiastic about taking on the challenge of the next top-team meeting.

How much detail should we drill for on actions?

I must acknowledge that some coaches would want to press for more detail on actions, for example, 'What exactly will you do by when?' Occasionally, that's appropriate and, as coach, you need to judge this yourself. In the above example, I assume Trey is a mature person, running a successful team, and he's capable of keeping his commitment. It feels a little patronising to insist on a detailed list of tasks and timescales. I'm guessing he is capable of what he's decided to do. I also know that some of the benefit of the session has been in his realisations and they will continue after the session. Plus, the situation is important to him and for him to avoid acting from his own fresh insights is unlikely. Now, it may be that, in the next session, he reports little action or progress. Since all the indicators are against that happening, it's a risk I'm happy to take. Remember, we operate from a principle that the coachee is responsible for the results they create. Trey is in the driving seat and must continue to steer his own course.

Here's a balanced way of ending this segment:

Coach: All right, I've got the following. Let's see if you agree:

1 Arrange to rehearse with your team. You want to get their input but also involve them more; make it about them as well.

2 Speak to Mike in preparation; gain his input, advice and ideas, especially in regard to how the group might respond.

3 Invite someone from your team into the next presentation, if that still seems appropriate.

Trey: Yes, what I'll probably do is ask Mike what he thinks about that first.

Coach: Great. Obviously, there's a shift in ways you want to think about it: the mental preparation. Do you want to note anything down about that?

Trey: No, it's not necessary. I might talk it through with my wife maybe, but it's fine; I've really got that one, I think.

Coach: Right. How might it be if I just pop those in an email to you, for our records?

Trey: That works for me.

At a Glance

Start an action statement with a verb

In written form especially, how we word or record actions can influence mutual understanding and so someone's tendency to complete them. An unclear or sloppy record of an action becomes less easy to recall over time and may lose meaning between sessions. Here are some ineffective examples:

1 Drinks list, acknowledge progress daily and weekly, keep simple.

2 Sunni Samson chair role discussed with values context and links – share.

3 On time and on plan; Ashley to chalk up quick wins.

These action notes are very vague when it comes to highlighting the point and this lack of clarity can happen when we write and talk at the same time. So, please stay conscious of what you've written down as a record of someone's actions during this stage of a conversation.

The wording of actions is clearer and feels more active when we begin them with a verb (a 'doing' word). Examples of typical verbs include: complete, identify, contact, build, create and adapt. It's a simple yet powerful switch; see how the previous actions transform in clarity and impact through use of a clear verb upfront and explicit statement of the requirement.

1 Write a list of drinks consumed every day, for example water, tea, coffee (raise own awareness).

2 Invite Sunni Samson to share the principles of her approach to chairing meetings and the natural links to company values.

3 Ask Ashley to summarise the quick wins gained in the early stages of the project and share those with our team.

It's a simple discipline to develop and, over time, will benefit your ongoing clarity. If at first you cannot write clear actions (starting with a verb) quickly, just make notes and then re-word them soon after. That way, when you begin your next session, you will have a good, clear understanding of what your coachee wanted to achieve between the sessions.

Sharing your note of their actions

Notice the coach has agreed to note the actions and send those to Trey. Not every coach will agree with this principle. Some coaches feel that the coachee should take all their own notes and record all their own actions, and that the coach should abstain from any responsibility. I feel that's often unhelpful and imprac- tical at this point. After all, the coach is there to serve the coachee. Immediately after a coaching conversation, the coachee might be tired and their ability to retain and record information is reduced. The coach will have been taking a few notes during the session. It's a simple matter for the coach to draft a quick email soon after the session as a record of agreements. As well as a courteous profes- sional gesture, it has the following benefits:

- It creates an accurate mutual record of what has been agreed.
- It can be used as a start-point in the next session.
- In the email you might also check if they are still happy after the session, maintain rapport, etc.

Stage five – completion/close

This final step is about drawing the conversation to a professional close. As in the first stage, you already have experience as to how to complete a conversation. You simply need to develop your own style of doing this in a coaching situation.

Figure 6.6 indicates where we are on The Coaching Path. Your objectives at this stage include:

- Summarise and indicate that the session is complete, for example no outstanding items.
- Emphasise a sense of progress made during the session.
- Help your coachee feel that the session is being handled in a professional, confident manner.
- Maintain mutual clarity, for example what happens after the session.
- Leave your coachee feeling comfortable about continuing items discussed following the session, without direct involvement from you.
- Close the session in a natural way.

Figure 6.6 Completion/close

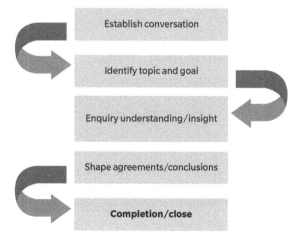

Establish conversation

Identify topic and goal

Enquiry understanding/insight

Shape agreements/conclusions

Completion/close

As you'd expect, there's no 'right' or 'wrong' way to close a session. Your own personal style will dictate your manner. Here is an example using the previous (abridged) scenario:

Coach: Okay, we're nearly there, I think, in terms of this session. Let me just check your original objectives. We had just one, which was this increasing confidence topic we've just covered. Was there anything else you wanted to talk through?

Trey: Nope, I'm happy with where we've got to.

Coach: Great! Has that been useful?

Trey: It has, actually; it's given me a few things to think about.

Coach: Good. So, the next session, shall I book that as usual through your office?

Trey: Yes, I'm away from the end of next week, but only for 10 days.

Coach: Work or pleasure?

Trey: Bit of both, I hope – over to Singapore, but with a quick stop-over in Hong Kong. Anyway, thanks for today. [shakes hands] As usual, very interesting.

Coach: You're welcome, I've enjoyed it too. Okay Trey, have a good few weeks and I'll see you in about a month or so. I'll confirm those actions by email this evening. As usual, if anything else crops up, do get in touch.

Trey: Lovely, thanks.

So, you see, all fairly natural and probably something you can imagine yourself doing.

General point: managing time

In all sessions, work at managing the session time effectively. This can be easier in short coaching sessions (30 minutes) than longer ones (two to three hours). In a short session, both parties are naturally focused on the time available. In long sessions, it's easier to get lost in the conversation and allow time to disappear. It's okay to be open about checking the time during a session. For example, at an appropriate moment, it's acceptable to say something like, 'Let's just check how we're doing for time here.' That way, the coachee also becomes aware of the need to stay focused and finish promptly.

One solution is to keep a clock or watch visible on the table and explain at the beginning of the session why it's there. My own choice is to wear a watch with a large/oversized face, which means that checking the time is easy and quick.

The Coaching Path: make this your own

Over time, you'll develop your own routines, habits and process to suit the way you work. For example:

- You might always begin sessions by revisiting the overall assignment objectives from your first session.
- Sometimes, you might call a tea/coffee break halfway through the session, to allow the coachee to 'rest' a little.
- You might begin/end each session with some type of routine to help your coachee relax and refocus, such as a breathing exercise or a 'verbal download' (where someone expresses their current thoughts, to clear their mind and become more present).
- You may choose to send a few notes from the conversation, plus a list of agreed actions.
- During this one, you could ask to schedule the next session, to create a clear and firm commitment.

It's important that you feel that you own the structure of your coaching conversations. However, I do encourage you to be consistent and self-disciplined. Consistency enables the coachee to trust in your professionalism and also be comfortable that they know what to expect.

Personal discipline promotes high standards of behaviour from yourself and your coachee. For example, if you say you'll call before the next session, make sure you call. If you offer to email some notes, make sure you send them. As previously described, the integrity and professionalism you demonstrate are vital to the ongoing relationship. Wherever possible, keep your word or make amends if, for some reason, that doesn't happen. I'm sure you'll find a way of working that creates a sense of balance you can maintain.

> **The integrity and professionalism you demonstrate are vital to the ongoing relationship**

In a Nutshell

Most formal coaching conversations can follow a similar path, with a common flow of activities and stages. Those stages are:

- Establish conversation – build rapport, sense of occasion, etc.
- Identify topic and goal – for the session.
- Enquiry, understanding and insight – regarding the topic and situation.
- Shape conclusions and agreements– arising from the 'fresh' understanding.
- Completion and close – checks, validations, end session.

The previous stages are activities, rather than 'tasks'. When you are aware of the basic stages and activities that underpin the conversation, you can facilitate your coachee through to an effective conclusion. Like all journeys involving pathways, sometimes we need to backtrack or retrace our steps. For example, we may need to revisit the goal for a conversation or check understanding.

At all times, your coachee needs to feel that they are in safe hands. So, it is important that you develop your own authentic style, which feels comfortable to you and more natural to your coachee. The Coaching Path is intended to encourage the development of your own personal style, while supporting an effective coaching conversation.

chapter 7

Coaching assignment: in three stages

'It is not in the stars to hold our destiny, but in ourselves.'

William Shakespeare

This chapter offers a supporting structure for a coaching assignment. By an assignment, I mean a series of coaching sessions, to work on agreed topics and themes. For example, six sessions over a period of ten months, perhaps to help the coachee realise a goal or focus generally on their personal development.

As a coach, when you think in terms of an overall assignment, you can plan and structure your involvement, which helps you to:

- create the foundation for an effective coaching experience for your coachee
- establish principles of success, for example, 'Here's how we will work together'
- explain and predict costs for potential clients

- promote your approach to working as organised, professional and distinct from other coaches in the field

- maintain your own sense of personal organisation and efficiency, for example, 'We're now halfway through, which means I need to facilitate a review.'

A framework for coaching

Figure 7.1 summarises a framework for a coaching assignment and can be useful both as an initial overview and as a subsequent checklist. All activities are intended to occur in most coaching assignments in some way. For example, whether an assignment is two sessions long or ten sessions long, it's still possible to have some form of review or confirmation of learning, etc.

When you plan your approach, you'll need to consider:

- What is the nature of this assignment? Let the situation and your initial sense of purpose indicate what type of support is needed.

- Who else is involved in this situation and how do you need to interact with them? For example, in an organisation, the individual hiring you may not be the coachee themselves: it might be someone's boss, or an HR person.

- What are the practical considerations? For example, if your coachee is based in a different country from you, then you'll need to consider different types of interaction: phone, email, Zoom/Teams, etc.

Use the following checklist to help you plan an assignment.

At a Glance

How much structure do I need?

Q What do I already know of the purpose of this assignment and what else would I like to know? For example, what has happened previously to result in a request for coaching?

Q Who else is involved in this assignment – how should I involve them?

Q What are the criteria of success in this situation? How will I be judged as successful or effective?

Q What experience of coaching or training has this person had previously?

Q What are the expectations of how I will work? For example, am I expected to complete specific documentation or report my activity in a certain way?

Q Where should/can the coaching take place?

Q Ideally, how long should/can each session last?

Q What constraints might there be on this assignment? For example, number of sessions, costs?

Balance structure with a flexible approach

While some structure and rigour are helpful, too much can be overly controlling of your coachee's experience. For example, you may try to dictate that your assignments always contain five two-hour sessions but, sometimes, someone just requires a session or two to support a distinct situation. Or you may propose that sessions are four weeks apart but that doesn't match someone's work schedule, or the rate of progress they make between sessions. So, before an assignment starts, consider how much structure is helpful, and be willing to adapt your approach to your coachee's specific needs.

Three stages of a coaching assignment

There are three basic activities or stages that can be used as a foundation for effective assignments. These stages are illustrated in Figure 7.1, and are:

1 Create the context for coaching.

2 Increase awareness, purpose and action.

3 Completion and possibility.

Where a series of coaching sessions rarely develops according to an easy formula, these three stages offer a flexible framework for you to work from, during an assignment. Some of these stages happen more naturally, while others require you to make them happen.

Figure 7.1 Three stages of a coaching assignment

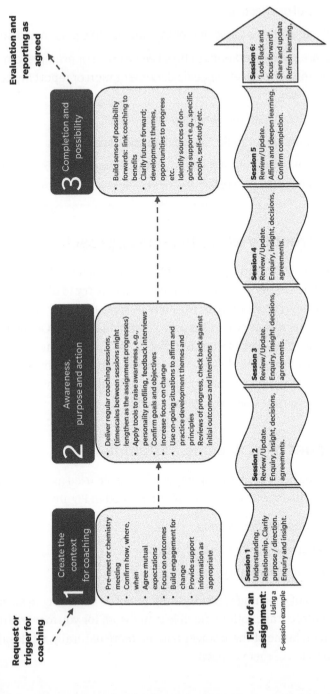

The order of coaching stages/activities

Our basic sequence of an assignment is based on what often makes sense, but it is not what always happens. For example, identifying ways that your coachee gains further support for their learning often sits within completion activity. However, it's also valid to promote learning from the outset and so you might decide to encourage that from the very first session.

Please note that one stage or activity does not necessarily equal one coaching session. In your initial coaching session, you will work to understand the coachee and their current goals, plus engage your coachee's commitment. This understanding and engagement is likely to continue throughout the assignment, just with a different emphasis or priority.

When an individual has no experience of either coaching or training, I might choose to spend a little more time explaining coaching or send them an overview of coaching as preparation. Or, if they have had personal training or coaching before, I'd simply ask them about that. Then we could acknowledge any differences we might expect from the coaching approach I am proposing.

Activities that develop over time

Once begun, activities are like plates that you must help keep spinning. Many of these activities are supported naturally, and all you need to do is maintain your attention on them. For example, while you create a focus on engagement from the outset, you will also maintain your awareness of the coachee's engagement throughout the assignment.

To try and portray how different activities may span practically across sessions, I suggest that you imagine that I'm describing an assignment that is six sessions long. Clearly, the number of sessions in your assignments may differ, according to your coachee's situation and need.

At a Glance

Explanation of terms

When planning an assignment, in addition to the person you are coaching, you sometimes need to involve or consider other people, for example if you are coaching in business and someone else is requesting your services, authorising payment, etc. The following will help as a general guide

▶

to the different roles you might encounter; sometimes, the names change so do make sure you understand what role a person is performing.

Coachee

The person being coached (sometimes called the client).

Sponsor

The person serving as the internal support or champion for the coaching. This is generally someone who initiates the coaching and assists its progress. This role doesn't exist on every assignment, but, when it does, you need to understand this individual's requirements – for reporting, principles and process, etc. Sometimes, a coachee's line manager is designated as sponsor, to encourage the manager to stay involved during the assignment.

Stakeholder(s)

This is anyone who is personally or professionally interested in the success of the assignment. In organisations, it might typically be a more senior colleague, or anyone who will be influenced in some way by the outcomes of the coaching. There may be many stakeholders to an assignment; you do not need to engage with all of them, you simply need to stay aware of those with most interest (or influence) and interact with them appropriately.

Line manager

The person your coachee reports to. In business, this person is a primary stakeholder to your assignment (and there may be more). As with all stakeholders, you need to understand how best to involve them on the assignment in a way that benefits your coachee and the assignment (while respecting the individual stakeholders' needs and situation).

Stage one – create the context for coaching

Here we build a supporting context within which to coach. By context, I mean anything surrounding the actual coaching conversations that might help or hinder those conversations. Here we also build expectations, principles and process that support the overall coaching assignment. This can range from physical aspects, such as the location, room, etc., to non-physical aspects, such as the coachee's understanding of what is happening and what will be expected of them. Let's look at the following activities within this first stage.

- Pre-meet or introductory conversation (begin to build relationship).
- Confirm logistics (how, where, when).
- Agree expectations (of each other).
- Focus on desired outcomes/results.
- Build a sense of engagement for change.

Again, while the above activities all require your attention, you may deal with some in a different order, or even all at once. For example, in an initial meeting or call with a potential client, you may discuss what they'd like to work on, what your approach is to coaching and also the logistics of location, meeting places, etc.

At a Glance

Negotiate an appropriate environment in which to coach

In face-to-face situations, coaching generally takes place in a room of some sort. Ideally, this room should be comfortable and not too cosy – it's important that you can both relax but also stay alert. The room should be able to support a relaxed and warm conversation, so not too big, not too small.

Unlike Goldilocks and her porridge, we don't always have a range of rooms to choose from. So, upfront, try to negotiate your requirements and, after that, improve things where you can. For example, I try to arrive early and, if needed, clear the space a little. I'll move chairs, declutter table surfaces and put any litter in the bin. Once the space is as good as I can get it, then I tell myself to simply relax and work with what I have.

For other ideas, see the previous checklist in Chapter 5 Barriers to coaching.

Pre-meet or introductory conversation (begin to build relationship)

I encourage you to arrange an introductory conversation as something separate from your first coaching session. This enables you to keep the administration-type discussions separate from your actual coaching sessions. This is, typically, a 30–60-minute-long conversation with a new or potential coachee and can be face-to-face, a telephone call or by Zoom/Teams, etc. The conversation has the following aims:

- To get to know each other a little – to learn about them and to share relevant information about yourself.
- To understand the background to coaching – what are the circumstances that have resulted in considering coaching?
- To understand the broad areas they'd like to focus on (delegation, business development, influence and impact, etc.).
- To talk generally about how coaching works, so that they know what to expect in terms of support and challenge.
- To discuss the potential logistics of the coaching process: where, how often, how long, etc.
- To answer any questions they might have, for example confidentiality.
- To understand requests of you, for example a need to send additional information or costs.
- To understand the way forward, or the best way to get started, for example their availability, etc.

At a Glance

Chemistry meetings: prepare to succeed

Chemistry meetings are increasingly popular to help someone choose a coach they want to work with. Typically, your potential coachee chooses from two to three coach profiles/CVs and then chemistry meetings are arranged. After the meetings, the coachee will choose the coach they want to work with.

Please prepare for these thoroughly – arrive ready to give an appropriate view of you and how you work as a coach. Remember, also, that any coach who spends the entire chemistry meeting talking about themselves is less likely to impress than one who demonstrates their typical style of coaching. Here is an ideal *opportunity for you to demonstrate effective listening, questioning, helpful observations*, etc. So, while the conversation should not become a coaching session, it is appropriate for you to display your typical coaching style, perhaps by offering them your observations of their situation, (arising from your listening and questioning).

Chemistry meetings are another reason why you might want to plan a simple structure to how you work, as it enables you to display clarity and professionalism in what is, ultimately, a sales situation.

Confirm logistics (how, where, when)

The basic practicalities of coaching are best agreed before you begin coaching sessions. For example:

- administration and logistics, location of sessions, room booking, invoicing, travel, etc.
- a basic or intended schedule of sessions (how many sessions over what period of time)
- other dependencies, for example who else needs to be involved in the process, in either an administration or participation role?
- key milestones or stages, for example, 'After three sessions, let's review progress'
- your outline approach to coaching, the methods and tools used, for example personality profiling, feedback interviews on someone's behalf, etc.

Nail the admin

While few of us enjoy extensive formal discussion related to admin and logistics, failure to create clarity at this point is likely to create issues later. So, as a minimum, before you begin the formal coaching, it is best to have agreed:

- the intended number of sessions in the assignment, plus the duration and location of those sessions
- any additional activities to the sessions that are likely, for example personality profiling
- the estimated cost of the assignment, including any expenses likely to be charged for
- how invoicing is carried out, for example are you charging upfront for the full assignment or after each session? Where/how will invoices be sent?
- any principles that impact on delivery of the coaching services, for example it must be completed within a certain timeframe, or the coaching must support their employer's values.

If you have had a pre-chat, then it's likely that much of the above has already been covered. Remember to create clarity with efficient use of time; always confirm key information by email to enable your coachee to digest it at their own pace.

Agree expectations (of each other)

Here you ensure that some simple and basic expectations are clear, to avoid any miscommunication later. For example, ensure that your coachee appreciates what coaching is, generally how it works and what they might expect during the coaching sessions. The following hints and tips item explains how you might do this in a written format to supplement an initial conversation or chemistry meeting.

> **Ensure that your coachee appreciates what coaching is, generally how it works and what they might expect during the coaching sessions**

Coaching overview document[1]

Before our first session, I sometimes send a new coachee a short overview of what coaching is and generally what to expect. It also encourages them to begin thinking about their goals, objectives, or sense of purpose. Some people welcome reading material to help them prepare, and some do not, but it's helpful to have this to hand and make the offer to share it.

When might I use it?
- During initial discussions about the potential of coaching.
- When beginning a new coaching relationship, to give a new coachee some background information or reading.
- In advance of the first coaching session.

What does it cover?
- A brief description of what coaching is.
- How coaching works, for example compared with other forms of learning or training.
- What situations are best suited to coaching and what are the typical benefits.
- What they can expect from you their coach, for example behaviours.
- What the coach will expect from the coachee.

Enough information to feel comfortable (and not overwhelmed)

Remember that too much information and explanation is counterproductive to your coachee's experience. Describing in detail how coaching methods work or what might happen is only necessary if someone requests more information to aid their understanding. You need to find a balance of information and explanation that will engage but not overwhelm the person.

At a Glance

First session – make coaching personal

From the outset, you need to form an appropriate level of understanding of your coachee as a person, their current circumstances, issues, etc. Basic information gathering ideally begins before the first coaching session and then continues during that initial session. By the end of my first session, I like to know:

- the coachee's full name and age
- what they do for a job/occupation
- their professional history, for example what did they do before this?
- where they live and where they work (and the type of journey in between)
- family circumstances: partner's name; number, names, and ages of children, etc.
- what general areas they would like to receive coaching in, for example confidence, productivity, health, finances
- anything else they feel is appropriate to this general fact-building part of the conversation.

I tend to gather the most basic details before the first session: name, occupation and, perhaps, areas they want to work on. Then, at the beginning of the first session, I will ask for information relating to their family, where they live/work, etc., as it is more personal or sensitive. People can be surprised that I'm interested in knowing their partner's name, their occupation, or even how long they've been married. However, most people happily accept that all these factors have a potential influence on the work we are embarking upon. On a more practical note, knowing

▶

> how many children someone has, and their approximate ages, avoids
> a potentially clunky conversation later in the assignment, for example,
> 'Ah – okay, so you have children?'
>
> Conversely, in the initial stages of coaching especially, I encourage you
> to volunteer only the most basic elements of your own personal informa-
> tion. This helps to keep the focus of the conversation on your coachee,
> keeps the conversation professional and avoids inappropriate 'chatting'.

Focus on desired outcomes/results

During the context stage, you also need a basic, shared understanding of what someone wants to get from a series of coaching sessions. Where you have a pre-conversation (or chemistry meeting), this surfaces naturally in discussion, for example, 'What brings you to coaching?' Your aim is that they arrive for the first session having prepared a little (but remember that they may not). If you've sent an overview of coaching, they will have had another opportunity to con-sider what they want to get from coaching. Hopefully, they've thought a little more about what areas they want to focus on, or simply have some questions based on the overview document.

Please don't expect someone to be crystal clear from the outset; that's less likely early on. For example, someone may initially have statements such as:

- 'I'm thinking of starting my own business, but I've no idea what's involved, and I need help thinking everything through.'
- 'I want to work on my management skills; I need to get better at building teams.'
- 'I need to decide what my next career move is; I don't have a plan and I'm con-cerned I'm just drifting.'
- 'I probably need to work on my influencing style; I've had feedback that some-times I don't communicate as effectively as I could.'
- 'I lack confidence in some areas and it's holding me back personally and pro-fessionally; I've tried everything, and I just need help with this.'

A need to incorporate external objectives and goals

When you coach within business, there are often objectives for an assignment that arise from other people or processes. For example, as part of a performance review, someone may have had development needs identified – perhaps a need to improve certain behaviours and skills or be supported over a difficult or stressful period.

If these objectives exist, please be aware of the need to incorporate them openly to maintain trust between you and your coachee, and your own integrity. For example, if your coachee's boss wants you to help improve your coachee's relationship skills, then your coachee needs to be aware of that. Options to encourage openness in these situations include:

- asking the manager to meet with the coachee before the coaching begins to explain why coaching is being offered

- asking that the objectives and topics for coaching are confirmed by document/email and forwarded to you and your coachee

- inviting the manager to be part of a coaching session to discuss their ideas and requests for the coaching (sometimes called a tripartite meeting).

Where a boss or third party is unwilling to disclose their own objectives or requests for the coaching, then your challenge is to maintain openness between the boss and you. You must explain that, since you have been given a third-party agenda for the coaching, you are unable to share openly, to try and coach those topics directly would cause a lack of integrity (and openness) in your relationship with the coachee. This creates what feels like a hidden agenda for the coaching, which communicates in some way to the coachee. In my experience, it's potentially a challenging conversation to have, and yet something that needs to happen if you are to retain your standards of professionalism.

At a Glance

Maintain direction within each session

The need to maintain a sense of purpose within each coaching session is also important. As in The Coaching Path, in the first part of each session, you will normally encourage a sense of direction, for example, 'What do you want to achieve in today's session?' By agreeing an intention for the session, you can reduce potential digressions or drifting, for example, 'You said you wanted to find ways of reducing your work hours because of the current pressure you're experiencing – are you happy to continue with this discussion of last week's presentation?'

The benefit of clear goals and outcomes

When you are supporting someone to achieve a desired outcome – to make something happen or to achieve something specific – you need a proper understanding of that outcome. For example, if your coachee says they want to get a new or better job, both of you need to understand the following:

- What specifically does 'better job' mean? Is that defined by an increase in salary, benefits, responsibility, working conditions, job content, working location, job title, training?

- What circumstances currently relate to their goal, for example money issues, tensions with current employer, contractual obligations, notice period?

- What are the coachee's reasons (motivators) for wanting the goal, for example financial security/freedom, lifestyle, personal profile, respect?

- What might stop, or form a barrier to, them achieving this goal, for example fear of change/risk, academic qualifications/work experience, peer pressure?

Often, just discussing what a coachee really wants and defining that with clarity can be of huge benefit. When someone develops a richer appreciation of the motivators, circumstances and issues that are involved in their goals, they create a shift in their perception. When a coachee is helped to gain this richer understanding, it's not uncommon for them to have a change of heart about what they want.

Story

When we don't want what we think we want

Matt, our coachee, wanted to find ways to support his son's education. Matt was frustrated at his son's lack of progress at school in some subjects (in particular, maths) and wanted to look at options, such as extra tuition or changing schools. Carla, our coach, decided to explore the situation a little more, for example not just what Matt was saying he wanted to provide for his son – a good education – but also what might be causing his frustration.

Through gentle enquiry, Matt realised that he didn't actually mind that his son was no good at maths. After all, his son was excelling in other areas that came more naturally to him. What frustrated Matt was that his son seemed so relaxed about the situation (instead of being worried or

---

stressed about it). He explained that his son loved English, history and sport, and saw maths as something to be 'tolerated'. This contrasted with Matt's values from his own childhood, when his strict father had taken education very seriously and taught Matt to worry a lot about any areas where he might be 'failing'.

During the conversation, Matt also saw that he didn't want to teach his son to worry or become stressed about things, such as his lack of natural ability for maths. Matt decided that teaching his son to live an enjoyable and productive life, one that fulfils him, was a lot more important. Strangely, Matt also began to see his son as someone he could learn from. He found that he actually admired the way his son could find real pleasure in being good at something. Conversely, his son could also accept things he's not good at and view them in a relaxed way.

This was quite a shift in perception for Matt, who tended to disregard all his own successes, and worry instead about the areas in his life where he thought he might be 'failing'. As Carla explored Matt's goals further, he was able to reach this conclusion fairly quickly. In addition, Matt now had a new goal that he felt better about: learning a new, relaxed way of being from his son.[2]

Build a sense of engagement for change

As we create the context for coaching, we also begin to build engagement. By engagement, we mean that the individual is interested, involved and actively part of what's going on. If someone isn't engaged in the experience of being coached, then they are much less likely to enjoy and benefit from it. When a coachee is highly engaged, they are noticeably committed to getting the most from the experience. And the more engaged an individual is, the more coachable they become. By coachable, I mean that they are more receptive to finding new ideas and fresh perspectives – they are more eager to learn and create change.

The more engaged an individual is, the more coachable they become

For you as a coach, the difference between coaching someone who's engaged in the coaching versus someone who's not engaged or 'bought in' can mean the difference between fantastic results and no results. Consequently, you must stay aware of factors that might affect your coachee's openness to being coached, from the outset of coaching. The following checklist is a guide of things to look out for.

At a Glance

Signs that your coachee is engaged in the coaching

- Your coachee's level of enthusiasm for the conversation feels high, for example their energy, tendency to offer ideas, the questions they ask.
- Their level of openness in discussion is high, for example they readily share their thoughts and feelings and appear willing to consider fresh approaches or ideas.
- They are active between sessions: they complete agreements, read background material and books and even over-perform on commitments made.
- They report tangible results to you, for example, 'This is getting much better,' or 'I'm noticing this is different.'
- You become aware that they discuss the coaching in positive terms with others or even recommend your services.

If any or all the previous checklist items are missing, this doesn't mean that someone will not become engaged over time. In the first couple of sessions especially, some people may not respond to coaching as you might hope. They might appear reluctant to discuss certain situations or appear to hesitate to implement changes or even seem to challenge your views as coach. Your challenge as a coach is to balance your commitment to create progress with sensitivity towards someone else's typical way of learning. Perhaps they are naturally cautious in their response to anything new, or simply need more time to process a very different style of conversation.

Let's look more at factors that might affect someone's level of engagement.

Who wants the coaching?

If someone has requested and paid for coaching themselves, you can usually assume that they want the coaching. However, if you coach in larger organisations, your coachee may not have requested support and may be sceptical and/or mistrustful of what this means. They may imagine coaching is happening because of a problem with them they aren't aware of. Or they may wonder if the coaching sessions are actually some kind of 'vetting' activity, for example for redundancy or promotion. They may also be concerned that what they say during sessions might be reported back to others.

If a different person or department has enlisted your services, please make sure that your coachee is aware of the opportunity that being coached presents and is comfortable about being coached. Also, while you might tell someone why you think they are having coaching, it's better that they hear this from their manager. That way they are more likely to trust the process as it appears an open one. As previously mentioned, I encourage the requesting manager to explain the arrangement and the reasons for it in person before my first session.

> **While you might tell someone why you think they are having coaching, it's better that they hear this from their manager**

If it's possible, as coach you might sit in on this session between the manager and the coachee. That way you can help the conversation to be effective, by asking questions or clarifying comments. And you also get to see the manager and the coachee together, which may provide you with useful insights into that relationship.

What is your coachee expecting?

It helps to be clear about your style and approach from the start. If your coachee expects you to give them answers and advice and you aren't doing that, this can cause them frustration, and they may not voice it. They may have had training in the past, or a mentor, and they may expect that you are some combination of that role. Mentioning that you will work with them to help them find their answers (rather than give them answers) helps your coachee to be open to this approach from the outset.

Another unhelpful expectation may express itself in the form of cynicism, perhaps where an individual has a negative view of coaching. This might be caused by their own poor experience of it (as mentioned in Chapter 4). Your options to help reduce someone's poor perception of coaching include an introductory/chemistry conversation plus sending them background reading such as a coaching overview document.[3]

Are they committed to change?

This question can relate to whether they really want the full experience of coaching (which includes the expectation upon them that they will be open to change). In my experience, some people say they want coaching, begin a coaching relationship, attend sessions, join in conversations – and don't actually want anything to change. As your coachee completes agreements and actions, their everyday experiences may inform their understanding further. For example, your coachee might say that they dislike their job with its lack of responsibility and inadequate salary. They might spend a long time explaining why it's awful and what kind of job they'd really like to get. Between coaching sessions, however, they might do nothing. During coaching sessions, the coach listens to the complaints and wonders why the coachee is not acting on the decisions they appear to be making.

The answer might lie in the fact that only part of them wants change, while another part of them doesn't. You see, to get a better, more responsible, higher-paid job might confront their ability to actually do that type of job. Maybe the thought of that scares them. Alternatively, the coachee has been discussing a subject that's easy for them to explore and non-confrontational in nature. They may have other issues that are more challenging, but they are not open to talking about those.

You need to decide:

- How material is their tendency (to complain but not act) to the success of the coaching?
- Is this situation likely to change without you approaching it directly?
- How are they likely to benefit from being made more aware of their tendency?

If you perceive a barrier that appears to be sabotaging what someone says they really want, at some point, you need to be open about that. By that, I mean give feedback as to what you observe is happening (in this example, a reluctance to embrace change). This enables you to help them understand the apparent block, for example, 'What do you think is causing this?' or 'What else does this link to?' Together, you can develop the awareness they need to make progress. It might mean that they need to consider what they really want more fully, or perhaps how they're stopping themselves from having it.

At a Glance

Increase engagement

If you feel someone's engagement for the coaching is low, consider the following options:

1 *Perform an informal review.* Try going back to someone's original purpose and intentions for coaching and check what progress they feel they are making, for example, 'As a direct result of our conversations, what's changed?' and 'What changes might you have hoped for that haven't happened?'

2 *Work to understand their viewpoint* better in order to support them. Explain that you are noticing a lack of engagement and give helpful examples of what you are seeing (or not seeing). Next, facilitate enquiry, for example, 'How do you see this?' 'What causes this?' Then encourage them to decide a way forward, for example, 'How important is this to you?' or 'What needs to happen then?'

3 *Consider your own levels of engagement,* and work to improve them. In my experience, as coaches, we can sometimes 'mirror' what's happening with someone else. For example, if someone appears lacklustre in conversation, we also feel a little dulled ourselves. Or, if someone appears uncertain of the coaching process, this may resonate with some level of uncertainty we also have. Try using the powerful questions technique (in Chapter 4 Five fundamental skills of coaching) to form more positive perspectives and ways to increase your own levels of engagement in relation to an assignment. I appreciate it feels a less logical place to look and, yet, my experience indicates that it's often worthwhile.

Stage two – increase awareness, purpose and action

The second stage of a coaching assignment creates a clearer emphasis on what your coachee wants to change and builds a stronger sense of purpose towards that. Here we focus squarely on enquiry (seeking to understand) to surface wisdom and insight. This can be done solely through coaching conversations or may be supplemented by additional activities and tools (such as personality profiling or seeking feedback from third parties). In my experience, a balanced combination of both is more effective.

Continue coaching conversations

Continuing the idea of our six-session assignment, in this stage, we are most often encompassing sessions two to four or even five. So, you continue to meet for coaching sessions in person (or by telephone, via Skype, etc.) and use the previous structure of The Coaching Path, if that's a helpful framework for your conversations. After the first couple of coaching sessions, hopefully, you will have settled into a routine where most of your conversations contain the following elements:

1 A quick review or reminder of the last session, for example, 'Here are the broad topics we covered; here's what you decided to do.'

2 An update since the last session, for example, 'So what's been happening?'

3 A discussion of relevant topics or events that inform the coachee's ongoing learning and development. From The Coaching Path, this is often prompted by you, for example, 'So what topics do you want to work on today? or 'What do you want to get from this session?'

4 Anything else they want to do, or that you have previously agreed to do, for example role-play a difficult conversation they want to have, or review the coaching process in some way.

5 A gently formal conclusion of the conversation, such as a list of key thoughts, decisions or actions. Again, often this will be prompted by you and you will do that in your own way. For example:

- 'Okay, so help me understand what you've got from this conversation.'
- 'What have you decided to do as a result of this conversation?'
- 'What would you like to note down as things you'd like to get done before the next session?'

At a Glance

During an update: do not 'police' their actions

When someone begins to update you on what has happened since your last session, or what they've been doing, this is not an opportunity for you to 'manage' or 'police' whether or not they completed their actions.

Remember, this is an 'adult-to-adult' conversation in which you assume they are responsible for the results they are getting.

If you do notice that they haven't completed an action and you feel it might be useful to explore what stopped them, then do so and remember to adopt all of our less directive principles, for example, 'So, I'm interested as to what stopped you having the conversation with Simone, as actually you seemed keen to do that last time. Would that be useful to talk through?' However, please do not develop a routine at the first part of each session which feels, for your coachee, like, 'Heck, this is where I need to look like I've made great progress, or else explain why I haven't.'

If you observe, over time, that someone has a noticeable tendency to avoid actions they have agreed during conversations, then you might decide to make that observation or give feedback at some point.

Use support activities and tools to raise awareness

Here we are using additional activities to increase someone's awareness, both of themselves and of the situations relating to their objectives. Please remember, any activity supplementary to coaching conversations is optional and you must decide what works for you and the people you work with. Examples of additional methods and tools you may adopt include:

1 *Personality or behavioural profiling.* Examples include MBTI, Colours Insights (DISC) profile, Enneagram or Belbin, etc.

2 *Obtain feedback from third parties.* This can be done via feedback interviews performed by your coachee themselves or that you perform on their behalf.

3 *Encourage self-study.* Your coachee might read books, watch TED talks, etc. on topics relevant to their goals.

4 *Written reflection.* Encourage someone to keep a learning diary, that is to regularly write down what has been happening with regard to the areas they're working on (this method accelerates learning).

5 *A regular practice that encourages awareness.* Try meditation, mindfulness (present moment awareness) and even mind–body practices such as yoga, breath work and tai chi.

Clearly, you must be guided by your coachee and the situation as to what methods you use or encourage. For example, in their work environment, someone may be used to personality profiling and even have existing reports to share with you during the coaching process. They may also welcome the idea of you interviewing colleagues on their behalf to understand how others perceive their strengths and development areas. Someone you coach outside of an organisational environment may, or may not, be less comfortable with this.

How support activities can help

Where your coaching assignment involves any of the above activities, the need to raise someone's awareness is naturally supported. For example, when a coachee receives feedback from someone outside of the coaching conversations, which acknowledges and values their strengths, they are likely to adapt or change their own views. Many of us aren't aware of our strengths and how valuable they are and so we don't harness their potential. It can mean that we don't feel as confident or capable as we might do. Or maybe someone is interested in the topic of leadership, or relationships, or what makes us happy. By reading a book or watching an inspiring speaker give a TED talk, they build their own awareness and engagement in the topic.

View your involvement as that of a facilitator in someone's own learning process, rather than as the cause of it

So, these methods of building awareness can really support learning and change. It also helps you, as coach, to view your involvement as that of a facilitator in someone's own learning process, rather than as the cause of it. Sometimes, as coaches, we can feel overly responsible for someone else's results and progress; this can provide a useful shift in viewpoint.

What if I don't use any additional activities or tools?

If you and/or your coachee choose not to use any of the optional list of activities and tools, then you rely more on the awareness developing from the coaching sessions, plus what happens between them, perhaps as your coachee completes agreements and actions as their everyday experiences inform their understanding further. For this reason, it's a good idea to begin each session with an update of what's been happening since the previous one, as that's where you will both notice that learning and awareness are developing. By noticing something, we can build on it, for example, 'Well it's great that you're feeling more comfortable running the team. What's causing that increased comfort, do you think?'

An opportunity to confirm someone's coaching objectives

Here you continue to maintain a focus on someone's objectives or desired outcomes. Remember, your coachee may decide to revise or change these but you will still maintain them as the background to your sessions. Assignments without a clear intention or sense of purpose can develop into cosy, chatty conversations with no real direction. Not that there's anything wrong with chatty conversations, I enjoy them – they're just not coaching.

> **Assignments without a clear intention or sense of purpose can develop into cosy, chatty conversations with no real direction**

Using the previous picture of a six-session assignment to illustrate, by the end of session two or three, I would expect myself and my coachee to be clear about what we are working on and what the opportunities and benefits available to them are. I'd also expect that these descriptions would be written down and shared in some way. As a minimum, this would take the form of a brief email sent to my coachee to confirm their objectives for the coaching. In a more formal organisational context, someone may be required to create a personal development plan (PDP), describing areas for development, desired outcomes, and benefits.[4] Again, you'll stay aware of the situation and needs of both the individual and the environment you are coaching in.

As someone's awareness develops through the process of coaching conversations, there's a natural clarifying of what they want to change or improve, plus their sense of purpose. This may result in a statement of a definite goal, for example, 'I want to earn twice my current salary.' Alternatively, it may be that they notice what isn't working for them and build a resolution to move towards what does, for example, 'I need to stop making other people's priorities more important than my own.' I find that this feels more like an evolving situation as, after a couple of coaching conversations, someone has been able to unpack their initial topics and themes and has an emerging sense of what's right for them.

Awareness tends to dawn (rather than jump) upon someone

Raising awareness is a gradual process and I'd encourage you not to rush this. For example, early on, someone may 'decide' that they have figured something out or realised something and be eager to action their ideas. However, through the ongoing activity within this second stage, they develop a much better understanding of themselves and the situation.

The following story illustrates this point.

Story

Dasia doesn't delegate

Dasia manages a busy team and feels like she's actually the busiest person in that team. Her workload means that she regularly starts early and stays late. Her own manager sees what's happening and also how Dasia appears to 'mother' her team a little, for example shield them from difficult tasks and issues by doing them herself. Her manager enlists your support as a coach.

Dasia arrives at a first session with you explaining that she knows she needs to get better at delegating, but she just doesn't know where to begin. You both discuss delegation, and its basic mechanics and Dasia is hugely enthusiastic about creating change. During the first session, Dasia decides on a list of requests she is going to make of individuals to enlist their help on key tasks.

However, during the second session's update, Dasia explains how difficult she has found making requests of people and that she really doesn't feel comfortable asking certain people in particular. It's obvious that there is more to understand about the situation and Dasia's unique perspective and relationship to it.

During subsequent sessions, Dasia realises that the issue is more complex than a need to simply go and ask people to do things for her. She realises that, actually, what stops her from delegating is a need to retain control or always know what's happening with a task. Dasia imagines that she is bothering people with difficult tasks and wants to avoid their discomfort or displeasure. In a later session, she shares her own discomfort with the idea of being a manager who sometimes needs to prioritise their own workload above someone else's feelings.

Over time, Dasia develops greater insight into what her beliefs and tendencies are and the issues she creates for herself and others. That increases and drives her sense of purpose to change. As Dasia's understanding increases, so does the maturity of her viewpoint, for example that she is not functioning well in this part of a manager's role and the overall performance of her team is reduced as a result.

Increase focus on 'how' change will happen

This topic is a natural continuation of the previous topics of raising awareness and clarifying the areas someone wants to change. Even when someone knows what they want to change and why, they also need to appreciate how to do so.

Again, using the illustration of a six-session assignment, I'd suggest that, by the middle of an assignment, your coachee needs to be clear about the simple things they need to focus on to become more effective. This might include:

- shaping behavioural change, for example, 'Do more of this, do less of that'
- implementing decisions they've made to change certain situations
- developing new skills, for example communicating more clearly with others
- increasing impact, for example leadership style
- building new relationships
- involving or working with others to create change
- enlisting the help or support of others.

Remember, the purpose of coaching is broadly to support someone to move away from something they don't want, and towards something that they do. That can encompass a vast array of situations, from something definite such as 'I want to be more confident at handling conflict' to 'I want to consider what's going to happen when I retire, so that I feel more comfortable about it.' However, any change requires some action to bring it into material reality and talking about a situation and understanding it is more the enabler of change than the evidence of it.

> **Any change requires some action to bring it into material reality**

Help someone turn insight into action

Maybe your coachee has realised that the reason they feel overwhelmed at work is because they tend to take on too much. Through the conversations with you, they also appreciate that their tendency is to make other people's priorities more important than their own. They see that the consequence of doing this is that they are working long hours, missing out on time with their family and generally building up feelings of frustration and resentment towards other people involved. They no longer want to quit their job; they simply want to create a situation where their workload is more manageable, and they have more time in their schedule to be creative again. So, now they have awareness and clarity of purpose. What they also need is a clear understanding of how they can create change.

Once someone knows what their block or issue is, and what they want to achieve, then the actions in some situations are obvious. For example, if someone realises that they don't sleep well because they drink too much coffee, then what they need to do is simple (although not necessarily easy). However, some situations require that you help your coachee make a clearer connection about what they need to do, for example by asking questions with the purpose of identifying and generating action:

- So, what needs to happen?
- What's it going to take for you to make your own priorities more important?
- What do you need to do more/less of?

Imagine that, like Dasia from our earlier story, your coachee has issues delegating. You use the above questions to help them decide to set clearer boundaries and become more comfortable with potentially disappointing people. Through conversation, they identify some simple ideas:

1 Make a list of my priorities, for example what I need to do to fulfil the needs of my job/role. Remind myself of those daily – keep a daily action list.

2 Decide on a list of criteria to help me judge if someone's request is something I should say 'yes' or 'no' to – or renegotiate in some way, for example, 'Not now but it may be possible later.'

3 Use my priorities as a way of renegotiating requests, for example, 'I'm working on "x" until the end of this week.'

Maintaining engagement and understanding to encourage action

For your coachee, some actions are simple to complete, and others require a higher level of engagement and a richer appreciation of the situation. Where there are interdependent factors in play, such as limiting beliefs or negative emotions, then the idea 'I need to say "no" more often' probably won't sustain change over time. For example, our overworked coachee has limiting beliefs that result in their becoming overwhelmed. They've realised that they enjoy the thanks they get when they help other people with their work, plus they don't like saying 'no' in case they displease someone. Also, they aren't sure how to say no constructively, in a way that sounds reasonable and appropriate.

So, as well as an appreciation of what they need to do, they also need to understand how to do it and also how to support themselves to cope with the challenges involved in sustaining change. As you facilitate their thought processes, your enquiry might include:

- What might stop you from doing this?
- What's important to you about this? For example, what will the benefits be when you have learned to create better boundaries?
- Who can you learn from here? Who does this really well?
- How can you support yourself to do this?
- When things become difficult or challenging, what do you need to do?

Please remember that coaching doesn't consist only of questions. Your ability to summarise someone's thinking, offer your own observations and provide supportive challenge can be appropriate ways to aid their thinking process. Of course, remember our principles of a less directive style of influence, and work from the basis of facilitating their thoughts and decisions, rather than trying

> **When you do decide to give someone an idea, please stay aware of your intention and neutral as to the outcome**

to get them to see a situation in the same way as you. During individual sessions, The Coaching Path can also help to guide you, as the model supports both the process of enquiry and also shaping agreements and conclusions.

At a Glance

What if I've had a good idea that I want to give someone?

Occasionally, it's valid for you to offer your coachee an idea, to help support their thinking or assist with their decision-making process. When you do decide to give someone an idea, please stay aware of your intention and neutral as to the outcome. Consider these questions:

- Am I telling them this for a constructive reason, for example it seems obvious, and they haven't spotted it, or because I keep wondering if it might help?
- Is my reason less constructive, for example I'll appear knowledgeable or smart, or because I'm getting frustrated at their lack of progress?
- What is the potential impact on their sense of empowerment if you offer them an idea in this conversation/situation?

By staying neutral, I mean that you offer the idea and are willing for it to be rejected or ignored by your coachee. It's a little like putting a gift on the table; you need to be as happy if someone doesn't accept it as you would be if they did.

Staying with our previous overworked coachee, when you have helped them to understand the factors that may inhibit action and progress, you can create a focus on how to overcome them. Using the previous topics of enquiry (how to set better boundaries), your coachee may decide on additional principles and actions, such as:

- Declare my intention to my manager, get her thoughts and ideas and check validity of some of my thinking.

- Develop my style of refusing requests to be more constructive by studying how Matt does it so elegantly, for example in emails, during meetings, etc. Come back to next session and discuss.

- Put a fun photo of my partner and children on my desk to remind me what I'm missing at home.

Regular reviews assist awareness, purpose and action

Throughout an assignment, you also need a way to ensure someone is comfortable with the process and can give you feedback or make additional requests of you. So, we use regular, informal reviews to reflect on progress more objectively. By an informal review, I simply mean a quick check every couple of sessions to gain an overall sense of the benefits someone is gaining from coaching. As you review, there is also a logical link to how active they are between sessions, which helps to increase their action focus.

So, regular reviews help maintain progress during a coaching assignment by exploring any or all of the following:

- How effective are the coaching sessions? Are they productive, worthwhile, etc.?

- What progress has been made with the coachee's goals?

- How effective does the coachee find the coach's style and approach?

- Are there any issues that need to be resolved, for example what's not working?

- How could the sessions be improved?

Your own reviews are also valid

The above questions are primarily intended for the coachee to answer as they are the person who places a value upon the coaching. After all, they are the focal point of the conversations and the person who should benefit from them.

However, you will also have views on all of the above, as well as your other coaching experience to draw upon. In addition, you may have your own goals during the assignment, such as improving your listening or questioning skills. It makes sense, therefore, that both you and your coachee have an opportunity to pause and reflect.

At a Glance

Methods to review coaching progress

- Ask for informal feedback from the coachee on an ad-hoc basis when it seems appropriate.
- Conduct regular, quick reviews with the coachee, for example at the end of each session.
- Give the coachee a questionnaire to complete between sessions.
- Use a questionnaire to conduct a structured review session with the coachee.
- Schedule an unstructured discussion with the coachee to explore the progress of the coaching.
- Complete a feedback questionnaire on your own experience (as coach).
- Supervision: arrange a coaching session with another coach to review progress (very useful when you are having some difficulty or issues with the assignment).

Deciding when and how to review

As a coach, you need to strike a balance between how much time you spend reviewing the coaching and how much time you spend in coaching conversation. Too many reviews can impair the flow of your conversations and cause an unnatural focus on the conversations themselves. Alternatively, if we disregard the review process, we risk missing an issue or an opportunity to improve the effectiveness of the sessions for our coachee.

There are no strict guidelines, although in any assignment more than five sessions long I like to schedule at least a couple of proper (obvious) reviews plus several quick checks. For example, the first part of the session will often contain some kind of update discussion and present an ideal point for a quick check. So here we can ask a couple of review-type questions, such as 'How are you finding the coaching generally, then?' or 'How are we doing, do you think?' If I want to encourage feedback, I might be more pointed, for example, 'I've been wondering, how can I support you more effectively, what can I do more or less of, do you think?' Obviously, that's not going to produce rigorous feedback but it will give me a general indication of how I'm doing from their perspective.

As a more obvious review, I'll verbally recap someone's original objectives for the coaching and use any notes or documentation that relate to that. For example, in a six-session assignment, I might do that at session five, or earlier if it seems appropriate. Types of questions I might encourage someone to reflect on include:

- How much progress has been made on their original objectives for the coaching?
- What else has happened? Is there anything that we didn't expect?
- What hasn't happened that they would have expected or hoped for?
- What needs to happen going forward?
- What else seems relevant?

I also like to send a request for feedback around six weeks after the coaching has finished. For example, I might mail someone a link to an electronic questionnaire in a tool such as Survey Monkey, containing questions that relate to their experience and opinion of the overall process. This remote review gives my coachee an opportunity to reflect and give feedback a short time after the coaching has ended. In addition, the activity of giving feedback reminds them of the insights and learning they have gained and, perhaps, encourages them to apply those lessons a little more rigorously.

I'll also do my own regular reviews of progress, by re-reading all my notes and any related documents or profiling information in the file I keep on my coachees during the time I'm providing them with coaching support.

If you keep paper notes and files, store them properly and destroy them once they are no longer required. For example, six months after an assignment is completed, shred or burn the coachee's file. While these routines may appear onerous, actually it's more a simple need to develop good habits – have a lock on your cupboard, check dates on old files, don't write or record anything that you wouldn't be happy for anyone to see, etc.

Using our original idea of a six-session assignment, Table 7.1 shows a typical schedule of reviews for you to consider what works for you.

At a Glance

Proper care of personal information/data

Whether you store information relating to your coachees on paper or electronic media – your laptop, tablet, computer, etc. – please develop practical routines to safeguard it and destroy it when it is no longer needed.

For example, ensure that electronic information is safeguarded by effective encryption, passwords and backups. I also recommend that you treat any free online storage or free cloud-type backup as unsecure. Also, that you protect extra-sensitive documentation as something that needs its own individual password. To decide what constitutes extra-sensitive, consider the implications of the item being made public, for example to anyone the information concerns, or their family, their employer, etc. Also be aware that any information you hold on someone is something they have a right to ask to see by law.

For further guidelines, check out General Data Protection Regulation (GDPR) at www.gdpr.eu and also the Data Protection Act at www.gov.uk.

Table 7.1 Typical schedule of reviews over a six-session coaching assignment

Stage	Nature of review	Comment
Pre-meet	During introductory conversation, describe the idea of informal and formal reviews. Explain that giving an update at the beginning of each session constitutes a natural, informal review.	Build positive expectations. Focus also on building rapport (see Chapter 4 Five fundamental skills of coaching).
Session one	Informal check at end of session, e.g., 'Was that what you expected?' Note down their key thoughts arising from the session, or any agreements/actions they've decided on. Send follow-up email with encouragement to give feedback, e.g. 'Let me know if we need to do anything differently next time.'	A little formality upfront can be helpful, e.g. email the key topics they want to work on and what they decided to do from this session. This also gives you something to review against.
Session two	During update at the start of the session, check: 'How were you after the last session?' At end of session, quick informal check, e.g., 'Was that a useful discussion to have?'	Remember not to 'drill' someone on their progress with their own actions (avoid parental tone).

▶

Stage	Nature of review	Comment
Session three	During update, using your notes, e.g. 'Let's have a look at how we're doing so far. I want to do a quick recap of your original objectives.' Acknowledge progress and ask for improvements, e.g. need to alter session times, focus more on work issues, etc.	Gentle, informal tone. Probably takes just a few minutes, e.g., 'How is this generally for you?' 'Is there anything we can improve?'
Session four	During update, informal check: 'How have you been since the last session?' At the end of session, e.g., 'Was that useful?' Flag the intention to review results more properly during the next session, e.g. 'What have you got from the sessions?' 'What haven't you got?' Encourage the coachee to prepare for next time.	Option: send them the formal review questions ahead of time.
Session five	More formal review of progress on goals, and recorded notes. For example: Q 'What's happened?' Q 'What progress have we made on your initial objectives?' Q 'What do you still want to make more progress with?'	Also: Q 'What is going less well?' Q 'What needs to happen?' Q 'How else can I support you?'
Session six	During initial update part of session, check well-being and progress, e.g. 'How have you been?' – plus a check against their intended progress since last session.	
Four to six weeks later	Obtain feedback from them of the effectiveness of the assignment process. Use questions that check their results plus your process: Q 'How effective was the organisation and scheduling of sessions?' Q 'How clear were you of the overall process during the assignment?' Q 'What would have worked even better for you?'	Send electronic feedback form for completion (or paper copy, if more appropriate).

You will develop your own style of managing sessions and the list of review options is intended to support that. Other options for reviews include a telephone call between sessions, or maybe an email to check how things are.

If the above appears to create a lot of reviewing, remember your coachee is likely only to notice the more formal stages, consisting of the review in session five plus the questionnaire, once the assignment is complete. For you, as coach, a lot of this happens naturally. For example, as I am filing someone's notes, I'll sometimes re-read the others that are there. This will often provoke me into thinking about what's happening with that coachee generally and I may choose to do something different in the next session because of that.

Stage three – completion and possibility

This is, logically, the final stage of coaching when we bring the coaching assignment to a conclusion. Our intention is to reach a point where our involvement with someone as their coach ends as they continue without our support. This does not mean that we cannot restart as their coach at some point in the future, merely that we need to fulfil the intentions of this agreed set of sessions, by bringing them to a close.

So here we acknowledge key points of progress and benefits, alongside requirements that have not been met or anything else that remains incomplete. We also encourage a sense of ongoing direction and possibility, for example, 'Here's what you're focused on, going forward.' This stage primarily takes place during the final session, but it may also require time spent on it before and after that session, perhaps as you prepare to complete ahead of time, or you remain available to your coachee after the final session, for a quick catch-up call or meeting.

The purpose of completion

As we work to complete an assignment, we aim to:

1 *Leave the coachee feeling that the coaching has been worthwhile, for example by acknowledging results.* In addition, where someone else has sponsored the coaching, the sponsor should also feel that they have received value from their investment.

2 *Identify the coachee's sense of future direction,* such as development themes, additional opportunities for change and progress, etc., that things continue to get better, sustained by a positive sense of what is possible.

3 *Ensure the coachee feels supported going forward.* Identify appropriate methods, such as people, self-study, courses, seminars, etc.

Begin with the end in mind

Preparing for completion actually starts at the beginning of a coaching relationship. As coach, you must operate from an assumption that your involvement with the coachee will have an end to it that fulfils the previous completion criteria. This requires you to think and act in ways that reduce the coachee's dependence on you and to consider their progress once your involvement has ended. For example, you might encourage the coachee to keep their own notes during sessions, create a personal development plan, or increase their tendency to ask others for feedback. Alternatively, you might offer book recommendations or other ways that they may gain additional inspiration and insight.

Let's look at each of our three completion criteria independently.

Leave the coachee feeling that the coaching has been worthwhile

This is an important feature of the completion stage, as we want to leave the coachee feeling buoyant about the experience and, so, more naturally engaged to continue their progress without our support. As they notice results, they also recognise the value of having engaged your services; that's good for them, you and our profession generally.

When you review the progress and results of coaching, you naturally confirm the benefits and create clear links between your conversations and the benefits your coachee is experiencing as a result. While this feature of completion doesn't necessarily require you to do anything additional (if you have already reviewed results), it is, however, important for you to judge the strength of the links made. Use the following questions to help you do this:

- Are the main benefits of the coaching visible to and understood by both myself and the coachee? (Consider the obvious and the less obvious.)

- How do the results and benefits of the coaching compare with the expectations of the coachee, for example compared with those they initially envisaged?

- Who else had expectations for this coaching and what perception do they now have of the benefits and value it has created?

What if there aren't any results?

Sometimes, the coaching doesn't produce the results that we hoped it would and it is important to recognise this. If we first identify that the coaching has had little or no lasting impact, we can then explore this with the coachee. Together, the coach and coachee can look at what's happening and why and decide if anything else is needed. Reasons for this lack of results might include:

1 The coachee became disengaged from the coaching process when things got challenging or difficult.

2 The coachee really needed support from a third party closer to their situation and they didn't get that.

3 The assignment lacked a clear structure, for example there were no clear links between the conversations and the coachee's – so conversations felt disconnected or like cosy chatting.

Balance support with a need to empower the coachee

Our intention here is not to create a problem, or to extend our involvement for our own gain. However, it's my experience that, when an individual recognises that the first reason has come into play, that is they disengaged because things got challenging, they might also request one or more further sessions. Here, I would recommend caution. While a further session or two may be effective, as coach, you need to step back at some point. In these cases, I might:

> **As coach, you need to step back at some point**

- agree to a limited number of additional shorter sessions (and charge for those)

- offer two or three short telephone calls to provide remote support for a clear set of actions (and I'd normally do those free of charge)

- dissuade them from continuing. Sometimes, a coachee needs to act independently of coaching support. Where I feel someone has all they need to make great progress (information, themes, other sources of support), I may do this, and check in with them at some future point to ensure their well-being.

Finally, if you are coaching in a business environment and the person contracting your services is not your coachee, then identifying and dealing with issues helps maintain your professional reputation with them as well.

What if the results are not good or the coachee feels worse?

Sometimes, an individual having coaching may find that things get worse before they can get better. This is a natural part of the learning cycle and both the coach and the coachee should be prepared for it as a possibility. The following story gives an example of this.

Story

Marco's management style got worse before it got better

Marco ran a busy chain of high-street coffee shops. Recognised for his high standards and results, he achieved these by making great demands of people and using controlling, sometimes aggressive, behaviours. Marco got results fast but found, over time, that colleagues gave him negative feedback, or simply avoided him. When a complaint of bullying reached his HR department, he was offered coaching to help him become more aware of the issues and develop a more constructive management style.

Marco arrived at the initial session genuinely upset about the negative feedback and also concerned at the accusation of bullying against him. He acknowledged his tendencies and wanted to learn better ways of making requests of people, to maintain relationships and support over time. Buoyed by a positive initial session, Marco retuned to work and stopped barking orders at people. He also stepped back from several situations that he would normally have become frustrated about. Unfortunately, standards in the coffee shops soon began to decline as employees felt neither engaged nor empowered to act without Marco's direction.

As the coaching continued, Marco realised that he wasn't actually fulfilling his role in maintaining standards of service and delivery in the coffee shops. Instead of delegating responsibility, he was simply abstaining from it. So, Marco practised new ways of making requests with his coach and also decided on ways to help people feel more comfortable acting on issues in his absence.

It took Marco some time to find the right balance between making a clear request of someone, engaging them in a need to carry out that request and doing so in a way that demonstrated respect and support for the individual. It also took Marco's team time to trust his new style and to learn how they needed to respond to it. While sometimes, progress felt like one step forward, two steps back, ultimately, Marco developed a consistently effective style, based on principles he'd agreed with his coach. The benefits were clear to everyone, most of all Marco, who felt he could achieve the high standards that drove him, while maintaining his sense of comfort about how he treated people who worked for him.

When you need more evidence of results

Sometimes, you might want to make a clearer link to the benefits of coaching, perhaps because of a general lack of clarity or a specific need to do so – for example to display the substance of your work to a new or potential coachee. Methods you might use include:

• Observing the individual in their workplace or anywhere that seems appropriate to view results, for example if they wanted to be better at public speaking, go and watch them.

• Collating the results of several reviews (such as those gathered via electronic surveys or on hard copy). Summarise data anonymously, to share with potential clients.

• Use your notes from structured review conversations with coachees and, again, collate these anonymously.

• Interview your coachee's colleagues or friends and ask for feedback on your coachee following the coaching. This works especially well if you have performed initial feedback interviews during the early stages of the assignment. Remember to maintain openness (and trust) – gain permission, share results with your coachee, etc.

• Ask coachees to write testimonials or ask their permission to share the results of any evaluation reviews they may have completed during their assignment.

• Request permission to video your coachee talking about what benefits they have gained, for example during an interview in person or via a remote link-up (such as a webinar). Share this only in situations where you have permission to do so.

Identify the coachee's sense of future direction: development themes and opportunities to progress

This stage is also about creating a sense of future direction and helping someone feel confident about continuing to make progress. After all, the benefits of coaching don't end when the sessions do and, actually, in some ways, the real work is just beginning. I find that, following a typical coaching assignment of five to seven sessions, people often achieve more widespread change after the assignment has ended.

> **The benefits of coaching don't end when the sessions do**

Short-term results are seeds that can grow in fertile earth

During the coaching conversations, your coachee is encouraged to try new behaviours, the rewards of which are immediate. However, more significant results seem to come from their shift in perspective, or the new principles they now operate from in all areas of their life. For example, I had one coachee who recognised a tendency to complain and moan and feel like a victim of circumstance. As a consequence, he was more passive or reactive to situations (rather than proactive), even when he was really annoyed about them. So, not much changed over time. When he became aware of that, he decided to stop complaining at work, at home, to himself, etc. Over time, his whole outlook shifted from one of 'life happens to me' towards 'if it's to be, then it's up to me'. His immediate career frustrations were soon reduced as he realised that he was the source of his own experience. As that idea took hold and grew roots, two years later, he felt a whole lot more powerful in his life generally and his circumstances reflected that.

So, it's important to build a sense of this future direction, in order to help the coachee:

- retain simple ideas and themes they can maintain a clear focus on
- know what they need to do with these to create steady and ongoing progress
- envisage a clear benefit from doing this, for example have a positive vision or sense of the future.

As you'd expect, there's no right or wrong way to encourage this sense of future direction and you will be guided by your own views as well as those of your coachee. Here you need to balance an appropriate sense of challenge with practicality. You also need to consider the individual and what they are likely to engage with most positively. Ideas and methods to consider include:

- discussing their key themes and actions and encouraging them to take some notes of the conversation
- discussing their themes (as above) and sending them your notes or a summary
- supporting them to construct a simple documented list of their key themes going forward, their updated objectives and actions. This document is something that can be reviewed and updated over time
- encouraging them to envisage how they'd like to view their situation, say a year from now – when they've continued to make progress and they are seeing the benefits all around them. On a blank piece of paper, ask them to

draw a picture of where they are now and another of their future situation. Let them know that anything they draw is great; it is simply an opportunity to play a little

- incorporating their ongoing objectives into a personal development plan (PDP), perhaps as something they might share with their manager or a mentor.

The full list of options is actually much longer, and you are limited only by your imagination. Remember that ideas need to be pragmatic and desirable for your coachee. It's no good suggesting books to people who don't like reading, or night school to someone who has to look after children each evening. Simple things work best, as they are most likely to be achieved. Someone who has a regular drive to work may find audiobooks or other recordings useful or, for those with a long train journey, a book might be a welcome distraction.

At a Glance

Key elements of a Personal Development Plan (PDP)[5]

A PDP forms a record for the coachee of the main areas in which they want to improve or goals on which they want to focus. They are especially useful in business, where they create a specific focus for someone's professional and career development. PDPs can also be used to request further training or support and can assist someone's career progress. The following are potential headings (or columns) within a PDP document. Not all headings are always necessary, so please decide what's useful for you.

1 Area of development

This is the general skill or competence, for example time management, financial awareness, health/well-being etc.

2 Development objectives (goals)

This is what the individual specifically wants to do, for example:

- Reduce my working day to eight hours.
- Develop proficiency to understand and manage financial reporting information relating to my area.
- Reduce my stress levels by improving my general sense of health and well-being.

▶

3 Behaviours to develop and demonstrate competency

This is what the individual will be doing more of when they start meeting their objective, for example:

- Use a weekly and daily action list to prioritise and schedule activity and review these plans regularly with one other person.
- Regularly review financial reports and discuss those with others, such as Pavel or Jenny in finance.
- Eat a healthy, light lunch every day; drink one glass of water for every tea or coffee; attend a yoga class at least once a week.

4 Actions to create progress

This is what the individual must do to really get into action on their objective, for example book a place on a course, arrange a meeting, find a mentor, etc. Agree on a date by which these arrangements should be completed. Using the three categories above, we might choose:

- Arrange meeting with Jo to agree what my current priorities really are (10/07).
- Arrange to see company accountant to understand what's important for me to focus on (03/07).
- Share my goal re. food, drink, classes with at least three other people and request support (05/08).

5 Date to complete or review the objective

Here we record the relevant dates for completion or review of the initial objective, for example, 'Reduce my working day to eight hours.' It's often a good idea to put a review date in before the final date, in order to check progress. For example, if my goal is to reduce my working day to eight hours within a three-month period, a review point after a month would make sense.

Ensure the coachee feels supported going forward

During an assignment you create a sense of involvement and support that your coachee welcomes and values over time. Sometimes, when that's gone, an individual may experience it as a withdrawal of support. To avoid this happening, we need to:

- prepare the coachee for the ending of the sessions
- identify other potential ways the coachee may get support, if needed
- check back on the coachee shortly after the coaching has ended.

Again, your preparation for the completion of the assignment begins long before the final coaching session. However, when the sessions are over, some sense of withdrawal may still be felt. One valid option is to make one or two phone calls a short time after the coaching has ended. These don't have to be coaching conversations, although there is an obvious opportunity to offer a little reassurance, guidance or encouragement, if needed.

If the individual still wants and, perhaps, needs support, then please consider other ways in which they might obtain that. For example, finding a 'buddy' or mentor might work, especially when the coaching has been done in a business environment. If the sponsor of the coaching is the coachee's manager, perhaps they might be willing to meet with the coachee on a regular basis to discuss their performance or progress. This option has some advantages in that the manager becomes more involved in what's happening with the individual who works for them. One disadvantage might be that the boss simply isn't the right person to listen to the coachee; maybe they're too busy, or perhaps the coachee doesn't feel able to discuss certain topics with them. Other alternatives within work might be a friend or colleague, or perhaps someone in the training or HR department, etc.

At a Glance

Why not just keep coaching someone?

No matter how great the benefits from the coaching have been or how enjoyable and stimulating the relationship is, each coaching assignment should have a clear end. Just as there's something very exciting for both parties about embarking upon the beginning of a coaching initiative, there can also be something very liberating about ending one.

As a coach, you are a catalyst, bringing fresh perspectives, different ideas, and a constant focus to the goals of the coachee. If you have regular sessions with the same person for a long period of time, perhaps even years, the value of that coaching will diminish over time. In addition, your coachee must assume ultimate responsibility for themselves and their circumstances. If they have the same coach as a constant companion, some of this sense of independence may be lost. So, while an assignment with a coach might easily be extended, I recommend that it does not become a permanent arrangement.

Of course, a coachee may choose to return to coaching when they need a clearer focus or more support over a period of time. Here they might usefully consider working with a different coach, one with potentially different strengths. Depending on their reasons for returning, it may be advisable to consider all the available options – there are many good coaches available.

Actual completion/sign-off

So, by now, you are ready to formally complete and, by that, I mean have a noticeable sense of an ending. Completion is mostly indicated by a sense we get, for example, 'This feels like it has reached a healthy ending, and nothing is left undone.' However, in reality, it may be indicated by your final session, a confirmation email or a catch-up call. In session terms, we are now either at the last of the six sessions or perhaps some time after that, for example, having a quick catch-up a few months after the sessions have ended.

Your final coaching session

One of the more formal elements of completion is your final coaching session and, so, using our imaginary assignment, we're now at session six. Here, you need to ensure that all our elements of completion are fulfilled (your coachee is feeling positive, has a clear sense of future direction, etc.).

In terms of timing, I would normally expect a longer gap between session five and six than any other sessions. For example, where other sessions have been four to six weeks apart, this session is likely to be 10 to 14 weeks after the previous one (sometimes longer). This is because, by session five, your coachee understands what they are working on and the core themes of the conversation are unlikely to change much. The coachee simply needs to apply these themes to everyday situations and challenges.

Depending on the length of your session, I'd expect an element of coaching to happen and so The Coaching Path is still a practical support for your conversation. For example, in a 90–120minute coaching session, I'd expect a blend of the following activities:

	Final session: activity	Comment
1	**Follow-up and update since last session:** 'How are you? What's been happening?', etc.	Light tone.
2	**Some direction setting for this session:** Agree topics and goals for the conversation. Add in any specific requirements for this final session, e.g. 'Let's discuss how you will maintain progress going forward.'	As indicated within The Coaching Path.
3	**Conversational enquiry:** Discuss topics agreed using coaching principles.	As indicated within The Coaching Path.

	Final session: activity	Comment
4	**Create a specific focus on completion:** Acknowledge the need to complete and check that all sessions within the assignment are fulfilled. Identify any outstanding actions required to complete, e.g. 'Let's have a 30-minute call in 6 months' time to see how you're getting on.'	Ensure coachee is happy to complete, e.g. is clear, feels empowered, etc.
5	**Session summary:** Summarise the way forward.	Combine coaching part of conversation with completion element.

Update any other roles within the assignment (sponsors, stakeholders, etc.)

Also consider anyone else who has been involved in the assignment, such as the coachee's manager. Here, you'll want to sign off or complete with these individuals in an open and professional manner. Remember to use any initial agreements created during your set-up stage and also to retain confidentiality, as always. I tend to report more on process and principle, for example, 'We've had six sessions over a nine-month period, and they've gone really well.' If I have permission, I may also confirm the topics we've worked on. When I email a stakeholder or sponsor to discuss a coachee in this way, I'll copy in the coachee so that they are both aware of and involved in the conversation. I'll also encourage them to talk with each other about the assignment. This helps any stakeholder understand what value the coachee has got from the process and also encourages them to support the coachee going forward.

Story

Great coaching plus poor communication equals poor perception

Jan was just one of a team of coaches hired regionally to coach as part of a major management development programme. Tomas was manager of a large branch of a high-street bank. The request for Jan to coach Tomas came from an administrator of the coaching who had found Jan on a website list of qualified coaches in her area. Jan was emailed some programme objectives for the coaching, which seemed broad, and a list of company values such as respect, trust, team building and performance. The administrator also put Jan in touch with Tomas's area manager, Mila, and explained that Mila was the sponsor of the coaching. Jan was given no formal requirements for reporting back to the scheme administrator and was told, 'Mila will be handling things.'

After positive initial telephone conversations, first with Mila and then Tomas, Jan agreed to coach Tomas for five two-hour coaching sessions over seven months. These face-to-face sessions mainly focused on Tomas's desire to develop a more impactful managing style. From Jan's perspective, the coaching sessions went really well and, during informal reviews, Tomas explained just how much value and benefit he got from the conversations. When it came to the fifth and final session, Tomas even brought Jan a small gift as personal thanks for having made such a positive difference to his managing style and ability to lift the spirits among his team. During that final session, Jan enquired as to the need to update Tomas's boss Mila, and Tomas offered to speak to Mila personally. Jan accepted the offer, confident that Tomas would give her a good recommendation.

Unfortunately, Tomas and Mila didn't have time for a proper conversation about the coaching, as the bank was going through a particularly busy period. Mila did notice that Tomas seemed to be in better spirits (certainly his results were up), but she wasn't aware of how that was linked to his involvement with Jan.

While the need for confidentiality meant Jan could not share the content of her sessions with Tomas, she could have easily kept Mila informed as to the process and principles, for example, 'We've completed three sessions, we've completed a review and results are positive, etc.' Jan might also have encouraged the importance of regular chats between Tomas and Mila, for example, 'I'm sure Tomas would appreciate your interest and support.' Jan might also have gained insight into the opportunities within the broader development programme, as that developed over time, for example, 'Here's what head office need help with, etc.'

Some weeks later, Tomas's manager Mila attended a business networking meeting. The owner of a local firm of solicitors asked everyone at her table if they could recommend a good coach with a credible, professional approach. Mila considered recommending Jan, but stayed quiet; after all, she wasn't entirely clear what the overall outcome of the coaching sessions had been.

The best approach is what is best for your coachee

How you complete an assignment is up to you; my only encouragement is that you view this from both your and your coachee's perspective. Personally, I like to stay in contact with someone a little beyond the last session; it's always lovely to catch up with them and hear their news. I also recognise that people value the additional support beyond any formal expectation or professional arrangement. To help you decide, use this checklist.

At a Glance

Are we complete?

At the closing stages of an assignment, use the following questions to help you consider the main elements of completion:

Q Have you had a conversation with your coachee to find out what they have got from the coaching?

Q Does your coachee now have other goals or learning objectives, for example how they might improve even more at something?

Q Is your coachee clear about how their learning can be supported from now on, for example asking for regular feedback from colleagues, finding a mentor, etc?

Q Is your coachee comfortable that the coaching is coming to an end?

Q Who else has played a role in the assignment and what is the appropriate way to involve them now – a simple email, three-way discussion, etc?

In a Nutshell

A simple, effective assignment structure offers the following benefits:

• Your approach contains the principles of success, for example clear direction and purpose, increased awareness and action, etc.

• Your coachee has clarity of expectation, for example they understand key information relating to the coaching, plus through discussion, the approach has been tailored to their needs.

▶

- You present yourself as professional, capable and effective – which has a positive impact on you and your coachee going forward.

By spending a little more time upfront planning your approach to an assignment, you can increase not only your effectiveness, but your enjoyment as well.

chapter 8

Emotional maturity – a key to coaching

'Change the way you look at things and the things you look at change.'

Dr Wayne Dyer

One of the benefits of effective coaching over time is the overall development of a coachee's emotional maturity. This chapter explains the term emotional maturity and its fundamental link to coaching. It also considers how we can develop emotional maturity as coaches; for, if our coaching conversations support change for others, then our own emotional maturity is a constant enabler of that change to happen.

What is emotional maturity?

Emotional maturity relates to our capacity to deal with our emotions. Our ability to interpret emotions, express emotions and let go of emotions are all functions of our emotional maturity. When we can do this effectively, we are described as emotionally mature. It is demonstrated in how we think, what we choose to believe and what we ultimately do because of that. More generally, our emotional maturity becomes our mastery of the skills of life. By that, I mean our ability to create conditions of happiness, success and fulfilment.

Our emotional maturity (or lack thereof) is often demonstrated by our manner or moods, as well as our behavioural responses. Table 8.1 illustrates how we might describe ourselves when we are being either mature or immature.

Table 8.1 Indicators of maturity and immaturity

Indication of maturity	Indication of less maturity
We can stay generally calm and relaxed. We can be flexible in our attitude and approach. We are typically less defensive.	We are uptight or tense more often. We have difficulty being flexible, perhaps seeming rigid. We can appear defensive.
We take responsibility for our own self and our own circumstances.	We blame others for our problems or situations, refusing to acknowledge our own influence in situations.
We have an appetite for learning; we evolve through our situations. We seek alternative views and information.	We appear resistant or slow to learn, either by rejecting new ideas or refusing to consider alternatives. We rarely change our attitudes or behaviour over time.
Our good humour is never far away; we can laugh at ourselves as well as our circumstances. We are comfortable with our self.	We use less humour, or perhaps only direct humour outwards. We find personal embarrassment very difficult to cope with. We are more self-conscious or less comfortable with our self.
We have a 'live and let live' approach to other people. We rarely criticise others.	We may take issue when people don't think and act in the same way as we do. We criticise others frequently.
We are able to deal with life's difficulties and setbacks, perhaps by expressing disappointment and moving on.	We struggle to cope with disappointment, failure or setback. We may get 'stuck' in the negative emotions of a situation, which inhibits our progress forward.
We are generally easy to deal with on a personal level. We build and maintain relationships easily.	We can be difficult to get along with, e.g. people may describe us as 'high-maintenance'.
We have learned optimism as something that sustains us through life. For example, we look for opportunity because we believe it exists.	We are determinedly pessimistic, sometimes refusing to acknowledge potential. We can sometimes filter out or miss opportunity through an assumption that it doesn't exist.

It is important to recognise that we do not always occupy one fixed place: sometimes, we are relaxed and resourceful; sometimes, we are uptight and critical. To be an effective coach, we want our general levels of emotional maturity in most circumstances to stay healthy. By 'healthy', I mean that our behaviours and responses create a mostly constructive effect over time.

Before we begin to help support the success and fulfilment of others, we need to consider our own emotional maturity. The following questions will help your own reflection before we look at the topic more closely.

Pause and Reflect

Where might you improve your emotional maturity?

First, answer the following questions for yourself, then get someone you know well and whose judgement you value to answer them about you. Compare your answers and reflect on the differences.

Q How self-aware are you; how well do you know yourself?

Q How well do you express and deal with your emotions?

Q How well do you handle yourself in difficult situations?

Q How good are you at relating to other people?

Q How well do you get along with other people?

Q How effective are you at influencing others?

Q How much do you operate from a principle of interdependency?[1]

What's in a name?

Although I prefer the term 'emotional maturity', the same concept is also referred to as 'emotional intelligence', as formed by psychologists John Mayer and Peter Salovey.[2] In a similar way to the assessment of IQ (intelligence quotient), emotional intelligence can be measured to produce a score known as EQ (emotional quotient). The studies to distinguish emotional intelligence to measure and understand it have created a wealth of information and the body of research in this area is now extensive. If you are interested in the formative work, look for titles by Daniel Goleman, including *Emotional Intelligence* and *Social Intelligence*.

Alternatively, as a taster, try *The Emotional Intelligence Quick Book* by Travis Bradberry and Jean Greaves (2005, Fireside).

The value of maturity vs intellect

Research suggests that our intelligence (our IQ) might account for just 20 per cent of our career success. The rest is down to our personality, (preferences, attitudes, postures, etc.) and, of course, emotional maturity. This is great news because, although personality and IQ remain fairly fixed over time, our emotional maturity is something we can always work on, to develop and improve. One way to do this is to actively focus on the four key 'skills of life' that make up emotional maturity, namely how self-aware you are; how you manage yourself in situations; how much you understand others; and how you good you are at building effective relationships with others (see Figure 8.1).

What are you feeling – and why?

Emotional maturity relates to our ability to process our experiences, our emotions and our learning. When we have this maturity, we can distinguish our emotions and express them appropriately. This relies on our ability to recognise what is going on.

Our emotions are not always easy to recognise. Sometimes, it is as simple as noticing, 'I'm a bit fed up about this, really,' while other feelings require more thought to understand them, for example, 'I should be delighted with this job offer, but somehow I'm not.' By learning to acknowledge and express our

Figure 8.1 Four elements of emotional competence*

Source: Adapted from Daniel Goleman's five components of emotional competence.

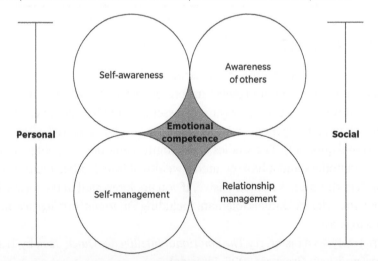

Note: * With acknowledgement to Daniel Goleman

emotions, even just to ourselves, we can understand and often release them. When we understand our emotions, we can distinguish ourselves as separate from them, which can promote a lighter sense of self.

It is a symptom of less mature people that they often get stuck in emotions. For example, they stay angry so that anger is never far away, and they lose their temper easily. To go through life not dealing with emotions may mean that emotions deal with you. In a mild way, it may simply be that we redirect emotions that we have suppressed from elsewhere, such as staying tolerant during a difficult day at work and then going home and taking it out on our partners, children or pets. This is probably healthier than never expressing frustration at all. And 'healthier' can mean just that. There is increasing acceptance of the links between our emotional states and our physical health. As we store up negative emotions, they can impact our physical well-being. For example, conditions such as acute stress, depression, chronic fatigue, etc. all take time to evolve. The denial or suppression of emotions can contribute to conditions of ill-health over time. If you are interested in studying or working more with this topic, I recommend a book called *The Journey* by Brandon Bays (2012, Harper Element).

Life – how do you handle it?

To process our emotions in a healthy way, it can help to work through situations by considering what happened, how we feel about what happened and what we can learn from it. For example:

- *Here's what happens.* You're out on a first date. You think it's gone well, and you'd like to see the person again; only they don't call. Then, when you manage to contact them, they make excuses. There will be no second date.

- *How do you feel about that?* Your emotions may range from humour, to ambivalence, to raging anger. It depends on you, doesn't it?

- *What have you learned?* This may range from absolutely nothing to lots of things. For example, when you reflect objectively on the evening, you become aware that you did all the talking (which is something you tend to do) or, alternatively, you did no talking, and you realise that may have been uncomfortable for them. Or you may notice a glaring difference of views on certain subjects or likes and dislikes. You may have previously disregarded all this information in your overall enthusiasm to be dating again. As usual, there are no rights and wrongs. To have no response to the situation may be a valid response. But what is true is that, if you have a good level of emotional maturity, you are likely to cope with the rejection or disappointment a lot better than someone with a lower level of emotional maturity.

Emotional maturity – four competences

As we've seen, there are four main areas that form the foundations of our emotional maturity, illustrated in Figure 8.1. These competences were first described in *Primal Leadership* by Daniel Goleman, *et al.* (2013, Harvard Business Review Press: Boston, MA) and are a practical way of understanding this topic. The four areas can be divided into the two main aspects of maturity: our ability to relate to ourselves (personal competence) and our ability to relate to others (social competence).

Within the four areas there are further skills, such as the ability to handle change, build relationships, work in teams, etc. However, to help with our perspectives for coaching, we'll simply focus on the main levels of the topic: self-awareness, self-management, awareness of others, relationship management.

It is possible that we are stronger in some of the above competences than others. For example, we *know* we tend to sulk after an argument with someone, which would demonstrate self-awareness. If, however, we don't seem to be able to stop doing that, this is related to self-management. It is also true that, in some situations, we demonstrate more 'maturity' than in others. For example, in a work situation, you may be consistently patient and calm. But if, on the 'wrong day', someone takes your parking space just as you are about to pull into it, you may just explode. We are all capable of maturity and we are all capable of immaturity.

> **We are all capable of maturity and we are all capable of immaturity**

I've mentioned briefly how emotional maturity can be good for the coach as well as for the coachee. For the coach, emotional maturity gives stability to their decisions and reflections, making them more effective in their role. For the coachee, the development of emotional maturity will allow them to deal with future situations, long after the initial situation that required a coaching relationship has been dealt with. Let's look at each area of competence with these two outcomes in mind.

Emotional competence 1: self-awareness

This first competence is summed up by the phrase 'know thyself'. It relates to your ability to accurately understand yourself either in the immediate moment or in general, for example your ability to interpret and describe your feelings accurately. It is also reflected in your strengths and weaknesses, your likes and dislikes, your good points, and your faults. Self-awareness can be in the moment, for example how do you feel right now? Or, more generally, how are you feeling about a certain subject, such as your social life, a certain relationship, etc?

Self-awareness: a link to you as a coach

As coaches, we need to maintain healthy levels of self-awareness to be effective. Our ability to express ourselves clearly, make decisions and know our own mind all demand this self-awareness. Within coaching sessions, our ability to stay flexible is also related to our own self-awareness. For example, in a session, this will help you understand what you are feeling, for example, 'I'm stressed – I need to relax.' That is pretty obvious to most of us; but it may also be more subtle, for example, 'I need to listen more.' Many of the *barriers to coaching* in Chapter 5 require self-awareness to avoid them, such as 'playing fix-it' or 'strategising'. If we don't know we are doing them, how can we stop? The other reason we need to be self-aware is so that we can be more appreciative of our effect on situations and conversations. Self-awareness informs us of our strengths, weaknesses and development needs. Use the questions below to help you consider this area further.

Please keep the note of your responses, so that you can use them later in this chapter.

Figure 8.2 Emotional competence: self-awareness*

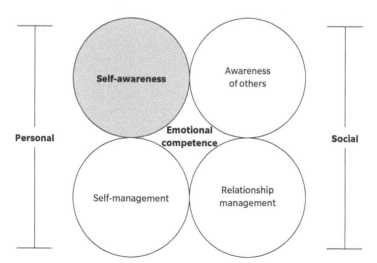

Note: * With acknowledgement to Daniel Goleman

Pause and Reflect

How self-aware are you?

Answer the following questions for yourself (and make a quick note of your answers). Then get someone you know well and whose judgement you value to answer them about you. If you have someone you have been coaching already, it might be a valuable way of getting some feedback. Compare your answers and reflect on the differences.

Q What are my strengths?

Q What is it that people really value me for?

Q What are my weaknesses; what do I need to get better at?

Q How do people experience me generally – how might they describe me during coaching sessions?

Q How am I different when I am under pressure, such as during interactions or conversations with others?

Q What three things could I stop doing that would make me more effective?

Q What three things do I need to start doing, or do more often?

Of course, when you lack self-awareness, it can work in different directions. You may believe you're better at something than you are, or not realise that actually you're very talented. Be open to the possibility of both!

Developing self-awareness

Ways to increase your self-awareness include:

- Complete a personality profiling exercise, for example Myers–Briggs, Belbin, the Enneagram, DISC, etc. Have your profile explained by someone who can help you get the most from the process, such as a qualified practitioner.

- Seek feedback on a regular basis, from clients, colleagues and other people with whom you have an important relationship, for example. But remember, feedback is just another person's perception; it is no more valid than your own perception and what you choose to do with the information is up to you. What is valuable is the additional information.

- Attend developmental courses that will help you reflect on both how you are now and how you might be in the future. Choose courses that intrigue you, interest you and that you believe will benefit your sense of clarity and confidence.

- Keep a learning diary; written reflection is a powerful learning tool over time.[3] Write a couple of pages regularly to describe your experiences, thoughts and feelings. Notice how your everyday attention and behaviours are shaped by the simple habit of writing.

- Read books and material related to practical psychology or human behaviour. Choose titles that you are interested in and enjoy the process. Reading is another activity that causes us to reflect. Reading also helps us view ourselves objectively in comparison to the thoughts and ideas we are being offered.[4]

Self-awareness: the link to the coachee

As a coach, self-awareness is something you nurture and encourage in the people you coach. By the process of enquiry, consideration and challenge, we encourage increased awareness in others. That awareness may include what they really think, how they really feel or what their values in a situation are. For example, when you ask someone, 'What's really important to you about this situation?', the answer the coachee gives may have previously lain buried under a stack of other information or emotion. This is when you might see a coachee struggle to answer your question. So, we must give the coachee time and space to consider what they really think. These thoughts and feelings surfaced from proper reflection increase the coachee's clarity and self-awareness relating to the situation.

As you work with a coachee over several sessions, their self-awareness tends to improve. For example, they might shift from being unclear about their development needs to realising what they really want to get better at. Alternatively, they may begin to appreciate some of the finer qualities and talents they have. The ways in which effective coaching raises a coachee's self-awareness include:

- Through the process of enquiry, the coachee realises what they really think (rather than what they've been saying automatically). For example, a quick response of 'Oh, I'm not really worried about the changes at work,' becomes 'Actually, there is quite a lot about this that's an issue for me.'

- As the coach uses tools of summary, reflection and feedback, the coachee gains a fresh perspective on themselves. For example, the coach reflects, 'You're spending a lot of time describing the problem, but appear reluctant to make a decision – what's causing that?' Over time, the coachee may realise they have a tendency to procrastinate, as a way of avoiding the tougher challenge of productive action.

- The coachee gains a better appreciation of who they are, who they are not and what they are capable of. For example, prior to coaching, the coachee may never have envisaged themselves as someone who might enjoy being self-employed. And they might be even more reluctant to imagine they could ever be very successful as a self-employed person. Or, vice versa, that:

- they might return to employment within a company and enjoy that even more than being a lone operator.

The early stages of the coaching assignment structure (discussed in Chapter 7) are designed to accelerate self-awareness, using tools such as personality profiling and feedback. These tools help the coachee to appreciate different views of themselves and build a fuller picture of who they are and who they might become.

Emotional competence 2: self-management

Self-management is the ability to influence ourselves: to choose our responses and behaviour. This relates both to the short term and to the longer term, for example your ability to:

- make a tough decision and stick with it

- adapt your natural behaviour for a 'greater good', for the longer-term benefit of yourself or others, for example staying patient with a naughty child

- do something you don't feel like doing, such as refusing a dessert in a restaurant, going for a run when you'd rather watch TV, or staying silent when you'd sooner speak your mind.

Self-management builds perfectly on the previous competence of self-awareness because it's one thing to be aware of your natural feelings or tendencies, but it's another to be able to choose consciously what to do in a situation. Sometimes, that means we'll choose to act 'in flow' with our feelings and, sometimes, it means doing the exact opposite – what we don't feel like doing.

Self-management: the link to you as coach

As a coach, your self-management affects many areas of the quality of service you deliver to your clients. Outside of coaching sessions, your ability to influence yourself includes:

- your basic self-discipline, such as your ability to work to consistent standards and quality, for example keeping appointments and agreements, staying focused and organised

Figure 8.3 Emotional competence: self-management*

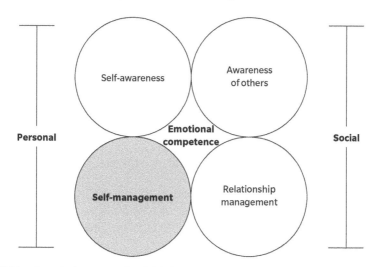

Note: * With acknowledgement to Daniel Goleman

- your ability to stay resourceful, for example your ability to motivate yourself to keep going when things get tough – maybe business isn't booming, and you need to stay optimistic and creative
- your ability to act on your own decisions and insights, for example, 'I need to find more work,' which means getting into action and contacting people
- your ability to handle pressure, for example you are really busy, and you need to find ways to accommodate all the demands upon you
- your ability to develop character traits that you value, such as patience, tolerance, humour or joyfulness (being happy is sometimes just a question of practice).

Inside coaching sessions, as a coach, the ability to influence ourselves enables us to:

- stay focused on the coaching conversation, for example to maintain concentration through a long session
- avoid displaying inappropriate characteristics to our coachee, such as frustration, nervousness, boredom
- avoid some of the barriers to effective coaching, such as talking too much, poor listening, seeking the 'perfect solution'
- display characteristics that support effective coaching, such as patience, flexibility, non-attachment to our own ideas or views, openness, warmth, generosity
- develop ourselves as better coaches, for example respond to feedback, learn from mistakes, push ourselves to try new things, etc.

Pause and Reflect

Where might you work at self-management?

For this one, you will need your responses to the previous activity – 'How self-aware are you?'

First, answer the following questions yourself. Then get someone you know well and whose judgement you value to answer them about you. Compare your answers and reflect on the differences.

Q What were the three things you identified in the previous list of questions that you wanted to stop doing?

Q What is it going to take for you to stop doing those?

Q What were the three things you identified that you want to do more of to improve your effectiveness?

Q What is it going to take for you to do those three things more often?

Q If you decided you wanted those two sets of three things as goals, how likely would you be to reach them?

Self-management: the link to your coachee

For your coachee, being coached will normally increase their ability to be self-managing around areas they want to improve. Just the simple act of focusing on issues, deciding on solutions, and making the commitment to take action between sessions helps. Coaching tends to have a motivational effect on people. By that, we mean having an increased sense of wanting to act, perhaps against some of their more usual tendencies. Also, if they fail to act upon their insights and decisions from coaching, you can help them to overcome unseen barriers to progress.

Perhaps your coachee decides they need to reshape their approach to their work in order to create more free time. They realise that they spend too long talking about what they're going to do instead of simply getting on and doing it. Sometimes, that discussion is with other people; sometimes, it's simply discussion with themselves (procrastination). After the initial coaching session, they attack the situation with relish, making decisions, getting into action and staying in action. The initial results are tremendous. The coachee's personal productivity and effectiveness go up, while their time spent at work goes down. Success! But, by the third coaching session, they find that they have returned pretty much to the original situation. They seem to be bogged down by a mountain of tasks and feel as if they are out of control again. Their work hours are back to their original length and they're frustrated with themselves. As coach, here's how you can help:

- You can act as a barometer or measure of the coachee's progress over time. By creating a constant focus on progress, the coach keeps productivity in the awareness of the coachee. By celebrating success, the coach encourages further success. By gently surfacing the issue of lack of progress, the coach is another source of commitment to the coachee's goal.

- You can explore what is causing the apparent regression, that is surface other values or motivations affecting the coachee's behaviour. For example, maybe the seduction of the old comfort zone of spending time in thought or discussion about tasks is too easy to return to. Or maybe your coachee struggles to maintain concentration for long periods of time and is fatigued by the process.

- You can revisit the original benefits of improving productivity or remind them of the cost of poor productivity. By increasing the coachee's awareness of both the cost of poor productivity and the benefits of great productivity, the coachee's natural motivation is encouraged.

- You can help find ways to return to a productive state: perhaps ask them how they might regain focus when they begin to procrastinate or help them find a solution to that.

- Over time, your coachee learns what drives and motivates them and what it's going to take for them to be more powerful. Through intention, commitment and practice, they develop the muscle of self-management.

Emotional competence 3: awareness of others

Awareness of others refers to our ability to observe other people and appreciate what is going on with them. This competence is linked to our ability to empathise (empathy is different from sympathy – see Chapter 5 Barriers to coaching) and means we can understand other people's emotional states and process that information effectively. It can be quite a sophisticated skill. For example, to notice that someone is angry because they are shouting is easy. But to notice that someone is angry when they are apparently 'not angry', for example quietly nodding, even smiling, demands greater awareness.

Awareness of others: the link to the coach

When coaching, this competence helps you relate to others. Your ability to notice and accurately interpret signals and behavioural cues from your coachee is significant for, if you do not demonstrate understanding, you are less likely to build rapport. Imagine it is your first coaching session and you mismatch your coachee's emotional state. Maybe they are cautious, mistrusting and fairly cynical about the process, but your focus and attention is on getting started and so you describe the coaching process, ask them for personal information, etc. While you are focused on the task, you miss warning signs – they are cautious and slightly worried. If your attention was more on them than on what you wanted to get done, you would have noticed behavioural clues: perhaps their clipped, business-like tone; their watchful expression; their tendency to fidget; frequently click their pen, etc.

It's difficult to describe how anyone displays an emotional state like 'worried' – we all do it differently. But to notice and be able to interpret what happens with other people is a skill you already have. Not only that, it is also a skill we can all hone further. The benefits of this are tangible: when you can judge or 'read' people more accurately, you are able to communicate with them more easily. Through your ability to empathise and relate to others on their own terms, you gain more access to their world. Here are some of the benefits of developing your awareness of others:

- You can interpret their thoughts and feelings quickly and effectively, for example, 'They're not comfortable with this.'

- You can demonstrate understanding, which helps build rapport, trust and openness, for example, 'You appear frustrated about that.' When we do that accurately, the coachee feels understood.

Figure 8.4 Emotional competence: awareness of others*

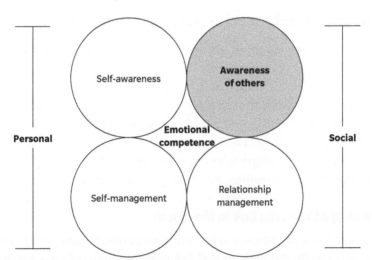

Note: * With acknowledgement to Daniel Goleman

- As real understanding is surfaced more quickly, the direction of the conversation can be guided more efficiently. There are fewer blind alleys. For example, 'Okay, it seems like that's something that's important to you – can we explore that more?'

- You can acknowledge and respect the coachee's thoughts and feelings, perhaps adapting your own style accordingly – increasing or decreasing pace, taking a break if they appear fatigued, etc.

- You are more able to help them deal with their feelings. For example, if you suspect your coachee is really worried about something, you can express that and look at ways to support them.

Pause and Reflect

Where might you work at your awareness of others?

Answer the following questions for yourself. Then get someone whose judgement you trust and value to answer them about you. If you have someone you've been coaching already, it might be a good way of getting some feedback. Compare your answers and reflect on the differences.

Q During conversations, how well are you able to interpret the emotional state of the person you are talking to?

Q How well do you 'read' people, that is gauge them correctly, interpret the meaning of their words, etc.?

Q During conversations, how much of your attention is focused on the words, story or content of the discussion, and how much is focused on the person themselves, such as their expressions, tonality, how they seem?

Q How quickly can you gain a true understanding of someone, for example what's important to them, what's not important to them, their temperament, typical attitudes and behaviours, etc.?

Q How accurately do you empathise with others, that is how well do you demonstrate an understanding of how things are for them or how they are feeling?

Developing awareness of others

Judging ourselves in relation to our competence here is obviously subjective. It's more useful to decide to focus on this area of expertise and develop our intention to improve our competence. In coaching, ways in which we can do this include the following:

- Write a reflection note after your coaching sessions, focusing on what was happening with your coachee. For example, try to guess their 'emotional journey' during the session: perhaps they arrived calm and engaged, surfaced some frustration, expressed discontent, got clearer, left brighter, etc.

- Engage in the process of being supervised by an experienced coach. Work on the subject together. The other coach will help you judge your ability to read or 'calibrate' the people you are working with.

- Study, or perhaps even gain a qualification in, an assessment tool, which will help you notice and interpret the behaviours of other people more accurately (for example, Myers–Briggs, DISC, Colours Insights). By having a thorough knowledge of a robust model, you will naturally develop your awareness of others. In addition, you will get better at predicting behaviour or noticing important clues or responses.

Awareness of others: the link to the coachee

Within coaching, the coachee can be encouraged to increase their awareness of others. For example, as a coach, you often encourage someone to pause and reflect on what is happening with others, either by enquiring into the coachee's awareness of other people's perspectives, or by challenging them. Maybe your coachee is protesting that someone is bullying them, and you offer an alternative view, for example, 'Maybe they simply aren't aware of how you feel . . . ' Table 8.2 illustrates this idea further.

People can learn the value of doing this through being coached and, over time, it becomes more natural for them to consider the thoughts, views and feelings of others.

Emotional competence 4: relationship management

This fourth competence brings together the previous three and builds on them. Relationship management refers to social skills such as building relationships, harmonising relationships, and sustaining relationships over time. It affects our ability to communicate clearly with others; collaborate with others; negotiate; deal with conflict; motivate and manage others, etc.

Table 8.2 Awareness of others

Objective/purpose	Question
Encourage the coachee to reflect on someone's thoughts or feelings in the past.	'What was Sara feeling/thinking at that point?'
Help the coachee develop their ability to interpret the responses of others.	'How did you know that you'd upset Sara?' or 'When have you seen her do that before?'
Reflect on the views of others.	'If Sara were here in the room now and I asked her what she really thought – what do you think she'd say?' or 'How aware is she of your feelings about this?'
Reflect on the values or motivations of others.	'What's really important to her about this situation, do you think?'
Help someone consider a future event in the same way.	'How might Sara react to that offer, do you think?'

When we demonstrate this competence, the other three competences are brought into play. Our ability to remain self-aware, self-managing and aware of others governs our ability to influence those around us, whether that's getting someone to make you a cup of coffee or help you win business. And your ability to manage others may not be as obvious as 'getting someone to do something'. It may be how people feel about you or understand and appreciate you. This is a social ability that describes how you build relationships and networks of support.

This is a social ability that describes how you build relationships and networks of support

Relationship management: the link to the coach

Any successful coach needs to be good at interacting with others. Whether employed, self-employed or a volunteer, our success as a coach rests on our ability to engage others in what we do and have them be supportive of us. If we are to build a successful coaching practice, we need to build and foster goodwill within our business relationships. For example, we need others:

- to listen to us as we explain our services
- to choose us over any other coach

- to value us and recognise the quality of service we deliver
- to encourage us to succeed, perhaps advising us, or offering constructive feedback
- to stay committed to using us as a coach over time (even if we make mistakes)
- to recommend us to others and champion our services.

Our ability to interact with the coachee is at the heart of an effective coaching session. Just a few of the benefits include the following:

- The coachee engages with us and commits to our coaching relationship.
- The coachee understands us, and we create clarity between us.
- The coachee will work with us, as a team, to make the coaching successful. For example, they will tolerate mistakes, or temporary lapses in quality, due to a broader appreciation of the overall quality we deliver.
- The coachee is more motivated to keep agreements between sessions, as a reflection of their commitment to our coaching.
- The coachee becomes an advocate of us as a coach and our business.

Ultimately, if the above is true, then the coachee will gain more from the coaching. Their commitment to the relationship over time will increase their investment and effort. The results they produce are likely to improve and the rewards they reap will mirror their own efforts.

Figure 8.5 Emotional competence: relationship management*

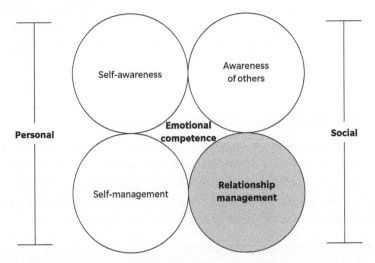

Note: * With acknowledgement to Daniel Goleman

Pause and Reflect

Where might you work at your influence of others?

Answer the following questions for yourself. Then find someone whose opinion you value and ask them to answer them for you as well. Compare and reflect on the answers afterwards.

Q How easily do you build new relationships?

Q How good are you at sustaining relationships over time?

Q How good are you at handling conflict?

Q Can you naturally get other people to support you?

Q How good are you at working within teams?

Q How good are you at influencing others? For example, if you make a request of someone, will they carry it out for you?

Q How good are you at negotiation?

When we consider these types of questions, we obviously need a good level of self-awareness. That's why it is helpful to ask the views of a trusted colleague or friend.

Improving competence: relationship management

Here are some ways to increase our ability in this area:

- Learn more about humans and how we interact, for example principles of communication, motivation, or relationships. Take time to consider what's behind our interactions and consider yourself in relationship to others. Find books or courses on subjects that interest you, such as negotiation skills, conflict resolution, influencing skills, or perhaps a broader study of psychology.

- Seek regular feedback on how people experience you, in order to appreciate better the perceptions you create in others based on your interactions with them.

- Consider two relationships you have had in the past. Pick a 'good' relationship and one where you have experienced issues. Find a way to reflect on them that helps you gain a broader perspective, if possible. For example, write about the relationship, the nature of that relationship, how it developed, what caused it to develop in that way, etc. Try to 'stand in the other person's shoes' to gain a more objective view; tell the 'story' from someone else's perspective. Get help from someone you trust, if that feels appropriate. Reflect on yourself in the two scenarios, for example how were your thoughts and behaviour different in each relationship? Consider how you were around each person and how that affected things. What would you do differently next time?

Relationship management: the link to the coachee

An effective coach uses techniques of enquiry, summary, reflection and feedback to encourage someone to improve their ability to relate to and influence others. The ways we might do this include the following:

- Help the coachee cope with other people's reactions more effectively, for example, 'If your customer is frustrated by the news, how might you deal with that?'

- Help them plan to negotiate, for example, 'What is going to convince them, do you think?' or 'What's most important to them?'

- Help them maintain commitment from others, for example, 'What do you need to do to sustain this relationship over time?'

- Help them recognise their patterns of behaviour, for example, 'Have you had a situation like this before?' or 'How similar is this relationship to the one we discussed earlier?'

- Help them influence constructively, for example, 'How will you gain the team's support for your plans?' or 'How will you sustain support for your plans over time?'

- Help them deal with conflict, for example, 'What caused the disagreement?' and 'What options do you have now?'

- Encourage learning, for example, 'What decisions are you making about your leadership style?' or 'How does your style of leadership need to develop going forward?'

In a Nutshell

Emotional maturity refers to our ability to deal with emotions, that is to interpret, express and process them. More broadly, our emotional maturity helps us cope with life. Our emotional maturity has a major impact on our ability to create the conditions for success, happiness and fulfilment over time. Another common term used for this concept is 'emotional intelligence'.

Like intelligence (IQ), we can measure emotional maturity (EQ). Unlike our rating of IQ, emotional maturity is something we can nurture and develop over time.

Emotional maturity has four main areas of competence:

- self-awareness
- self-management
- awareness of others
- relationship management.

It is our mastery of all areas that develops our overall emotional maturity and, in turn, it is our emotional maturity that enables us to foster and encourage maturity in others.

Emotional maturity impacts on our ability to be effective as a coach, which accelerates the self-development of the coachee and improves their emotional maturity. As your coachees learn these 'skills of life', they can continue to use them long after the coaching has been completed.

chapter 9

Become a coach

'Dreams don't work unless you do.'
John C. Maxwell

There are many reasons why you may be reading this book. Perhaps you are considering coaching as a way of providing income, or you want to add coaching to what you already do. Whatever your reason to explore coaching, this chapter is intended to help. I'll be asking you questions and explaining some principles to help facilitate your decision to become a coach and consider how you might make that happen. The questions that follow are intended to help you 'coach yourself' to become clearer about your situation and the changes you may need to make.

This chapter focuses mainly on your internal thought processes, so, to gain the most benefit, I encourage you to work through the groups of questions or 'mini assignments' in an open, calm state of mind. It will help to go somewhere quiet, switch off your phone and give yourself the gift of time and space to reflect and consider. You will get maximum value by writing down your answers. It's always tempting just to read through the questions and form mental answers, isn't it? That's fine, but you are likely to get a less satisfactory result, and you will know what's best for you.

What this chapter will not do is tell you how to write your business plan, what to charge or how to maximise revenue. My focus here is on whether coaching is right for you and on exploring your internal sense of how to move forward. If you are interested in the commercial elements of coaching, such as marketing, money management, etc., I encourage you to find a book that specifically deals with this subject, such as *The Prosperous Coach* by Steve Chandler and Ritch Litvin (2013, Maurice Bassett).

What do we mean by 'become a coach'?

First, let's begin by saying that you don't have to declare yourself as a coach to the world in order to engage in the activity of coaching people. However, if you want to be regularly engaged in coaching, then you will benefit from having your own personal sense of 'being a coach'. It's as though being a coach is part of your identity (who you think you are). Over time, this aspect of you develops; you know you're a coach and for you to coach others is a natural form of self-expression. This self-conception sits alongside other aspects of your identity, as a daughter, son, partner, nurse, teacher, project manager, etc. When part of your identity includes being a coach, this strengthens and supports your ability to coach others. When you have an inner sense of alignment that comes from knowing you are a coach, your confidence, surety and energy flow more naturally in conversations. The questions that follow will help you notice the part of you that can be called a coach.

Pause and Reflect

Become a coach

Please reflect upon, and then write answers to, the following:

Q How have you been drawn towards coaching? For example, what are the events, people or circumstances that have brought you to this point?

Q How would you describe coaching? For example, what difference does it make to people? Why is it valuable? How do you feel about it?

Q What will becoming a coach do for you?

Q What are your current thoughts and considerations about being a coach?

Q What are the questions you need to answer?

Okay, so that's got you thinking. Please know that, whatever you write, it is relevant and useful. The 'right' answers are whatever is true for you. Pause a while and look at your answers before continuing. Why not keep them to read in a few years' time?

So, you want to be a coach?

There are many reasons why you might consider becoming a coach. While no reason is right or wrong, some reasons are better than others. For example, if you have recently quit your graphic design job in anger and just want a job with flexible hours, then you may want to think that through a little more. If, however, you've felt drawn to coaching for some time, find yourself naturally supportive of others and find the idea of being a coach both interesting and challenging, then this path might be more in alignment with your values and goals. But not necessarily! The following questions are intended to help with your thoughts and decision-making processes.

Pause and Reflect

Your values and goals

Please reflect upon, and then write answers to, the following:

Q Think about your previous occupations, the jobs or roles that you've had. Think about what you've enjoyed, been good at, not enjoyed, not been good at, etc.

Q For you to enjoy and be fulfilled by your work, what has to be true about the work that you do? For example, it's creative, it's got variety, there are opportunities for travel, etc.

Q What special talents do you think you have to offer? What abilities do you have?

Q What do people really value you for?

Q Spend a few minutes imagining yourself as a coach, either as part of what you already do, or as something new. As you think about what that might be like, what might you be doing, seeing, thinking, etc.? How does it make you feel?

Q How will things be different for you when you're a coach? Think about your day-to-day life, the effect on people around you, etc.

Q How do you feel about becoming a coach now?

These questions are intended to increase your level of self-awareness and allow you to blend your experience with your expectations. As you reflect on your answers, you will, I hope, be moving closer to the decision of whether coaching is a good way forward for you. Coaching as a profession needs to align with your values, your talents and your interests. If coaching contradicts what is important to you, then you need to consider what you want to do with that lack of balance. For example, if you love working in teams, can you still do that? Or, if people value you as an expert, and you love being in that role, you may want to reflect on how becoming a coach will impact on that. Let's continue with the process.

Paid coach or unpaid coach?

In the process towards becoming a coach, you have several decisions to make. These decisions include whether to make coaching something you receive payment for. Before we consider that further, let's revisit our definition of coaching:

> *Coaching is a conversation, or series of conversations, that one person has with another. What distinguishes the conversation from any other is the impact the conversation has on the person being coached (the coachee).*

I know you'll have some life experiences that fit into the above description, where you have positively influenced someone through conversation, and they have valued you for that. So, clearly, it's possible to coach others without giving up anything else that you do or making any radical life changes. Maybe you simply want to develop your ability to adopt a coaching style of response more often. Remember, coaching can be both a distinct activity and a style of behaviour. For you, becoming a coach may simply mean shaping your general day-to-day behaviour using coaching principles and guidelines. Maybe you will develop a tendency to listen to people more deeply, use purpose-based questions, offer reflective feedback more often, etc. And these forms of coaching may take place while you're employed in a job that's unrelated to coaching, or maybe you're not employed at all.

Remember, coaching can be both a distinct activity and a style of behaviour

For example, you may run a small theatre production company. While you're pursuing the business of keeping the theatre running smoothly, you may choose to hold formal coaching sessions in a quiet setting with people who are happy to receive coaching from you. Those relationships may develop over time and you may enjoy being recognised as that person's 'coach'. It may not say 'coach others' on your job description, but that's not going to inhibit you from doing what you feel is worthwhile. You're choosing to coach anyway and are getting on with your everyday life while adopting a coaching approach.

It's a worthwhile decision to make for, in that simple commitment to 'be a coach', you have also committed to make a positive contribution to the people around you. You are making the well-being and development of others important. Your contribution is based on nothing more than your own sense that it's a better way to be. Imagine a world where we all used the powerful principles that underpin coaching. We might support each other to do better, be better and create more. What an encouraging world we might live in. Perhaps that's where the potential of coaching really lies.

Use the following questions to help you become clearer about the decision to become a professional coach or else a coach who coaches within their current professional occupation.

Pause and Reflect

Paid or unpaid coach?

Q What are your thoughts and feelings on this? Do you see yourself charging for your coaching or not?

Q Take a moment to imagine choosing to coach people professionally – how does that feel?

Q If you did want to coach professionally (and charge for your services), what changes would you have to make to your working life to allow that to happen?

Q What else is affecting your thinking here? For example, who else is involved?

Q What are the less tangible things impacting on your thinking? Are you, for example, creating any barriers in your mind?

Professional coaching – 'just coach' or 'coach and also . . . '?

You may have decided that you do, indeed, want to become a professional coach, that is someone who performs coaching for part or all their income. So, now your decisions include whether to be a full-time coach ('just coach') or, if coaching will be just one part of your paid work ('coach and also . . . '). I'd like you first to consider becoming a coach who also does other things, for I suspect that any professional coach benefits from having a varied career that includes other activities, occupations and work experience. Part of your contribution as a coach is your nature and true self. As we are enriched by diversity and shrunk by stagnation, it seems healthy to engage in work-related activities that do not involve coaching. It doesn't have to be a feat of superhuman endeavour, just something to broaden your horizons. Maybe you perform coaching during some of your working week and, at other times, you help out at a local restaurant. Or maybe, in between coaching sessions, you design and deliver training, write music, or sing. Whatever enlivens you will be an asset to your coaching. Here are some potential benefits from thinking more broadly about your involvement as a coach:

> **Whatever enlivens you will be an asset to your coaching**

- Coaching people is an intense activity that requires recuperation time to enable the coach to stay mentally alert and well-balanced. Doing nothing is one way to help yourself rest and recuperate. Doing something completely different is another (note that it is not necessarily better than doing nothing – just different).

- Any coach benefits from a rich life experience, filled with personal challenge, creative endeavour and collaboration, just as anyone is enriched by such a life. The added benefit for a coach is that they develop a broader viewpoint on the world, which can inform their coaching conversations.

- A sole focus on one-to-one interaction with others may prove limiting over time, through the lack of personal stimulation, learning or more varied challenges.

I recognise that some coaches decide that they want to dedicate themselves solely to the activity of coaching. Their commitment is to build a client base that will sustain both their income and their time. Their sole professional occupation becomes coaching, and they spend most of their working week in personal coaching sessions. I can imagine that, for some people, this is a perfect choice. If you are one of these people, I wish you fulfilment and good fortune. I'll also remind you, however, that such a focused occupation may be demanding on you and your system. Sitting in one-on-one sessions concentrating for long periods can be draining and can dull the senses. Of course, it is frequently energising and rewarding – your art will be to achieve a good balance. For example, how will you stay fresh and resourceful for your clients? Here are some ways that anyone deciding to 'just coach' may balance any negative effects:

- Schedule appropriate breaks between sessions, for example 15–20 minutes before and after a 2-hour session. If you're coaching all day, make sure you have a lunch break of at least 45 minutes.

- Reduce your travelling time – especially driving time – as much as possible, for example arrange to meet halfway, coach from your home, travel the night before.

- Consider the benefits of coaching supervision, for example getting your own mentor or coach to talk through your assignments confidentially, and give you guidance and support with issues or challenges.

- Maintain a strong focus on your own personal development, for example attend courses and seminars, read developmental books.

- Ensure a healthy work–life balance: rest a lot, play a lot, engage in hobbies or interests that you find relaxing, stimulating, creative, etc.

Interestingly, the above list also provides a great set of principles for anyone, whether we are in the category of 'just coach' or 'coach and also . . . '.

At a Glance

No time to coach?

Q I'm a busy manager. I'd like to coach my team – how do I make the time?

Please don't be put off from beginning to use coaching behaviours just because you think you simply don't have the time. First, consider the following:

Q What are the potential benefits of you developing the ability to coach others, both personally and professionally?

▶

Q How could you begin to use the ideas and principles of coaching in everyday situations? For example, asking more open questions to help people think and act for themselves.

Q What other situations give you an opportunity to develop coaching skills? For example, developing deeper listening, building better empathy and rapport.

Q How could you make this simple? What could you do in your very next conversation that would apply coaching principles and beliefs?

Q What other reasons/excuses do you have for not getting started with this?

Many everyday conversations offer you the opportunity to engage in some coaching-type activities (and the exercises in this book are based on this principle). As a manager, your rewards over time include colleagues who act with an increased sense of responsibility and empowerment. Most people prefer to work for someone who engages with them in this way. Your challenge is to merge the coaching ideas that make most sense for you into your everyday style.

One of my other books, *Brilliant Coaching*, is targeted at managers who want to 'manage less and coach more'. It is a short, pacey read and the models and examples are specific to the role and objectives of a manager.

What kind of coach are you?

There are many different styles and types of coach. It's important that, over time, you develop your own style and approach to be an authentic expression of you. By authentic, I mean that the type of coaching work that you do, and the way that you do it, suits you as a person and is compatible with your talents and personality. Furthermore, when offering or selling your services, you will want to distinguish yourself from other coaches. So, it's good to know what circumstances are best suited to what you offer and what value you will add. Being clear about who you are as a coach helps with both your confidence and your ongoing success as a coach. When you're describing your coaching services to potential clients, you will sound clear and aligned about what you plan to do. That will give your client the assurance that they would be in safe hands and that, in turn, is one of the main reasons they will engage your services. Obviously, your awareness of yourself as a coach will develop over time, as your coaching identity emerges. In the meantime, you'll want to spend a little time building your own picture of the type of coaching that might suit you.

Begin from where you are now

To develop this sense of yourself as a coach, start from where you already are. In other words, don't look into the distance at some other professional coach and decide you need to model yourself on what they do. You may learn from other coaches, but please let any change you make to your style or approach be something you feel is right for you. For example, you may see another coach accessing lots of government-funded work by coaching young people who want to get into full-time employment. If that 'speaks' to you as something you'd love to do, and you feel you've got something to offer those young people, then great. But if, in truth, you'd be frustrated at the nature of the conversations, or don't relate to the challenges of that community, then perhaps reconsider. Based on your background, what you enjoy and are good at, you may find that there is better work waiting for you. And, of course, in the meantime, you might decide to try working with the youngsters – who knows, you could find that you enjoy the challenge!

> **Let any change you make to your style or approach be something you feel is right for you**

Build on what you have now

I sometimes hear from people wanting to enter the coaching profession who are in danger of ignoring all their existing talents and experience. They assume they need to make radical changes to become a coach, such as change the industry they operate in, or reinvent their professional profile in some way. Some people leave their existing jobs to focus totally on building a coaching career. It's quite a commitment to make and I'm not qualified to judge the wisdom of that for anyone. Instead, I encourage you to reflect on the potential of your existing resources, such as skills, experience, relationships and network of contacts. Maybe you're a sales professional; maybe you manage tech projects; or maybe, before you had children, you worked in recruitment. Look at your existing skills and experience. That's often the best place for you as a coach to emerge from. It's also

> **Reflect on the potential of your existing resources, such as skills, experience, relationships and network of contacts**

a potential source of immediate work opportunities, for example maybe you can coach salespeople, or other project managers. Perhaps you can find agencies who want some coaching for their recruitment agents. It may be that there are coaching opportunities that are looking you right in the face, if only you stopped scanning the horizon!

As before, please take some time to reflect on the following questions and write down your responses.

Pause and Reflect

Your existing assets and resources

Q What work experience do you have? For example, what type of businesses or situations have you already worked in?

Q What type of roles have you had? For example, administration, selling, training.

Q What are the common themes that seem to run through your professional experience? For example, my role is often about getting people to work together, or about introducing change, or day-to-day running of small businesses.

Q What other life experience have you had? For example, raising a family, organising a household, arranging large events. Please think of everything; look in every corner, uncover every formative period of your life.

Q List all the people, companies or communities you know of that might benefit from your services as a coach. Some people might be potential clients and coachees, others may sponsor your coaching assignments. Think through your existing network of contacts and those individuals or groups just outside your network.

Q What kind of coaching would you be good at? For example, what kind of people, with what kind of objectives and goals? In what kind of environment or circumstances?

Q Let's assume that your previous experience provides the perfect foundation on which you're going to build work as a coach. How does your experience and skill affect the kind of coach you might be?

> These questions are intended to help you appreciate the resources you
> have already and the opportunity that they create for you now. They are
> also designed to encourage you to realise how the steps you might take
> forward can be simple, logical steps, rather than dramatic 'giant' strides.
>
> Finally, spend a few minutes reflecting on your responses to the previ-
> ous sets of questions as well as those on this list. What thoughts are you
> having now?

Let's acknowledge that you cannot know all the answers. A world of possibility
exists in front of you and, of course, there is an element of the unknown that you
are venturing into. But I do believe that, as you journey into uncharted territory,
it's useful to remind yourself how capable you already are, and how you may be
better prepared for the adventure than you perhaps thought.

How do you equip yourself to be a great coach?

When you describe yourself as 'a coach', you will want to feel confident and
clear that you have the authority to declare that as a fact. Ultimately, the person who decides if you are fully equipped to begin coaching others (formally or
informally) is you. However, a combination of study and experience fuels your
confidence and ability and so you need to consider what development path is
best for you.

There is continual and ongoing discussion within the field of coaching that
relates to the formal qualification needed for a person to be able to coach. As
yet, no single organisation has any universally accepted authority, and I'm not
sure this will ever happen. However, there are a few associations who appear to
be central to the debate. For example, the International Coach Federation (ICF)
and the European Mentoring and Coaching Council (EMCC). Most coaching
bodies seem well-intended and provide a wealth of information, resources and
backup, which help support the ongoing development of coaching everywhere.
Others seem more commercially motivated and orientated to the provision of
paid-for services only. Spend a little time surfing the internet and I'm sure you'll
find them all.

Personally, I applaud any organisation that helps coaches to develop high personal standards. I am less enthusiastic at the idea of the coaching field appearing

exclusive, expensive and overwhelming in the standards they set for aspiring coaches. If you choose to gain a formal qualification, it must be because it will create tangible benefits for you – for example, if you think your clients may want you to have a formal qualification, or if your ability or confidence will increase.

How are you going to equip yourself to be a great coach?

So, rather than engage in a discussion of 'What's the best training course to become a coach?', let's consider the question 'How are you going to equip yourself to be a great coach?' The following questions may take a little time to answer, but I hope you'll find it a worthwhile activity:

Pause and Reflect

Equip yourself to coach

1 Identify the specific skills you need to develop

Q Which skills do you need right now? And which can you develop over time (some will fall into both categories)?

Q What are the different ways you can develop those skills?

Q Who do you know that has these skills? (Be willing to ask for help!)

2 Start developing your coaching ability quickly

Q How can you increase your experience of coaching styles of conversations (both as a coach and as someone being coached)?

Q What everyday conversations are appropriate to try out the principles, for example adopt a coaching posture, practise listening, ask open questions, etc?

Q What else will help you develop your coaching skills, for example life experiences, self-development courses, mind-body work (yoga, tai chi, etc.)?

3 Get practical, build productivity and focus

Q How could you build, develop and then strengthen your personal vision?

Q What are the practical 'tools of the trade' you might need, for example a description of you and your services, website, business cards, pricing structure, etc? Remember – you decide what's appropriate.

Q What is your simple action plan and what are the priorities?

---

4 Maintain focus and motivation over time

Q What simple routines might help you stay on track e.g., reflection notes, early morning action log etc?

Q Who or what might be able to support you to stay in action?

5 Strengthen your identity as a coach

Q What is it going to take before you feel really equipped to coach other people? For example, a certain number of sessions or assignments, a level of qualification, a stronger sense of self-belief, etc.

Q How can you strengthen your own confidence and identify as a coach?

Some people may feel a training course specifically focused on coaching is what they want. But you do have other options. For example, you might study counselling first, or learn more about personality profiling, language patterns or motivational theory. There are lots of specialist skills that you may feel interested in or drawn to, which might enhance you as a coach. Instead of focusing on core coaching skills, you may choose a self-development route to focus more squarely on your emotional maturity. You may consider getting coached yourself or studying an area such as NLP (neuro-linguistic programming). Both these routes will help you develop yourself, while improving your coaching ability. You can also find useful resources in the LearnStarr area of my website: www.starrcoaching.co.uk.

This book is obviously intended to equip you and support you as you develop as a coach. Of course, reading will only help you so far and there is no substitute for real coaching practice. To sustain you through your own personal journey, you will also need the intention to succeed and the determination to keep going when you meet challenges along the way. While my own journey to becoming a coach has been certainly challenging, it has also been a worthwhile adventure. What's sustained me is the belief that I am both 'good enough' and also still capable of more – and I know that's true for you, too.

> **You will also need the intention to succeed and the determination to keep going when you meet challenges along the way**

In a Nutshell

Anyone who wants to support others by coaching them will benefit from a clear personal sense that they are a coach. There are different expressions of being a coach, including:

- adding coaching as a style of behaviour to your existing occupation, that is the job you already do
- solely performing professional coaching for a living (and having no other paid occupations)
- as an additional source of income or service that you offer, that is offering formal coaching sessions and getting paid for it.

No one choice is better than any other. What is important is that you work through the facts of your situation in a way that is logical for you. By surfacing your own thoughts and feelings about the options available, you can decide what is best for you.

Too often, we disregard all that we already are. So, take time to consider what existing resources you have, such as skills, experience, contacts and opportunities to coach. Also reflect upon what resources you may need to create a basis for a successful coaching practice. These resources might include your website, LinkedIn profile, YouTube page, etc. They may also include new skills, support from others, or simply more experience of coaching.

Whatever you decide, and whichever point on the horizon you choose to navigate by, I wish you every good luck and good fortune.

chapter 10

Consolidate your learning

'Confine yourself to the present.'

Marcus Aurelius

What follows is a gathering of the major ideas and principles within this book to bring together formative ideas into one place. My intention here is to provide you with an 'at a glance' guide, so that you might check your understanding and comfort with each topic, plus help you decide where to go next. Perhaps you may choose to revisit a topic or, as you are reminded of your interest, decide to pursue that, for example, 'I want to find something that goes deeper into emotional maturity,' etc. This chapter also completes this current stage of your coaching journey and signals the arrival of the next and so, as you review the principles and headlines here, I hope you will notice just how far you have already come.

Key points of learning

Collaborative coaching is an effective, respectful approach

Collaborative coaching is effective because of the underlying principles that support it, namely:

- The relationship is based on equality, which encourages openness and trust. The coach does not claim to have all the answers and the coachee feels their contribution is valuable.
- The coachee appreciates being really listened to and the effort the coach makes to understand them.
- Coaching conversations have a clear emphasis on enquiry, and the coach works to facilitate the coachee's understanding of their situation to increase awareness and surface insight or clarity.
- Solutions are normally of greater relevance and effectiveness as they emerge from the understanding of the person experiencing the situation.
- As more ideas and insights come from the coachee, responsibility to complete actions also rests more naturally with them.
- If an idea does not get the result the coachee wanted, the coachee still feels ownership of the idea and so will be more willing to work to get a better result.
- Connecting thoughts and ideas provoke ongoing learning. Like a pebble thrown into a pond, good coaching triggers an ongoing reaction. Sometimes, responses are immediate, while others take time to emerge. In this way, coaching conversations are beneficial long after the session has ended.

When we adopt a less directive style of conversation, we emphasise the internal learning processes of the coachee. We also respectfully maintain the responsibility of the coachee for their situation, which empowers them over time. Coaching conversations are, ultimately, a 'call to action' as they provoke an awareness of what needs to happen to improve a situation, move towards a goal or create positive change.

As a coach, the principles you operate from inform what you do

The principles we operate from create a foundation for everything we do. A collaborative coach is guided by the following personal principles:

- I will maintain noticeable commitment to support the individual.

- My coaching relationships are built upon truth, openness and trust.
- The coachee is responsible for the results they are creating.
- The coachee is capable of much better results than they are currently creating.
- I maintain a focus on what the coachee thinks and experiences.
- I know that coachees can generate perfect solutions.
- My coaching conversations are based on equality.

These principles can have more impact than our technical skill. For example, operating with a commitment to openness, honesty and trust often can do more for our coaching relationship than conscious rapport-building techniques.

Coaching rests on core skills and you can develop them

The core skills of a collaborative coach are highlighted again in Figure 10.1. These skills and disciplines are behaviours that we must learn and constantly develop over time.

Some coaches have better access to these skills naturally, either because of their basic personality or because of previous experience and training. Some skills require more technical competence, such as asking questions, and gaining these requires a more focused, disciplined approach. Once acquired, these skills must be practised. Many everyday situations present opportunities to develop or maintain these skills, such as natural conversations with colleagues or friends.

Figure 10.1 Skills Star: Fundamental skills of coaching

Building rapport
and relationship

Constructive
feedback

Focused levels
of listening

Asking effective
questions

Use of
intuition

BELIEFS WE OPERATE FROM

Be aware of barriers to effective coaching, to avoid them

Common barriers to effective coaching relate to your environment, your personal well-being, and your behaviour, or they combine all three. This might include the suitability of the location you are coaching in, your mood and how both of those influence your behaviour in a particular situation.

Certain behaviours or principles of behaviour also form barriers to the development and flow of an effective coaching conversation. They include:

- talking too much
- adopting too much control over the direction or content of a conversation
- playing 'fix-it'
    - strategising in the conversation
- looking for the amazing moment
- wanting to look good in the conversation
    - needing to be 'right' or appear infallible
- assuming your previous knowledge and experience is relevant
- focusing on what not to do.

Some of these behaviours are simple traps that any of us might fall into, no matter how experienced we are. Many arise from natural human tendencies such as being enthusiastic or enjoying solving other people's problems. So, when we're coaching, we need to develop a three-step process:

1 Become aware that we are doing or thinking something that's not working.

2 Acknowledge that – and give it up, that is let the thought go.

3 Substitute or refocus with another more effective intention or behaviour.

The Coaching Path supports most formal coaching conversations

The Coaching Path can support most typical coaching conversations, whether they are planned or unplanned, formal or informal. The Coaching Path is illustrated in Figure 10.2.

The different stages along The Coaching Path are activities to focus on, rather than tasks to be completed. As a coach, you must fulfil the simple intention of each stage, while staying aware of the needs of your coachee. Some activities might need revisiting, such as the coachee's goals for the conversation, if the direction of the discussion has changed.

Figure 10.2 The Coaching Path

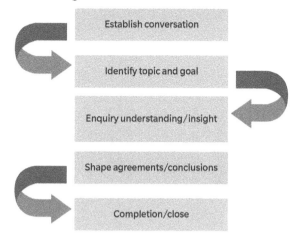

Your role as coach is to facilitate the session through to its conclusion, while encouraging a less directive style of conversation. That demands an awareness both of which point the discussion has reached on The Coaching Path and of where the coachee needs to be guided towards next. The coachee needs to feel they are in safe hands, so that they can focus on the content of the discussion, rather than the process of the session.

While the structure may require your initial focus and attention, with practice, it will help you develop a style that is effective and naturally your own.

Assignments are more effective when supported by simple structure and process

An ongoing coaching relationship (called an assignment) is made more effective by planning and preparation. By considering the key stages or components of the coaching process, we can balance the amount of time we spend on these activities. These three stages are highlighted in Figure 10.3.

It makes sense to consider these stages in the logical order they are indicated, even though that's not always how they will occur. Once the stages have begun, they become themes that develop throughout the coaching assignment. For example, once we've defined initial goals and a sense of direction for the assignment, we must maintain these over time.

Emotional maturity empowers you and your coachee

Emotional maturity refers to our ability to deal with emotions, that is interpret, express, and process them. Our ability to stay resourceful, to manage ourselves, to build or harmonise relationships are all life skills that are embraced under the

Figure 10.3 Three stages of a coaching assignment

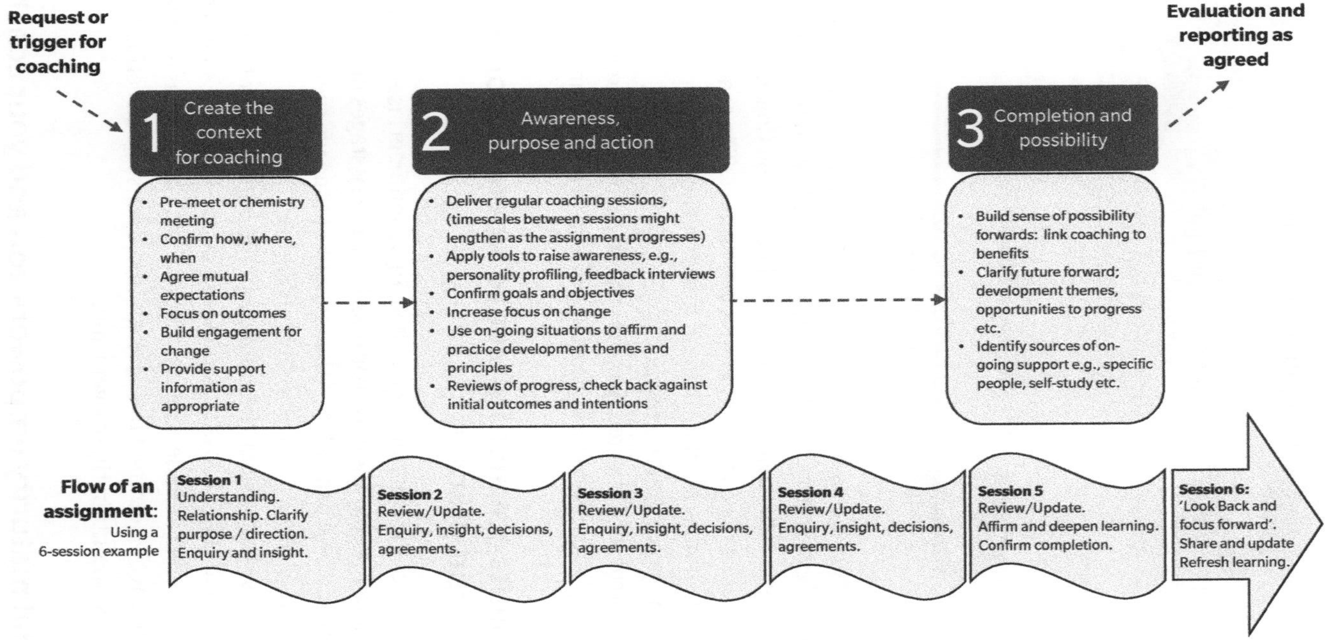

Request or trigger for coaching

1 Create the context for coaching
- Pre-meet or chemistry meeting
- Confirm how, where, when
- Agree mutual expectations
- Focus on outcomes
- Build engagement for change
- Provide support information as appropriate

2 Awareness, purpose and action
- Deliver regular coaching sessions, (timescales between sessions might lengthen as the assignment progresses)
- Apply tools to raise awareness, e.g., personality profiling, feedback interviews
- Confirm goals and objectives
- Increase focus on change
- Use on-going situations to affirm and practice development themes and principles
- Reviews of progress, check back against initial outcomes and intentions

3 Completion and possibility
- Build sense of possibility forwards: link coaching to benefits
- Clarify future forward; development themes, opportunities to progress etc.
- Identify sources of on-going support e.g., specific people, self-study etc.

Evaluation and reporting as agreed

Flow of an assignment:
Using a 6-session example

Session 1
Understanding. Relationship. Clarify purpose / direction. Enquiry and insight.

Session 2
Review/Update. Enquiry, insight, decisions, agreements.

Session 3
Review/Update. Enquiry, insight, decisions, agreements.

Session 4
Review/Update. Enquiry, insight, decisions, agreements.

Session 5
Review/Update. Affirm and deepen learning. Confirm completion.

Session 6:
'Look Back and focus forward'. Share and update. Refresh learning.

heading of emotional maturity. More broadly, our emotional maturity helps us cope with life. Our levels of emotional maturity have a significant impact on our ability to create the conditions of success, happiness and fulfilment over time. Another common term used for this concept is 'emotional intelligence' (EI).

Signs of emotional maturity or immaturity can be reflected in our typical behavioural responses. Instinctively, when we describe someone's behaviour as 'mature' or 'immature', we are often referring to their apparent levels of emotional maturity. Like intelligence (IQ), we can measure emotional maturity in a rating called EQ. Unlike our IQ rating, emotional maturity is something we can nurture and increase over time.

Emotional maturity has four main areas (see Figure 10.4):

- self-awareness
- self-management
- awareness of others
- relationship management.

It is our mastery of all areas that develops our overall emotional maturity. And it is our overall emotional maturity that enables us to foster and encourage maturity in others.

Figure 10.4 Four elements of emotional competence*

Source: Adapted from Daniel Goleman's five components of emotional competence.

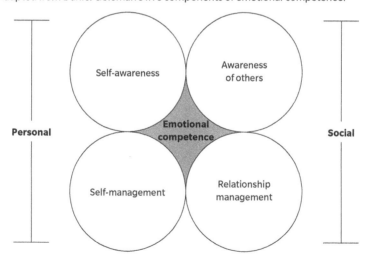

Note: * With acknowledgement to Daniel Goleman

Good coaches make a great difference

Above average levels of emotional maturity enable any coach to be more skilled and get better results. Effective coaching also helps increase the emotional maturity of a coachee as they learn new principles of thought and behaviour during coaching. As the coachee learns these 'skills of life', they can continue to develop them long after the coaching has ended.

Become a coach

Anyone who wants coaching to be something they are good at benefits from a personal sense of being a coach. Someone may declare themselves a coach whether they charge for their coaching services or not. There are three main expressions of 'being a coach'. They are:

- To integrate coaching as a style of behaviour that enhances your current job or role, so that what you do remains broadly the same, but how you do it is sometimes in a less directive coaching style.

- To avoid any other occupations and devote yourself to earning an income purely through coaching.

- To supplement or combine your current methods of earning income with coaching. For example, declare yourself as offering coaching services and charge people for those coaching services while, at the same time, continuing to work in another profession.

There is no 'right' way to become a coach. Each of us must reflect on our own circumstances and objectives to find the best way forward for us. What is important is that you develop your own style and application of coaching, which aligns with who you are as a person. In that way, you develop your coaching as an authentic expression of you, guided by a set of universal principles and skills.

When we first venture into coaching, we often disregard all the resources we already have. Those resources include skills, qualifications, experience and our existing network of relationships and contacts. We often have immediate opportunities to coach around us, or at least within close reach. By reflecting on our existing resources, we can also decide what else we need, for example skills, experience or support from others. As a guiding principle, the idea that we are 'enough', and can also be much more, can help sustain us as we embark upon the journey ahead.

The future of coaching

The personal coaching field has grown significantly during the past 30 years, and it continues to grow. No longer do we think of coaches as being associated only with the field of sports. There are coaches in business, life coaches, coaches for presidents and politicians – wherever people are striving to attain success and fulfilment, coaches are often at work. Clients are becoming more aware of the potential benefits of coaching, and more aware of what they are looking for in a coach.

So, the field of coaching is firmly established and is growing. It still, however, needs to be more clearly (and simply) defined. Too much of what distinguishes quality coaching remains a mystery to both clients and coaches alike. Where a lack of clear definition exists, coaches waste valuable time and take unnecessary risks with coachees, trying to learn for themselves what works and what doesn't. Great coaching can be transformational, causing dramatic improvements in both professional and personal situations. Poor-quality coaching does no one any good, least of all the coaching profession itself.

The simple ideas of coaching build from an understanding of our basic inter-dependency and of our need to support each other's success. The more accessible we can make coaching behaviours to everyone, the better. Anyone interested in coaching as an activity or profession needs clear guidelines and principles to operate from. Coaches also need simple supporting structures, processes and tools upon which to build a great coaching practice. However, too many rules, principles and codes of conduct are confusing and create imagined barriers to coaching. As in life, achieving balance is the key.

Take your learning forward

The person who ultimately benefits most from your learning and development as a coach is you. The skills gained within coaching – of awareness, communication, analysis and insight – are incredibly fulfilling. They are also invaluable life skills and help all of us in our own situations and relationships.

As a profession, or simply as part of what you already do, coaching offers you an opportunity to make a positive contribution to others. Good coaches can make a great difference. And no matter how experienced or skilled we are, there is always more to learn. Fresh perspectives and

> **Good coaches can make a great difference**

new ideas emerge constantly to keep us challenged and engaged in our own development. I hope this text has added to your own learning (I know it's added to mine). I encourage you to stay committed to your own self-development and I wish you enjoyment and success with that.

Always an end before a beginning

For both the coach and the coachee, coaching is, ultimately, a journey of discovery. For any coach, this is no ordinary work but a labour of love: often demanding, sometimes frustrating – always worthwhile. And, if you accept the challenge of coaching, it's a lifelong journey of learning, where we experience the circle of giving and receiving often. And, if you've got this far, I suspect you're already a traveller on that journey and, so, allow me to end with a warm welcome.

Free resources

Practise coaching skills and build successful assignments

This section provides you with ways to improve your coaching ability as well as short pieces intended to help you build coaching assignments.

- *Part 1 Strengthen your skills* are activities that enable you to practise core principles of behaviour. These exercises are a little more detailed than those in the previous chapters of this book.
- *Part 2 Building blocks* contains items to help as you coach more formally, for example to construct a coaching assignment.

Use the following tables to find what you need:

Part 1 Strengthen your skills

Practice item/Activity	Purpose and benefit
1.1 Help someone find their answer	Practise a core coaching principle of helping someone else surface their own ideas and conclusions.
1.2 Develop effective attention	Develop a 'still mind' needed to coach effectively. Strengthens your use of attention with intention to help you focus effectively.

▶

Practice item/Activity	Purpose and benefit
1.3 Develop deeper listening	Develop the attention you need to coach effectively.
1.4 Get some feedback	Learn the principles of giving constructive feedback, by receiving some feedback yourself.
1.5 Build a clearer goal	Help someone get clearer about what they want in a situation and become more motivated towards getting that.
1.6 Questions for reflection (coach)	Prompts to help guide your reflection and accelerate your learning.

Part 2 Building blocks

Name of building block	Purpose and benefit
2.1 Coaching overview document	A document you might give to a new coachee or client to help them understand and prepare for coaching as you begin an assignment.
2.2 Starting a first session	Helping you plan and prepare for a first coaching session.
2.3 Summary of a first session	An overview of what happened in a first coaching session, to help you imagine a typical conversation.
2.4 Summary of a feedback interview process	An overview of both the approach and content of a conversation a coach has had with someone nominated by their coachee, where the coach gathers feedback on their behalf (as input to a coaching assignment).
2.5 Questions for reflection (coachee)	Prompts to help guide your coachee's reflection and accelerate their progress.
2.6 Personal development plan	A document that creates a clearer focus on, and record of, your coachee's goals and objectives.

Free Resources Online

The following resources can also be found in the LearnStarr area of my website, www.starrcoaching.co.uk. There, you can register to access downloads, watch video clips, read articles, etc. All items are free for your personal use and I request that you do not charge for these.

Part 1 Strengthen your skills

Activity 1.1 Help someone find their answer

What is this?	A way to help you practise being less directive during an informal conversation.
When might I use it?	When you want to begin coaching and aren't sure how to. Or when you have realised that you are giving your coachees too much advice or controlling the direction of conversations.
Why would I use this?	To experience a different style of conversation and the simple power of the less directive principle for yourself.
	To get better at coaching and facilitation generally.
	To help let go of any cynicism you might have about the principles of collaborative coaching.

Set-up

Choose a casual conversation where someone is discussing an issue or complaining in some way. It will be a conversation where the other person is not asking you to solve their problem; they are just talking or complaining about it. For example, perhaps they are too busy, or in conflict with someone, unhappy with a situation, etc. You can have this conversation by asking someone to talk about their issue, or you could wait for the next time such a conversation occurs naturally.

Key principle: don't fix, don't coach . . .

During the conversation, you *must not* give them any advice or suggestions for a way forward. No matter how great your ideas or advice, act from an assumption that you don't have an answer – and they do.

Step one – display the relevant facts: enquiry

Use an intention of enquiry to create a conversation where the relevant facts and features of the situation are displayed. Ask those questions, use silence and summaries until you've (both) heard what you feel to be the 'key' facts that clarify the situation, for example, 'What's causing this?', 'How supportive is your boss?', 'What actually is the real problem here?' Where observations work better than questions, then use them, for example, 'You seem to be spending a lot of time out of the office.'

Step two – reveal their answer

When you feel you have got enough information for them to answer the following questions, use whichever seems appropriate:

Q 'What are you thinking of doing, then?'

Q 'What needs to happen?'

Q 'How will you/are you going to sort this out?'

Q 'What can you do to improve things, then?'

Q 'So, what options do you have?'

Or any other question that requires them to focus on a solution.

Step three – optional

This next step is optional, and I discourage you from using it! If you are still 100 per cent convinced that you have a better answer, the right answer, and that they will benefit greatly from hearing it, then tell them. Use one of the following phrases to link to the previous part:

- 'Can I offer an idea?'
- 'As you were talking, I thought of something that might help. What if . . . '
- 'You know, I'm wondering if another answer might be to . . . '

Sanity warning

We can feel quite awkward or uncomfortable not 'fixing' things for people. So, if the conversation isn't going well, for example:

- the discussion isn't flowing naturally
- you can't think of the right questions or observations
- they really (definitely) can't think of any ways forward

then give up and have a go another day! Go back to having a normal, casual conversation – give your own views, experience, ideas, etc.

Alternatively, do step one on its own, then add step two when it feels right. Simply ask a few more questions than you would normally, before suggesting something. Before long, you'll find that feels more natural, as you feel less compelled to give your idea or advice. Then, when that bit feels comfortable, simply ask them what their solution is, perhaps using some of the suggestions in step two.

Resource Summary

Help someone find their answer

This can be a difficult exercise – especially if you're used to solving other people's problems for them! If you find this uncomfortable at first, please relax as it's perfectly normal. Simply use the principles and prompts to gain greater self-awareness and, over time, build from the insight you gain from even trying to do this. Remember, the foundation of your coaching practice builds from this simple idea and so it is worth persevering with this one.

Activity 1.2 Develop effective attention

What is this?	A way to practise letting go of the judgements/evaluations we make about others and developing a focus more effective for coaching.
When might I use it?	Whenever you can observe someone else. For example: • someone making a speech or presentation • someone who's talking to someone else • someone involved in a group discussion, such as a business meeting.
Why would I use this?	To develop a more objective view of someone else's situation. To help you relate to someone else more closely, e.g. when coaching them. To create a more still, clear mind when listening.

Stage one – become aware

1 Find someone appropriate to observe. You will be in the same room or setting as they are and be able to see and hear them clearly. Ideally, you should be able to observe them without being disturbed, for example by having to speak or join a discussion.

2 Remain relaxed and focused. Let your breathing be steady and your posture relaxed yet upright. Begin to watch or take notice of the other person.

3 As you watch the person you're studying, begin to notice your own thoughts. What are you thinking or saying to yourself? Just notice, that's all. For example:

- I like/don't like . . .
- He/she reminds me of . . .
- This is my impression of them . . .

Notice your own thoughts with detachment, almost as if they weren't yours, as though you are observing yourself observing.

Stage two – let go of your own thoughts

4 As you notice your thoughts, let them go. Acknowledge a thought, then let it pass. Like a stick floating down a stream, notice it there and watch it go again. If it helps, write down any thoughts as you notice them and then allow them to pass.

Stage three – use intention to guide your attention

5 Use one or two of the following to guide and refocus your thoughts:
- What is this person saying?
- How does this person feel about this?
- What is important to this person?

Resource Summary

Develop effective attention

Our minds are often busy and reducing the number or rate of distracting thoughts can be difficult.

The benefits are totally worth the effort, however. If you're finding it difficult to do stages one to three all in one go, perhaps just do the first one

---

for a while. When that becomes easier, add the second stage. Finally, when you have mastered stages one and two, add stage three.

The key is to develop an awareness and detachment of our own thoughts and judgements. It's similar to meditation as it follows the same principles – observing our own thoughts and allowing them to pass. Another way to develop your focused attention would be simply to practise meditation.

Once we allow ourselves to detach from our own thoughts or judgements about another person, we can create a better focus of attention, which helps us to listen and coach more effectively.

If you are interested in practising this technique more fully, I recommend the work of Jon Kabat-Zinn.

Activity 1.3 Develop deeper listening

What is this?	An exercise for listening to someone that creates a deeper understanding of them and their thoughts.
How would I use it?	You'll need to do this with someone who knows what you're doing and why, so that you can ask them for feedback and learn faster. They will be your practice partner for this activity.
	Once you are comfortable with this style of listening, you can use it anywhere you like. It's especially useful for coaches to be able to listen in this way during coaching sessions. Alternatively, put it into practice any time you want to give someone the gift of being really listened to.
Why would I use this?	As the quality of your listening improves, you will benefit from:
	• a clearer understanding of other people, their situations, thoughts and issues
	• an ability to develop better rapport or relationships with others
	• a more relaxed style of conversation with others.
How long will it take?	Approximately 45–60 minutes, depending on what the person you are working with wants to discuss.

Set-up

Ask your partner to think of three situations around which they'd like to create change. These might be problems, minor frustrations, or goals and objectives they already have. If they can only think of a couple, that's okay – a third often pops up during the conversation. You are going to ask your partner to talk about each of the three situations or issues, one after another. Your role is that of listener, and your practice partner is the speaker.

The conversation – step by step

1 Ask your partner to talk about three things (problems or situations they want to change) with you. This might take about 30–40 minutes. During this time, you need to ask questions, acknowledge points raised, clarify information, etc.

2 You should then take about 10 minutes to summarise back to your partner:

   • what the three issues or situations are

   • how they feel about them

   • what else wasn't actually said but seemed relevant to the conversation.

3 Then, ask your partner to give you feedback, specifically:

   • How 'listened to' did they feel? For example, how well did they feel you gave them your full attention as they were speaking, and how well did they think you understood them?

   • What effect did your 'listening' have upon the speaker? For example, 'It made me talk more, made me feel like this . . . '

   • How did the conversation affect how the speaker now feels about the three things?

During feedback, the speaker should give both their experience, for example what they felt – and what caused that experience. For example, the speaker might say, 'I felt listened to because you asked me questions to help you understand what I was saying.'

Your role as the listener

Your primary aim as listener is to understand what the speaker is saying. By a process of listening, questioning, summarising or clarifying, you aim to do the following:

• Understand what the situations or problems really are. For example, if the speaker is not happy with their job, identify some of the causes of that. If they want a closer relationship with their stepchildren, find out the driving factors behind that, what is currently in the way, etc.

- Understand how they feel about the situations and be able to tell them afterwards. For example, 'I think this situation is frustrating you and also perhaps upsetting you a little.'

- Be able to fill in gaps in the conversation, that is what wasn't said. For example, 'I wonder if you're uncertain as to how your step-children's mother might react.'

Ground rules for you as the listener

During the conversation, do not:

- attempt to give the speaker ideas, solutions or suggestions relating to the situations they are discussing

- refer to or discuss any of your own similar circumstances, experiences or feelings

- attempt to control the direction or content of the conversation

- seek to look good or impress the other person in any way, such as by asking 'clever' questions, by offering impressive facts or information, etc.

- imagine that you are a coach and you are coaching them – that won't help!

Resource Summary

Develop deeper listening

This exercise is great for developing a different listening perspective. As listener, your simple aim is to really understand and relate to the other person, nothing else.

This exercise enables us to become aware of how much we are programmed to want to put 'something of ourselves' into a conversation with another person. We might do this by solving their problems for them, showing them how much we know about what they're talking about, or even taking over the conversation completely.

Once you have experienced this way of listening, you can then practise it again and again, whenever you like. The other person doesn't have to know what you're doing, unless you want feedback. At some point during your practising, you are likely to experience a greater sense of what's really going on with the speaker, including those thoughts or feelings that aren't actually spoken. That's deep listening!

Activity 1.4 Get some feedback

What is this?	A way to learn how to give effective feedback, through the experience of receiving some.
What does it do?	Helps you learn what works and what does not work, plus how it feels to be focused on in this way.
When would I use it?	When you decide it's time to improve your skills at giving feedback messages to others.
	When you want to accelerate your own learning or self-awareness in a specific area, e.g. 'How professional do I appear to others?'

Set-up

Choose someone who knows you well (whom you trust); they will be your practice partner for this activity. As a word of caution, there can be no guarantees that you'll like what you hear or agree with what's said. Remember, in order to give supportive feedback yourself, you need to know what works and what doesn't.

Stage one – establish a clear topic

Ask your practice partner to consider your behaviour and tendencies in an area you're comfortable to discuss, for example:

- your managing style at work
- your parenting style at home
- your ability to build warm and supportive relationships.

Alternatively, you could choose another area that you're interested in getting better at. If you'd like a more challenging set-up, ask them to think about how they experience you generally, as a person.

Stage two – the questions

Ask them to consider the following three questions, regarding the topic or area you've requested feedback on:

- What am I good at? What do I do well? What are my strengths, etc?
- What am I not so good at?
- What could I do differently to improve?

When your partner has answers for each section, continue to stage three.

Stage three – have a feedback conversation

Ask your partner to give you their responses to each question in turn. Make sure that you understand each response, and use questions to clarify if necessary, for example, 'Can you tell me a little more about that?' or 'Can you think of an example?' Receive all feedback graciously and maturely, and don't contradict the other person's view – after all, it's just their view. If they say something that you don't like or disagree with, simply find out a little more about what may have caused them to have this view. When your partner has finished, thank them.

Stage four – take the learning

Now, on your own, sit down with a piece of paper and write answers/notes to the following questions:

- What did I learn about myself from that conversation?
- What will I do differently as a result of that conversation?
- What was good about the way they gave me feedback?
- What didn't work about the way they gave me feedback?
- What can I learn from that? For example, what principles will I use when giving feedback now?

Think also about how the conversation was useful to you generally. What was it like seeing yourself through the eyes of the other person?

Stage five (optional) – share your learning

If you feel it is appropriate and useful, share your answers to the above questions with your practice partner. Ask them first if they'd like to hear them, as a way of sharing your learning. Remember, you'll now be in the position of giving feedback yourself, so please employ all your learning and care!

Resource Summary

Get some feedback

This is an exercise where what you get might be something different from what you imagined, for example self-awareness or a desire to adapt some of your behaviour in some situations. Remember, one of the key benefits of coaching conversations is emotional maturity, and the giving and receiving of feedback demands emotional maturity in either situation.

Activity 1.5 Build a clearer goal

What is this?	A way to help someone define a goal or objective more clearly.
What does it do?	Helps someone gain a fuller understanding of their goal. Explores the motivation behind their goal. Either: • increases their motivation towards their goal, or • helps them realise they might want something else instead. Identifies situations or barriers that might stop them from reaching their goal. Agrees immediate actions related to the goal.
When might I use it?	During initial coaching sessions, when discussing what goals the coachee wants to work on. Any time that someone seems to have a vague goal or 'wish', e.g. 'I wish I had a better job.'

Parts of this exercise can be used separately, that is some questions work well on their own in general conversation.

Learning guidance

The stages that follow (state the goal, get specific, etc.) can be used in the sequence you find them here, or you can change that if you need to. It's more important to create a conversation that flows naturally. The best way to learn the parts of the conversation is to write a checklist, that is make a note of the headings, then tick each one when you've covered it. You will soon remember them and be able to hold the conversation naturally without the checklist.

You might cover some stages quickly, while other areas require further discussion. For example, someone might know exactly what they want, but need help understanding why they want it.

The 'coaching questions' are suggestions you might find useful. Just use those questions that work for you and the situation you are discussing. During the conversation, remain flexible. For example, if the person changes their mind about what they want, go back a few steps to create a clear view of the revised goal.

State the goal in positive terms

The goal must be stated in terms of what the individual wants to do rather than what they don't want, for example:

- What they want to stop doing: 'Stop losing my temper so often.'
- What they want to do instead: 'Keep calm and relaxed in difficult situations.'

Coaching questions – to encourage positive statements

- 'What is it you actually do want?'
- 'What do you want?'
- 'What would you rather have be true?'
- 'What do you want instead?'

If someone keeps restating what they don't want, try this: 'I can hear what you don't want, and I'm interested – what is it that you *do* want?'

Get specific! What, where, when, with whom?

To be really clear about the goal, we need to build more detail. For example, 'I want more energy' is too vague. We need to understand when, where and with whom, for example, 'I want more energy to be able to play sports with my children after work.' If there's a timescale involved, find out what it is, for example within three months.

Coaching questions – be specific

- 'When do you want more energy specifically?'
- 'What does having more energy mean to you?'
- 'When might you not need more energy?'

Occasionally, you might want to challenge the person a little, to improve either their goal or their level of commitment. Please exercise care and use your judgement wisely; the person will normally know what constitutes a stretch for them. Sometimes, a simple question will identify whether the goal is challenging enough, for example, 'How much of a challenge is that for you?' Remember to focus on what they want and not what you think would be good, for example, 'Wouldn't more energy help you to play sports with your children at the weekend?'

Use imagination to pull it closer

Using other senses, for example sight, sound, etc., helps the individual to create images or ways of representing the goal, to enable them to understand it more easily. It is even more powerful to ask these questions from a position of assuming they already have the goal.

Coaching questions – pull it closer

- 'How wtill you know when you have your dream job?'
  - 'Imagine you have your dream job – what do you feel like?'
- 'How are things different now that you have your dream job?'
- 'How does this affect the way you look?'
- 'What are you saying to yourself now that you have this dream job?'
- 'So, imagine you wake up tomorrow and you have this dream job – now tell me what that's like.'

The other benefit to these questions is that you may spot 'something missing', for example they don't seem as thrilled as you expected. Their response might be a prompt for you to double-check that they do actually want what they say or seek to understand their hesitation.

Check their power to influence

A goal is more easily reached when it is within the natural influence of the individual who wants it. For example, I can't get my boss or partner to stop acting stressed around me, but I can have the goal of responding in a relaxed, resourceful way to their behaviour. I can control my own actions – not those of others. I can't have a goal for someone else. Also, when someone else has a goal for me, I need to want it as well to be really motivated to make it happen.

So, we need to discuss the goal in a way that establishes a clear responsibility, or influence, over the goal.

Coaching questions – check influence

- 'How much influence do you have over this?'
- 'Are you responsible for making your goal happen?'
- 'What can you do to achieve it?'
- 'Is it within your power to influence this?'
- 'Who else wants this for you?'

Check that the goal is in balance

We want to make sure that it's okay for the individual to have this goal, in relation to the rest of their life. For example, if someone wants to travel more with their job and they have young children, they need to look at the effect of travel upon their home life. By exploring the impact of their goal on other situations, we work to maintain balance. We are also respecting other parts of their life, relationships and circumstances by considering any knock-on effects elsewhere.

Coaching questions – check balance

- 'What are the wider effects/consequences of reaching this goal/making this happen?'
- 'Are there any negative consequences of reaching this goal?'
- 'How would achieving this affect your home life (or your family, or your friends)?'
- 'How does this affect other people at work?'
- 'How does this affect other things that are important to you?'

Increase motivation

Here we refer to someone's basic values and understand their goal in relation to those. For example, if variety and challenge are important to you, you may notice that it doesn't 'feel good' to imagine doing exactly the same job for the next three years. However, if security and stability are more important to you, you may view three years in the same job as perfect. In this check, we also identify potential barriers, either internal or external, with the aim of eliminating them.

Coaching questions – increase motivation

- 'What would achieving this do for you?'
- 'What higher purpose does this fulfil?'
- 'If you have this, what sort of person will that make you?'
- 'If you have this, what else will you get?'
- 'What is stopping you from having this?'
- 'What might stop you from having this?'
- 'As you think about the journey towards this – what might stand in your way?'
- 'If you could have this right now, would you take it?'

That final question is a clever one, as it works with people's gut instinct. Ask that question to someone who says they want to quit smoking. For example, 'If I could make you a non-smoker right now, would you let me?' If they hesitate, that's usually because they have some doubt. Once you've identified the hesitation, you can explore the cause.

Identify action – do it now!

This check identifies someone's next logical action in relation to achieving their goal. Here, we move from understanding what the goal is and what it means towards what someone needs to do to achieve it. For example, 'I want to study for my degree' becomes 'I'm going to call three colleges to get their current syllabus.' You may choose to support the individual further by gaining a more formal agreement to taking this action, for example which colleges, by when – and agree to check in later to hear how they've progressed.

Coaching questions – identify action

- 'What can you do to achieve this goal?'
- 'What is the next/first step for you now?'
- 'What's the next logical thing you would do to achieve this?'
- 'What one (or two, or three) thing(s) could you be doing right now that would have tremendous impact on your progress towards this goal?'

Resource Summary

Build a clearer goal

When you help someone consider different perspectives on their goals, you help them to feel clearer, more optimistic and, perhaps, more determined or motivated as a result. By strengthening their sense of being connected to their goal, you increase the likelihood of them attaining it. Try the clarification process for yourself, to see if this is true for you.

Alternatively, they might have discarded the original goal completely, having realised that it wasn't something that they really wanted or would benefit from. Maybe they've replaced it with a new goal, or maybe they need to go away and do some more thinking. In either instance, you now know more about the person's thinking and can support them more effectively.

Activity 1.6 Questions for reflection (coach)

What is this?	A writing method to help you to reflect on your learning, as part of your skills development and practice. You'll need a paper and pen for this one.
What does it do?	Helps to accelerate your learning and ability as a coach, by provoking your own enquiry and reflection.
When might I use it?	Any time you feel you want to accelerate your learning and progress generally.
	If you have a specific issue or behavioural barrier to work through.
	To support your involvement with coaching supervision, e.g. you might share your notes with your supervisor.

Your options: write freestyle or use questions

You might write freestyle as in a diary ('Here's what just happened') or you might use questions to help you to write. For example, helpful reflection questions you might use include:

Q What happened during that conversation that seemed important to notice?

Q As a coach, what did I do well during that conversation? For example, what was I pleased with?

Q What was I less pleased with – that I'd like to do better next time?

Q Generally, in these types of conversations, what do I want to do more of/less of?

Q What am I thinking now?

A more rigorous form of reflection is to write session summaries. For an example of this, see the later Building block 2.3 Summary of a first session.

Resource Summary

Questions for reflection (coach)

Reflection is a valuable way to accelerate our awareness, learning and behavioural change. This is an optional tool to support your learning and progress after and between sessions. As you become accustomed to the method and its benefits, it becomes a natural way to support yourself over time.

To download a Reflection Note Template you can complete by hand, see the free resources in the LearnStarr area of www.starrcoaching.co.uk.

Part 2 Building blocks

Building block 2.1 Coaching overview document

What is this?	An overview of coaching.
What does it do?	Gives someone an initial understanding of coaching, what it is, possible benefits, etc.
	Establishes mutual expectations, such as what your coachee can expect from you and what you will expect from them.
	Encourages a coachee to begin thinking about any goals or objectives they might have.
When might I use it?	During initial discussions about the potential of coaching.
	When beginning a new coaching relationship, to give a new coachee some background information or reading.

Introduction

This document is intended to:

- explain personal coaching, what it is, how it works and its potential benefits
- describe what you can expect from your coach and what your coach will expect from you
- encourage you to think about how coaching might benefit you.

What is personal coaching?

Coaching is a form of learning, where a person (a coach) supports someone else (sometimes called a coachee) to make progress in some way. Progress might include reaching a goal, solving problems, or creating learning and change. Coaching is normally a conversation, or series of conversations, that one person has with another. The coach works to create a conversation that will benefit the other person in a way that relates to their objectives. Coaching conversations might happen in different ways, and in different environments, for example in person, by telephone, over Zoom, etc.

How does coaching work?

An effective coach blends the skills of questioning, listening, observation and feedback to create a conversation rich in insight and learning. The coachee experiences a focus and attention on their own circumstances that helps them develop greater awareness and understanding. In addition, they'll also learn fresh ways to resolve issues, produce better results and achieve their goals more effectively.

Common benefits people experience from coaching include:

- improved sense of direction and focus
- accelerated learning around a distinct topic, such as managing people, relationship, influence
- improved performance in a distinct area, such as professionally, health, finances, etc.
- increased knowledge of self/self-awareness
- improved personal effectiveness, such as focused effort on priorities
- increased motivation or sense of personal engagement
- increased resourcefulness/resilience, such as ability to handle change.

What coaching is not

Coaching is none of the following:

- **Structured training, for example classroom learning**
  Structured training relates to a fixed agenda of learning, and a prepared approach to make learning happen. For example, if you are being trained in a classroom to use a computer, the trainer would use a planned approach to ensure you learned a certain amount of information within a certain time frame.

  Coaching follows a more flexible format, according to someone's objectives. Both the individual and the coach influence the direction and content of sessions. Coaching also places responsibility for learning on the individual and encourages learning to continue after the session, such as through an agreed set of actions.

- **Therapy, psychoanalysis, psychotherapy**
  Some issues are best handled by someone trained to support a specific issue with a specific set of skills, principles and approaches. For example, addiction or mental health issues (depression, compulsive disorders, etc.) are best supported by someone trained to deal with them specifically.

  While coaching is not therapy, and is not viewed as therapy, it does provide a viable alternative to people who may have previously considered some form of counselling to resolve a situation. For example, milder forms of anxiety, crises of confidence or self-doubt might all be effectively supported by a qualified and experienced coach. This is because coaching promotes a greater self-awareness and fuller appreciation of our own situations and circumstances. Sometimes, we know our own answers and simply need support to implement our own solutions.

- **A way of someone else solving your problems for you**
  Coaching assumes that an individual is ultimately responsible for the results they create. While you may argue that this is not always true, it is normally a more effective idea to operate from. If we acknowledge that we are responsible for something, it follows that we have power and influence over it. For example, if you're not getting the results at work that you want, a coach might encourage you to:

  - understand the situation more clearly
  - develop new ideas or approaches for those situations
  - take constructive action that gets you the results you want.

What an effective coach will *not* do is instruct you to do something specific or go and do it for you. If they did, the coach would be taking responsibility (and so power) away from you. An effective coach aims to empower you by supporting you to act, rather than acting on your behalf.

What you can expect from your coach

A coaching relationship is like no other, simply because of its combination of objective detachment and commitment to the goals of the individual. It's a distinct form of support where someone creates a focus on your situation with an attention and commitment that you rarely experience anywhere else. An effective coach will listen to you with a genuine curiosity to understand who you are, what you think and generally how you experience the world. They will also reflect back to you with an objective sense of assessment and challenge that creates real clarity.

Confidentiality

All qualified coaches have agreed to a code of ethics which protects the privacy of the people they coach and so the content of coaching discussions is confidential. Where a third party has requested the coaching, for example as part of a company-sponsored assignment, a coach will agree with you the best way to keep any interested third parties involved or updated.

What your coach will expect from you

In return, your coach will encourage you to stay committed to the coaching process. That means showing up for sessions, taking your own notes where appropriate and keeping any agreements you make during sessions.

In addition, your coach needs you to be open to the potential of coaching. That means contributing to conversations honestly and openly. The strength and power of coaching relates directly to the level of openness and trust in this relationship.

Prepare for coaching

Please consider your own objectives for coaching before you meet your coach. Also decide how you might increase the effectiveness of your coaching involvement by reflecting on factors that may support it. Use the following questions to think through these two topics:

1 What areas or topics might be most useful to work on with a coach? For example, you might consider personal or professional goals, or simply those related to general learning and development.

2 What simple goals do you have right now that you'd like to make more progress with? For example, is there anything you would like to achieve or make happen?

3 What learning and self-development goals do you have? For example, do you aim to get better at something or express certain qualities more (or less) often?

4 Of the factors under your own influence, which might stop your involvement with a coach from being successful? For example, are there any distractions in your life, or do you tend to procrastinate?

5 What thoughts are you having now about getting started with a coach?

While the intention of the previous questions is simply to encourage your own thoughts and evaluations, you may also find that ideas, questions, or actions arise from your thinking. That's great: simply make a note of them and, if appropriate, take them to your first session with your coach.

Summary

Hopefully, you'll now have gained a better understanding of the opportunities that coaching offers. Perhaps you've also begun to think about your own situation and goals, and can imagine how coaching might support you.

Resource Summary

Coaching overview document

This document can be a useful way to help someone understand key information relating to coaching and also help them orientate and prepare for a first session. Some people prefer to read and digest information in written form as it allows them to recap and reflect. It's also a good way of ensuring that someone understands what will be expected of them and what they can expect of you. While the content of this document may not be totally appropriate for the people you work with, it will help you decide how to create your own.

To download a PDF version of this document, see the free resources in the LearnStarr area of www.starrcoaching.co.uk.

Building block 2.2 Starting a first session

What is this?	A checklist to help you 'get going' in the first coaching session of a new assignment.
What does it do?	Helps you think about what you need to focus on. Helps you plan your approach. Helps you feel comfortable about the session.
When might I use it?	When beginning a new coaching relationship. When you're less sure about how to handle the initial stages of a conversation. When you want to remind yourself of the principles of beginning a first session.

It's good to begin any initial conversation with a coachee on a firm footing. So, a little advance thought and preparation will help set you up for success. For example, perhaps consider the following questions:

- What seems important for you to do well during this first session?
- How will I know that the session has been a success?
- What might stop the session from being a success?
- What do I want the coachee's experience to be?
- What simple principle or belief do I want to remember during the session?

For further help, see the checklist in Chapter 7: 'How much structure do I need?'

Relax the conversation, build rapport

Introduce yourself, if necessary (if you've not met before); lighten the situation by discussing something familiar and easy for your coachee – something about the company, their colleagues, maybe your journey or the physical environment you're in. Make sure to notice their pace, their energy and match that in some way. Don't rush this; take the time to connect and ensure that they're comfortable.

Check that the coachee is orientated to the conversation

Make sure they've had all the information they need as background, for example, 'Did you have a chance to read the coaching overview – was that helpful?' List the main objectives of the session as you see them, for example to understand the coachee, their background and the initial themes for coaching. Explain what's going to happen in this first session, for example, 'So, I'm hoping to spend the next couple of hours getting to know a little bit more about you and what you'd like to get out of coaching – is that okay?' Give them the opportunity to add anything they need to, for example, 'Do you have any specific requirements of me or this process at this point?'

Get to know them

Record some basic personal details (where they live, if they have a partner, children, etc.), for example, 'Can I ask you a few basic facts, so I know a little more about you?' This is an obvious place to create some more easy conversation – take a genuine interest in what they're telling you, ask a little bit more about their home life, etc.

Explore what they think they'd like to get from the coaching

If some of these goals are already known, then acknowledge them, for example, 'You mentioned, during our initial conversation, you'd like to focus on developing better influence – could you perhaps tell me a little more about that?' If no goals have been discussed yet, start with something gentle like, 'What kinds of things were you thinking of working on?' Sometimes, the coachee either doesn't know or isn't yet comfortable enough to discuss goals. In this instance, simply have a general discussion, for example, 'Perhaps begin then by telling me a little more about yourself,' or 'Okay, can you tell me a little more about what you do at work?'

Once you've found something that they are comfortable discussing, that's it, you're off! You can then use all your skills of listening, questioning, observation and feedback to begin to support them. Use The Coaching Path to support you as you facilitate them through the conversation.

Resource Summary

Starting a first session

The key elements of an initial coaching conversation are to:

- relax the conversation and build rapport
- confirm that the coachee has an appropriate awareness and expectation of coaching
- continue to get to know them properly (as a person)
- confirm and explore what they want to get from coaching
- give the coachee confidence in you, that is because you know what you are doing.

A little preparation ahead of time will help you be effective, plus help you to stay comfortable, too.

Building block 2.3 Summary of a first session

What is this?	An imaginary summary of the first session of a coaching assignment.
What does it do?	Displays the key points, the flow of the discussion and a little content from the discussion. It is not a scripted account of the conversation, nor a guide to the 'perfect' first session.
	Detailed facts of the discussion are intentionally reduced, to enable us to focus on the key points and general flow.
When would I use it?	As general background reading to enhance your learning.
	As a guide to writing your own session summaries, if you feel that would be of benefit.

To confirm, what follows is fictional, and simply serves as an illustration of the content and approach to a first session.

Coach: Carla Foster	**Coachee:** Jannis Jannisovich
Date of session: 3 May	**Duration:** 2½ hours
Location: London	

Session objectives

- To learn a little more about Jannis.
- To identify some initial goals for the assignment.
- To discuss how the coaching assignment might be structured over time (currently estimated at five sessions over six months).
- To discuss some of Jannis's current issues and challenges.
- To agree a way forward, for example actions following this session.

Background

- Joined Global Autoparts Ltd seven years ago (has over twenty years in manufacturing).
- 44 years old.
- Originally from Kraków, Poland.
- Married to Elizabeth for 15 years.
- Has two children, Pawel (seven) and Aneta (ten months).
- Still has both parents: Alex (retired teacher) and Zdzisia.
- Brother Mathius is older by three years (accountant).
- Sister Silvie younger by five years (teacher).

Jannis is the project director of the Pyramid Programme, set up six months ago. The Pyramid Programme aims to create environmentally friendly processes for the manufacture of car parts. It is a two-year project with a budget of £2.7 million. This project is already the subject of media attention and represents a new direction for the company. This means the Pyramid Programme is high-profile and the source of a potentially pressurised situation. Jannis's industry knowledge and entrepreneurial ability were the main reasons he was chosen for the role. He has a fairly senior team of five people. These people are all new to him and he has needed to build working relationships quickly. Each member of his team has their own team reporting to them. The overall project team is around 45 people.

Jannis is married and has a young family. He lives on his own during the week and travels home at weekends. This is a new situation for him and one that both he and his family are getting used to.

Initial objectives for coaching

Jannis is interested in three areas:

1 His ability to manage performance, for example in terms of his ability to deliver. He admires anyone who can do this naturally:

- 'I see people who are better at this than me.'
- 'I don't feel strong in this area. I have trouble letting go sometimes.'
- 'It's especially difficult with such a senior team – we've got some strong characters.'

2 His ability to 'stay at the appropriate level' – be the guardian of the vision and create leadership for others, rather than getting 'lost in the detail':

- 'I need to manage my time better – that's an immediate opportunity.'

3 He'd like to find ways to foster better relationships, both within the team and with some of the suppliers:

- 'Manufacturing is pretty cut-throat.'
- 'This project is high-profile so our approach must be different.'
- 'The environmental conversation is an issue for everyone. We need to be collaborative.'

Jannis's objectives for the project

- 'I want the vision for the programme to be owned by the whole team – I want people to engage at an individual level, to feel that we're doing something worthwhile.'
- 'That we stay aligned over time – what we're doing and how we're doing it.'
- 'I want to feel that we're harmonising our approaches; that people are really pulling together, supporting each other.'
- 'That, technically, we maintain quality. That we get the specifications side of the manufacturing process right. That's where we have the experience – I want to see that count.'
- 'I'd like to see more creativity around some of our solutions; this is a new area for us, and we need to display a fresh approach.'

A need for a more consistent style

Jannis acknowledged that his attitude towards the individuals in the team can vary. For example, if he believes in someone's ability from the outset, that person will get his commitment and support. That person will experience him as open, friendly and supportive. But, if someone makes a poor first impression, he is likely to make assumptions based on their overall ability. He may even withdraw support from them over time, simply by being less communicative or warm towards them.

This person's performance could then degrade, which might go unnoticed for a period, until Jannis's attention is drawn to the situation. This person may have needed support and not been getting it, or concealing issues, which later cause difficult situations. Jannis has recently had one such example, where a serious issue arose, 'The guy had been off doing his own thing – I just hadn't seen the mistakes being made.'

Through discussion, Jannis decided that a more structured, consistent management style would improve this situation over time. For example:

- Regular, structured group reporting sessions.
- Monitoring measures of performance more closely, for example delivery against plan.
- Regular, structured one-to-one meetings, based on coaching principles.

Jannis explained that he has various styles of managing, dependent on the individual. Sometimes this works and sometimes it doesn't. For example, some people had regular one-to-ones with him, while others did not. He identified this irregular contact with some people as one of the causes of his 'blind spots'.

Structuring time

Jannis explained that he also wants to manage his time more effectively, to focus on the priority tasks. We quickly estimated how Jannis spends his time using simple blocks of activity, for example planning, organising, leading, managing, etc..

Jannis saw opportunities to improve the allocation of his own time and his team's time. For example, Jannis wanted to spend less time being interrupted at his desk in ad-hoc conversations. One way he thought this could be possible was to have regular, structured conversations with each of his team. He also saw benefits from involving the team more in some of his own activities, such as during the early stages of generating ideas, sharing his workload, etc. One obvious area was to have the team take more responsibility for liaison with suppliers, once they are more aware of its importance.

Jannis decided that he wanted to spend time identifying what activities are needed for increasing performance across the team. Then he can work out how to focus more time on those activities.

Creating 'head space'

Jannis explained he'd like more 'time to think'. When we explored this further, he realised that what he actually wanted was a feeling of 'free space' in his head, which is a slightly different idea. For example, if he felt the project was well organised, well structured, running well, he'd feel like he was 'on top of things'. Automatically, that would mean that his thought processes would be clearer, and he'd feel he had more time to consider things. He explained that he often felt 'on his back foot' and had a background concern of having forgotten something.

Conclusions

Jannis valued the time spent talking about his situations and challenges. Together, we agreed the initial focus of the coaching and his objectives for it. He also agreed it would be useful to gather some feedback from his current and previous project team. Carla will gather this on his behalf. He would also be interested in seeking feedback on the project generally from some of his suppliers but would like his own team to gather it.

Let's gather feedback

We agreed to interview some of Jannis's colleagues to gain feedback about Jannis's strengths and development needs. Jannis will make requests of the following people:

1 Bob Barker

2 Simon Breau

3 Nicolas Roget

Jannis will confirm contact details by email (Carla will then interview them by telephone).

Actions

1 Jannis to construct a 'list of priorities' and refocus his time against those priorities, for example meetings with his team.

2 Jannis to contact the three people for Carla to interview and send contact details.

3 Jannis to confirm how many coaching sessions he'd like and over what approximate time period.

4 Carla to send email of actions agreed, plus book recommendations, for example *The 7 Habits of Highly Effective People* by Stephen R. Covey.

5 Carla to contact Jannis's PA to schedule next session in approximately four weeks' time.

Resource Summary

Summary of a first session

A first coaching session needs to build rapport, gather initial information, and create a sense of direction for the future assignment. This information and direction form the base on which further conversations can build. It is not necessary to 'learn everything' about your coachee or, indeed, 'solve all problems'. More important is that trust and openness are developed between you and your coachee.

Remember that the process of conversation is a catalyst, as thoughts and ideas will continue to emerge for your coachee over time. So, the simple 'laying out' of facts and objectives is often more valuable than we might anticipate. As coach, you add value by gently navigating through the conversation, establishing background information and key goals for the assignment, and then surfacing discussion on your coachee's areas of interest.

By the end of the session, you should both be left with a clear sense of the approach and the way forward. Where you have agreed to follow up in any way, such as emailing key discussion points, or arranging the next meeting, this needs to be handled quickly and professionally.

Building block 2.4 Summary of a feedback interview process

What is this?	A way for you to conduct feedback interviews (and document those) on behalf of your coachee.
What does it do?	This type of interview: • gathers perceptions of the coachee from people the coachee has nominated for feedback • gathers feedback on the strengths and development areas of a coachee • provides the coachee with additional sources of reflection or observation to support their development • helps raise the self-awareness of the coachee.
When might I use it?	• In the early stages of an assignment, e.g. after the first session. • Any time you determine that to gather feedback for your coachee is useful.

Collecting feedback on someone's behalf must be done sensitively and as openly as possible. Anyone that you interview must be aware that the feedback summary document will be attributed to them. They must, therefore, also have a chance to review and change the document before it is shared in the coaching session.

Your role as a coach is to collect the feedback in a way that is both efficient and effective, for example interviewing people in a professional manner, recording comments in a way that distils the message clearly and handling the approval process quickly. You can also 'coach' the interviewee to offer comments in an appropriate way (which, generally, people want to do). The other value you add is in the delivery of the feedback. For example, you help your coachee to hear and digest the messages before they decide what they want to do because of the feedback.

Guidelines for interviewing people, writing up the session and gaining approval to use the document can be found later in this section.

Gathering feedback: the approach

Early in an assignment, I agree on three or four individuals it would be useful for me to speak to. I normally agree the individuals with the coachee, although, occasionally, the coachee's manager may also propose names for consideration. As well as close colleagues whom the coachee knows and trusts, I also encourage them to nominate someone with whom they perhaps have a less comfortable relationship (or even some tension). I normally interview the coachee's manager, as they are both a stakeholder and influencer in the coachee's success.

All interviews are conducted either in person or by telephone and normally take around 30 minutes. During feedback interviews, I use the following questions:

- What is this person (my coachee) good at?
- What do you value most about them?
- What do they need to get better at?
- What do they need to do to be successful in their current situation or role?
- Do you have any other messages for this person?

All messages are attributed, that is the coachee hears both what was said and who said it (obviously, it's important to make that clear to everyone).

Recording and gaining approval for disclosure

After the interview, I summarise the conversation in a document and send it to the person I have interviewed, so that they can review, edit and approve it for open use. People might change or reshape their comments, making them clearer or more helpful. Once the individual is happy for me to use their feedback, I can share the same document with the coachee. An example of this summary document (based on real interviews adapted for this purpose) is what follows.

Coachee name: Simon Everett	
Input name: Helena Franco	
Date of interview: 17 March	
Date approved for use: 25 March	

Q1 What is Simon good at?

I think, generally, Simon brings skills we really need to the role – he's got relevant experience and qualifications and it shows. He's experienced in both building strong teams and managing projects; he's a professional. When things get awkward, such as when we've got technical issues, Simon can usually contribute. He's also pretty objective and remains focused when things get stressful – I wish I could say that of more people around here. Plus, he's a nice guy to have around, generally – it's fair to say he's well liked.

Q2 What do you value most about him?

On reflection, it's probably his ability to focus on solutions, rather than problems. We have some pretty difficult individuals here who like to apportion blame. Simon seems to stay out of all that; he automatically seeks the resolution, for example, 'Okay, that's how it is – so what can we do now?' I think I've come to really rely on him for that.

Q3 What does he need to get better at?

Generally, I think I'd like to see Simon speaking up more, making a bigger impact. He tends to stay quiet sometimes. Like I said, he's often got a lot to add to the conversation but can sometimes get 'drowned out' by the bigger personalities in the room. I don't know if it's a confidence thing; he seems pretty confident. I wonder if it's about avoiding conflict – not sure. In a fast-moving environment, we need people to get in fast with views and opinions. It's just not a culture here where people seek out consensus or listen patiently to quiet voices.

A smaller point is that he sometimes seems preoccupied with detail. In discussions, it sometimes feels like he's over-explaining things. He needs to either find a way to communicate the key data more quickly, or else make more generalised points. Keep the conversation at an appropriate level. It's fine to tell us that the plan is going to be changed, but, as an operational area, we don't need always to understand the finer detail of what led us to that decision. We're more concerned about what's going to happen most of the time – if we want the detail, I guess we can always ask. On matters of planning and scheduling, we trust his judgement – maybe he doesn't appreciate that?

Q4 What does he need to do to be successful in his current situation or role?

I think he's already doing a good job, so I would say that he's already fairly successful. I think if he wants to bring true value to the role, he could use his position to act more as a 'bridge' between departments. For example, he sits between the customer-facing departments and the more technical functions. He's in an ideal position to mediate some of our issues or facilitate discussions for us more. His ability to remain calm in a crisis (or a row) makes him ideal. But that's going to mean stepping forward more often into those situations, which may cause him discomfort.

Q5 Do you have any other messages for him?

Just that I'm pleased to have been asked to do this. Simon is someone I'm incredibly supportive of – we really value his contribution. If there's any of this feedback he wants to discuss with me, I'd be glad to – I'll even buy the coffee!

Gather feedback that is clear, supportive and constructive

During interviews, I encourage people to make statements in a balanced, constructive manner and eliminate any overly harsh or insulting language. While I rarely hear insulting language, if I do, I'll ask for a more helpful version of the statement. For example, if someone tells me, 'Anna's team is making a fool out of her, instead of her managing them – it's the other way round,' I may say, 'Okay, that sounds a tough message, what's appropriate for me to record here?' The person will normally give me something more constructive, like, 'She needs to lead from the front more and find a way to keep the stronger characters following her lead.'

So, as a coach, you need to help people give feedback that is clear, objective and balanced. You are a natural 'filter' in the process and your job is to encourage openness, clarity and constructive comment. It may surprise you that, in my many years of using this approach, no coachee has ever responded badly when receiving this type of feedback. When the more challenging messages are stated constructively and balanced with praise and acknowledgement, most people respond very well and are grateful for the additional information and input.

Deliver feedback messages in a considerate, constructive manner

I aim to deliver all feedback to my coachee in person and to share all feedback gathered at the same time. This helps to illustrate common themes or messages, across multiple viewpoints. When delivering feedback to the coachee, it's important to remind them that all comments are reflecting a perception that has been created. People's comments are not 'true' – they are simply that person's perception of the coachee. For example, in the feedback, a colleague may have described my coachee as 'disorganised'. That does not necessarily mean that the coachee is disorganised (although they may admit to that!), but it does mean that they have created the *perception* of being disorganised with the person giving the feedback. The coachee is more likely to accept responsibility for having created the impression of chaos than that admit they are truly 'disorganised'.

Read directly from the document

After telling the coachee a little about what to expect, I'll read out directly from the document. I'll also add any positive or balancing statements I think will help, for example, 'This person is clearly a supporter of yours and wants to see you do well . . . ' While I don't want to tell the coachee how to respond, I do feel I can help them distil key messages or keep messages in perspective.

When a coachee hears the interview summaries, they can be informative and thought-provoking. Rarely do we see ourselves through the eyes of others. The coachee may be surprised by how other people experience them, and the feedback can lead to breakthroughs in someone's understanding. For example, a coachee is frustrated with her lack of acknowledgement or promotion at work. When her feedback is returned, she gains information that helps her understand why. Her manager and colleagues view her as happy, contented and unambitious. In addition, she is perceived as someone who prefers a small group of colleagues and does not actively seek new friends or contacts. By receiving this feedback, the coachee can decide for themselves what the important messages are and what they want to do about those. Their goals for the coaching assignment can be refined or changed, for example, 'I need to promote myself and my goals more. I also need to develop relationships with a much broader group of people.'

Leave paper copies with your coachee

After the conversation, I leave paper copies with my coachee, so that they can work through them again after the session. I also encourage my coachee to contact those interviewed to acknowledge their input and also discuss the feedback further, if that's helpful.

This method requires that you deliver the messages from the interviews in a supportive, sensitive manner. Clearly, you need to be able to give effective feedback. For further guidance, please refer to the supportive feedback section in Chapter 4 Five fundamental skills of coaching.

Resource Summary

Summary of feedback interview process

Gathering constructive feedback can be a valuable way to support coaching. The additional perspectives or views are often new information for the coachee. The information creates useful discussion with your coachee and helps them become clear about their development goals. As a coach, it's important to appreciate the principles of gathering the feedback plus those for recording, approval and delivery. When you are well-prepared, you add value to the process and improve the benefits of the feedback for your coachee.

Building block 2.5 Questions for reflection (coachee)

What is this?	A writing method to help your coachee reflect on their sessions and their learning. They will need a paper and pen.
What does it do?	Helps to accelerate their ongoing clarity and engagement in the learning by provoking further enquiry and reflection.
When might I use it?	You might offer the method for your coachee to use at any time, most obviously after a coaching session. They can also use it any time they feel they want to examine their own progress; perhaps where they feel something is missing, or they have an issue to work through.

Two options – write freestyle or use questions

Your coachee can choose to write freestyle ('here's what just happened') and that's often called a learning diary. Or they might use questions to help them write. For example, reflection questions they might use include:

1 What happened during that conversation that seemed important to notice?

2 What are my key thoughts arising from that session, for example what ideas or insights do I want to focus on now?

3 What actions or decisions do I want to take because of this conversation?

4 What might stop me? (Or how might I stop myself?)

5 What else do I want to remember?

Resource Summary

Questions for reflection (coachee)

Reflection is a valuable way to accelerate our awareness, learning and behavioural change. This is an optional tool you might offer your coachee as a way of supporting them to make progress after and between sessions.

To download a blank reflection note template for your coachee's use, check out the free resources in the LearnStarr area of www.starrcoaching. co.uk.

Building block 2.6 Personal development plan

What is this?	A document that outlines someone's development areas.
What does it do?	Helps to maintain a focus on someone's goals and objectives throughout a coaching assignment (and beyond).
When might I use it?	This can be offered to your coachee to complete at any time, for example at the beginning of an assignment to help focus their goals and objectives, or at the completion stage to help them stay focused once the assignment has ended.

Short summaries that maintain focus

Try to use brief, succinct statements that explain the topic and goal in summary detail only; they can always record further detail separately. Descriptions are intended to be a simple record to support action planning and discussion. The document is intended to be updated regularly as progress is made and objectives develop further.

Please discourage too many development objectives or goals. For example, between three and five can work well, while seven to ten is too many, as they become difficult to remember and potentially overwhelming to focus on.

Development objective/goal	Benefit/opportunity	Actions to create progress
1 Increase tolerance to, and appetite for, risk. Increase comfort in situations where infallibility is less guaranteed, e.g. 'This is a balanced risk (and still a risk).'	Increased flexibility, e.g., willingness to accommodate the unknown/uncertain. Increase ability to maintain progress rather than 'stop and stall'.	Stay aware of all available options. Use a structured way to evaluate risk (find a method). Be willing to commit to a path forward, despite some ambiguity.
2 Develop a pathway and plan forward to become self-employed within next 12 months.	Enables fulfilment of personal and professional goals. Enables a focus on topics of personal fulfilment, e.g. supporting others, creativity, etc. Provides personal challenge and growth.	Consider personal, domestic and professional aspects/impact. Identify support and resources required. Create a robust business plan for appraisal by professionals, such as the bank and business mentors.
3 Build a broader network of business relationships and contacts. Increase personal impact, raise profile: e.g. 'This is what I'm doing/this is what I'm involved in.'	Builds greater awareness of the business marketplace. Increases potential for career success/choice. Enlarges potential contribution. Increases sense of self-expression and enjoyment.	List key areas of focus and contribution. Identify (and communicate with) groups, communities and networks of individuals with natural resonance and synergy to own goals. Build awareness of ways to communicate more broadly, such as social networking, blogging, etc.

Decide what works for your situation

There is no one correct method for creating a development plan; simply aim for what best supports the needs and situation of your coachee (and any stakeholders). You'll notice that item 1 reads like more of a personal development objective while item 2 is more of a personal goal. Item 3 incorporates both, that is, in order to build a broader network, the individual is going to have to learn and grow personally.

Why not try completing a row for one of your own objectives or goals and see what feels helpful for you?

Resource Summary

Personal development plan

This can be a useful document to help create mutual clarity of the aims and focus of a coaching assignment. It can also be a useful way of documenting someone's way forward once a coaching assignment has ended. It is intended to be a short, succinct document that creates a quick reference or point of discussion. The document is best kept fresh over time, by revisiting and revising the content fairly regularly.

To download a PDF version of this document, see the online free resources in the LearnStarr area of www.starrcoaching.co.uk.

End notes

Chapter 3

1 To help you practise, check out the exercise 'Develop effective attention' in the Free resources section.

2 For an exercise to help you to develop this essential skill, see the exercise 'Help someone find their answer' in the Free resources section.

Chapter 4

1 De Haan, E., Duckworth, A., Birch, D. and Jones, C. (2013) 'Executive coaching outcome research: the predictive value of common factors such as relationship, personality match and self-efficacy', *Consulting Psychology Journal: Practice and Research,* 65.1, 40–57.

2 To improve your listening, try the item 'Develop deeper listening' in the Free resources section.

3 To assist your own reflection, download the reflection note template called 'Questions for reflection (coach)' from the LearnStarr area of www.starrcoaching.co.uk.

4 For a way to do this, see the item 'Get some feedback' in the Free resources section.

Chapter 5

1 Acknowledgement to Kevin Billett, co-author, Bays, B. and Billett, K. (2009) *The Journey – Consciousness: The New Currency.* Journey Publications.

Chapter 6

1 See also the Free resources item 'Summary of a first session', at the back of this book.

2 For a way to help someone build a clearer sense of objective, see the free resource 'Build a clear goal' in the Free resources section.

3 To help you practise your style and approach, check out the exercise 'Develop deeper listening' in the Free resources section.

Chapter 7

1 To print or download a version of this overview, see the Free resources item 'Coaching Overview' in the LearnStarr area of www.starrcoaching.co.uk.

2 For further support on setting clearer goals, check out 'Build a clear goal' item, in the Free resources section.

3 To print or download a version of this overview, see the free online resource 'Coaching Overview' in the LearnStarr area of www.starrcoaching.co.uk.

4 I've put further explanation of the previous list of activities in the Free resources, where you'll find the following: a feedback interview document (with guidance for completion); a template for a reflection note (coachee); an example of a personal development plan.

5 For a simple version of a PDP, see the free resources in the LearnStarr area of www.starrcoaching.co.uk.

Chapter 8

1 When we are interdependent, we view ourselves as part of a system; we are effective by working *with* other people (rather than being dependent or independent).

2 Salovey, P. and Mayer, J.D. (1990) 'Emotional intelligence', *Imagination, Cognition and Personality*, 9, pp. 185–211.

3 For a reflection note template, see the Free resources section.

4 For a recommended reading list, see the LearnStarr area of www.starrcoaching .co.uk.

Index